The Wisdom of the Word

The Wisdom of the Word

BIBLICAL ANSWERS TO
TEN PRESSING QUESTIONS
ABOUT CATHOLICISM

MICHAEL DAUPHINAIS

AND

MATTHEW LEVERING

WORD ON FIRE
INSTITUTE

Published by the Word on Fire Institute, an imprint of
Word on Fire, Park Ridge, IL 60068
© 2021 by Word on Fire Catholic Ministries
Printed in the United States of America
All rights reserved.

Cover design by Rozann Lee and Cassie Pease.
Layout by Anna Manhart.

24 23 22 21 1 2 3 4

ISBN: 978-1-943243-76-1

Library of Congress Control Number: 2020925975

Dauphinais, Michael, 1973–

Levering, Matthew, 1971–

To **Nancy Dauphinais** and **Joy Levering**

"The LORD bless you and keep you;
The LORD make his face to shine upon you, and be gracious to you;
The LORD lift up his countenance upon you, and give you peace."
—Numbers 6:24–26

CONTENTS

ACKNOWLEDGMENTS ix

INTRODUCTION xi

Chapter 1 **Why Believe in God and in Jesus Christ?**   1
"The Author of life, whom God raised from the dead"
(Acts 3:15)

Chapter 2 **Why Listen to the Church?**   33
"The obedience of faith" (Romans 1:5)

Chapter 3 **Does the Holy Spirit Actually Transform Christians?**   65
*"You shall receive power when the Holy Spirit has
come upon you"* (Acts 1:8)

Chapter 4 **How Can Christ's Blood Be Good News?**   97
"A sharing in the blood of Christ"
(1 Corinthians 10:16)

Chapter 5 **Why Would God Hold Our Faults Against Us?**   127
"Be reconciled to God" (2 Corinthians 5:20)

Chapter 6 **Why Not Live and Think Like Everyone Else?**   161
"Do not be conformed to this world" (Romans 12:2)

Chapter 7 **Why Care for the Poor?**   193
"There was not a needy person among them" (Acts 4:34)

Chapter 8 **Why Is the Church So Strict about Sex?**   221
"Glorify God in your body" (1 Corinthians 6:20)

Chapter 9 **Why Do Catholics Fight So Much with Each Other?**   253
"Do not speak evil against one another" (James 4:11)

Chapter 10 **Are the Saints of the Church Too Strange to Be Relevant?** 273
"So great a cloud of witnesses" (Hebrews 12:1)

CONCLUSION 303

ACKNOWLEDGMENTS

Proverbs 3:7 teaches, "Do not be wise in your own eyes." We benefitted greatly from the wisdom of others correcting and improving our insights and writing. Our first thanks goes to the biblical scholar James Prothro, now of the Augustine Institute, who is not responsible for the weaknesses of the book but who is responsible for many strengths. We are grateful to him for reading and commenting upon an early draft of the whole manuscript. Second, we owe thanks to many current and former students of Michael Dauphinais at Ave Maria University. Their critical and constructive feedback was invaluable. We should especially mention Kara Logan, Michael De Salvo, Jose Quiceno, Joan Crawford, Mary Hailey Derrick, Clara Paloucek, Peter Atkinson, Tyler Rosser, Megan Magyar, and Catherine Lagarde. We also thank the professional copyeditors of the manuscript. It was a privilege to work with them and to benefit from their skills. At Word on Fire, Brandon Vogt saw an early version of the manuscript, and his encouragement and support have been crucial. Matthew Becklo and Daniel Seseske gave excellent help in bringing the manuscript to publication. Bishop Robert Barron inspired the manuscript in many ways. May God bless his ministry and sustain his marvelous joy in the Gospel. We dedicate this book with love and gratitude to our beloved wives, Nancy Dauphinais and Joy Levering.

INTRODUCTION

In this book, we propose that Catholic faith has a strong basis for its claims—and that a central way to discover this is through the Bible, as canonized in the Church, proclaimed in the liturgy, professed in the Creeds, and embodied in the lives of the saints. We invite Catholics who are thinking about leaving the Church, or who are confused about elements of Catholic faith and practice, to pause and give the Bible a chance to illuminate the most challenging questions that the Church faces today.

In addition to the evils of the sexual abuse scandals—which the Church needs to address with deep repentance and spiritual renewal, marked by accountability and attentiveness to the victims[1]—we see other signs that the Church is suffering from malaise and confusion. In our experience, at many if not most American parishes, only a minority of Catholics believe that *all* the Church's most solemn teachings about faith and morality are true. It seems reasonable to conclude that the crisis that the Church is experiencing among its members is caused not least by a *loss of faith in Jesus Christ as the Son of God and Savior* whose words and deeds have been faithfully communicated to us through Sacred Scripture as handed on and interpreted by the Catholic Church.

Once people no longer believe that the Catholic faith communicates the Word of God who has come to save us from sin and death and for everlasting intimacy with God, then Catholicism is no longer of real interest. This is the core of the crisis of faith that we face today. Put simply, such faith becomes salt that has "lost its taste" and "is

---

1. For an important start, see Robert Barron, *Letter to a Suffering Church: A Bishop Speaks on the Sexual Abuse Crisis* (Park Ridge, IL: Word on Fire, 2019).

no longer good for anything, but is thrown out and trampled under foot" (Matt. 5:13).

Bishop Robert Barron has succinctly named the problem: "Young people are quitting the Church because they don't believe in the teachings of classical Christianity."[2] Barron is especially attentive to the phenomenon of "nones"—people with no religious affiliation. He states that today "fully forty percent of those classed as millennials (born 1981 to 1996) are 'nones,' and among Catholics in that age group, fully fifty percent have left the Church. This means that every other Catholic child baptized or confirmed these last thirty years now no longer participates in the life of the Church."[3] This is a heartrending statistic, one that we have personally experienced in our lives.

A young Catholic priest, Fr. Josh Johnson, provides a perspective on the real people behind the numbers: "I remembered my older brothers' responses to being confirmed: They immediately stopped setting foot in a Catholic Church. For them, confirmation was like 'graduating' from the Church."[4] But when we listen to the Bible and gather around the Eucharistic table, we share in God's love story for us. How can this truth be rediscovered?

Pope Francis, in his first encyclical *The Light of Faith*, probes the roots of the loss of belief in divine revelation. He observes that, to many contemporary Catholics, faith appears to be "an illusory light, preventing mankind from boldly setting out in quest of knowledge"

---

2. Robert Barron, "The USCCB Meeting, Jordan Peterson, and the 'Nones,' Catholic World Report, June 18, 2019, https://www.catholicworldreport.com/2019/06/18/the-usccb-meeting-jordan-peterson-and-the-nones/.

3. Robert Barron, "Evangelizing the Nones," in *Renewing Our Hope: An Essay on the New Evangelization* (Washington, DC: The Catholic University of America Press, 2020), 22.

4. Fr. Joshua Johnson, *Broken and Blessed: An Invitation to My Generation* (West Chester, PA: Ascension, 2018), 29. Likewise, the young Catholic theologian Stephen Bullivant, in his recent book *Mass Exodus: Catholic Disaffiliation in Britain and America Since Vatican II* (Oxford: Oxford University Press, 2019), offers a helpful diagnosis and confirmation of this same trend.

and entrapping the faithful in a pre-modern and pre-scientific superstition.[5] In his apostolic exhortation *The Joy of the Gospel*, he makes these concerns more concrete: "In the case of the popular cultures of Catholic peoples, we can see deficiencies which need to be healed by the Gospel: machismo, alcoholism, domestic violence, low Mass attendance, fatalistic or superstitious notions which lead to sorcery, and the like."[6] Many once-Catholic cultures, he says, are today marked by "a growing deterioration of ethics, a weakening of the sense of personal and collective sin, and a steady increase in relativism."[7] Divine revelation is neither believed nor lived.

In response to this problem of faith, recent popes consistently urge the whole Church to turn more deeply to Scripture. According to Pope St. John Paul II, the Bible teaches us saving truth by offering "a vision of the human being and the world which has exceptional philosophical density."[8] Pope Benedict XVI expresses his own confidence in Scripture: "The Church lives in the certainty that her Lord, who spoke in the past, continues today to communicate his word in her living Tradition and in sacred Scripture."[9] He eloquently summarizes the stance of the Church toward the Bible: "I trust the Gospels."[10]

5. Pope Francis, *Lumen Fidei*, 2, encyclical letter, Vatican website, June 29, 2013, http://www.vatican.va/content/francesco/en/encyclicals/documents/papa-francesco_20130629_enciclica-lumen-fidei.html.

6. Pope Francis, *Evangelii Gaudium*, 69, apostolic exhortation, Vatican website, November 24, 2013, http://www.vatican.va/content/francesco/en/apost_exhortations/documents/papa-francesco_esortazione-ap_20131124_evangelii-gaudium.html.

7. Pope Francis, *Evangelii Gaudium*, 64. The pope underlines the role of the Bible in renewing the Church: "It is essential that the revealed word radically enrich our catechesis and all our efforts to pass on the faith" (no. 175).

8. Pope John Paul II, *Fides et Ratio*, 80, encyclical letter, Vatican website, September 14, 1998, http://www.vatican.va/content/john-paul-ii/en/encyclicals/documents/hf_jp-ii_enc_14091998_fides-et-ratio.html.

9. Pope Benedict XVI, *Verbum Domini*, 18, apostolic exhortation, Vatican website, September 30, 2010, http://www.vatican.va/content/benedict-xvi/en/apost_exhortations/documents/hf_ben-xvi_exh_20100930_verbum-domini.html.

10. Joseph Ratzinger, *Jesus of Nazareth: From the Baptism in the Jordan to the Transfiguration* (New York: Doubleday, 2007), xxi.

Pope Francis reminds us to let God speak to us in the Bible: "The prayerful reading of God's Word, which is 'sweeter than honey' (Ps. 119:103) yet a 'two-edged sword' (Heb. 4:12), enables us to pause and listen to the voice of the Master. It becomes a lamp for our steps and a light for our path (cf. Ps. 119:105)."[11] Under the guidance of the tradition and teaching of the Church, the Bible is a source of truth for our lives. When we listen to the Bible, we hear the voice of Jesus Christ leading us on our life's journey.

Why so much focus on the Bible? Such a biblically-focused approach to Catholicism may appear questionable to readers who imagine that they already know what the Bible teaches or, alternatively, suppose that the Bible is too confusing and thus only known by experts.[12] Moreover, isn't Catholicism the religion, not of a book, but of a living person, Jesus Christ?[13] This is so, but a central way that Jesus invites us to meet him is through the words of Sacred Scripture, which reveal the meaning of our existence. God our Creator loves us and comes to meet us in Jesus Christ, so as to lift us into his everlasting light and life in the Holy Spirit. As Catholic theologian Leonardo

---

11. Pope Francis, *Gaudete et Exsultate*, 156, apostolic exhortation, Vatican website, March 19, 2018, http://www.vatican.va/content/francesco/en/apost_exhortations/documents/papa-francesco_esortazione-ap_20180319_gaudete-et-exsultate.html.

12. In the present book, we treat the Bible as an ecclesial, canonical, inspired text that prepares the people of Israel for the coming of Jesus Christ and that proclaims the truth about him and about our life in Christ. With the exception of some footnotes, we do not take up historical-critical questions regarding authorship, ancient genres, or whether a particular story has a historical referent "behind the text" or simply has a typological import in God's plan for his scriptural word. Taken as a whole, the historical truth of the people of Israel under their kings, priests, and prophets and the historical truth of Jesus Christ's public ministry, crucifixion, and glorious Resurrection ground our analysis. For further discussion of these issues, see Matthew Levering, *Engaging the Doctrine of Revelation: The Mediation of the Gospel through Church and Scripture* (Grand Rapids, MI: Baker Academic, 2014). See also Brant Pitre and John Bergsma, *A Catholic Introduction to the Bible: The Old Testament* (San Francisco: Ignatius Press, 2018).

13. See *Catechism of the Catholic Church*, no. 108: "The Christian faith is not a 'religion of the book.' Christianity is the religion of the 'Word' of God, a word which is 'not a written and mute word, but the Word which is incarnate and living'" (*Catechism of the Catholic Church*, 2nd ed. [Washington, DC: USCCB Publishing, 1997], 31).

DeLorenzo aptly expresses the matter, the Bible draws us out of our-selves and teaches us "how to know Jesus on God's terms."[14]

It is not for nothing that the Second Vatican Council empha-sized that the Church receives the Scriptures, taken together with Sacred Tradition, "as the supreme rule of faith, since, as inspired by God and committed once and for all to writing, they impart the word of God Himself without change, and make the voice of the Holy Spirit resound in the words of the prophets and Apostles."[15] Through the Bible, the Holy Spirit speaks authoritatively, offering a faithful witness to help us understand our experience and discover how to embrace Christ's redemptive love and to live in communion with God. The council insists that "like the Christian religion itself, all the preaching of the Church must be nourished and regulated by Sacred Scripture."[16]

Faced with the challenging questions of our time that cause prob-lems for handing on the faith, the Second Vatican Council's instruc-tion should inspire us. After all, as we hope to show, when read with a sense for the unity of the Old and New Testaments, Scripture pro-vides answers to questions that frequently lead people to abandon faith. As Bishop Barron says, "God's definitive revelation through the Bible—the showing forth of his unique manner of being—constitutes . . . a world of meaning, a new way of imagining ourselves, a matrix of thought, action, and value otherwise unavailable to us."[17]

---

14. Leonard J. DeLorenzo, *What Matters Most: Empowering Young Catholics for Life's Big Decisions* (Notre Dame: Ave Maria Press, 2018), 87, 95.

15. *Dei Verbum*, no. 21, in *The Word on Fire Vatican II Collection* (Park Ridge, IL: Word on Fire Institute, 2021), 35. Commenting on *Dei Verbum*, Pope John Paul II distinguishes the full Catholic view of "the unity which the Spirit has created between Sacred Tradition, Sacred Scripture, and the Magisterium of the Church" from an erroneous "'biblicism' which tends to make the reading and exegesis of Sacred Scripture the sole criterion of truth" (*Fides et Ratio*, 55).

16. *Dei Verbum*, no. 21, 35.

17. Robert Barron, *The Priority of Christ: Toward a Postliberal Catholicism* (Grand Rapids, MI: Brazos Press, 2007), 272. For an exemplar of the mode of reading that we pursue in the present book, see Barron's "Training in the Divine School: Hebrews 12:5–11," in *Word on Fire: Proclaiming the Power of Christ* (New York: Crossroad, 2008), 28–34.

The purpose of this book is to invite people to enter into this biblical "world of meaning."[18]

We have identified ten major difficulties that Catholics who are falling away or have fallen away from the Church often have with respect to the Catholic faith:

1. They no longer believe in a Creator God, let alone one who became incarnate in Jesus Christ and rose from the dead.

2. They no longer think of faith as involving authoritative divinely revealed truth, and so "obedience" to the Word of God as mediated by the Church no longer makes sense.

3. It appears to them that the "power" of the Holy Spirit is too weak to transform our hearts. After all, the Church's leaders and members are so sinful.

4. They take what they have heard about the saving power of the cross and the truth of the Eucharist to be disturbing. Surely, they think, God doesn't need the bloody sacrifice of his Son, and neither do we need to commune sacramentally in Jesus' Body and Blood.

5. God's offer of forgiveness and reconciliation in Christ no longer appears necessary to them. Many think that God does not take our deeds, good or bad, very seriously.

6. They no longer find meaning in the Church's call for believers to be distinct from the world and avoid "worldliness." The world's moral standards make sense to them, and they see the Church's rules as absurd and outdated.

7. They admire the Church's care for the poor but reject the Church's other doctrines. On this view, Catholic concern for the under-

---

18. For an overview of the Bible, see our earlier book *Holy People, Holy Land: A Theological Introduction to the Bible* (Grand Rapids, MI: Brazos Press, 2005).

privileged merely means the attempt to change unjust economic and political structures.

8. Catholic teachings on sex and marriage appear especially unreasonable, oppressive, and contrary to reality.

9. The infighting and arguments among Catholics seem to invalidate the claims of Christian faith to bring peace and reconciliation.

10. They find the great heroes and saints of the Catholic tradition to be difficult to relate to and irrelevant to modern life.

In response to these ten major difficulties, each of the following chapters selects an emblematic biblical verse and, on this basis, turns to explore the wisdom of the Bible. The biblical answers we provide are not the sort that can be looked up quickly on the internet or summarized in a short message, for we aim to open up the reader's understanding and imagination. We employ a meditative approach of unfolding the biblical narrative and examining key themes, central stories, and pivotal figures. The answers to the above difficulties arise from within this attentive exposition. The answers we offer are meant to be, not the final word, but rather a step on a lifelong journey toward joyfully believing and practicing the Catholic faith. Sometimes the Bible's answers are rather blunt. Inevitably, those who dare to learn from the Bible must be willing to be challenged and stretched.

Who is the audience for this book? Pastors, professors, teachers, parents, seminarians, students, and anyone who wants to know how the Bible helps answer their deepest and most urgent questions. Do you, or someone you know, think that certain elements of the Catholic faith just don't make sense? As part of seeking answers, are you willing to take a deep dive into the Bible, trusting that it may well be a source of wisdom? Are you bold enough to give the wisdom of sacred Scripture a chance? If so, we have written this book for you. Together, let us ask Jesus to enable us—as after his Resurrection he enabled his Apostles—"to understand the scriptures" (Luke 24:45).

CHAPTER 1

Why Believe in God and in Jesus Christ?

*"The Author of life, whom God raised
from the dead"* (Acts 3:15)

Does God exist? It has become almost popular today to answer
"No." Some who claim to be atheists or agnostics may feel that what
we know about science leaves no room for religious belief. Even a
number of baptized Catholics are unsure whether God exists and
whether Jesus Christ is truly the Son of God who rose from the dead.
One recent study of this phenomenon quotes a young man who,
having left the Church, explains: "I lost my faith studying science at
school and beginning to think for myself about the plausibility of the
existence of God and the context in which religions were established.
I concluded that Christianity . . . was just a cultural creation based
on beliefs held by people two thousand years ago, when they didn't
have scientific explanations for seemingly divine occurrences."[1] And
another young man comments, "When I try to justify my belief in a
supernatural being or in Christ as a felt presence in my life, I feel silly."[2]
Bishop Robert Barron has found that many young people, even if
raised as Christians, have a "fundamental conviction that religion is
finally irrational, a matter of complexes and fantasies."[3] *The cosmos*

---

1. Stephen Bullivant, Catherine Knowles, Hannah Vaughan-Spruce, and Bernadette
Durcan, *Why Catholics Leave, What They Miss, and How They Might Return* (New York:
Paulist Press, 2019), 39. Another ex-Catholic young woman remarks: "Now that we have
such scientific advances we no longer need a higher being to explain why we came to be on
this Earth" (39).

2. Bullivant et al., *Why Catholics Leave, What They Miss, and How They Might Return*, 40.

3. Robert Barron, *Arguing Religion: A Bishop Speaks at Facebook and Google* (Park Ridge,
IL: Word on Fire, 2018), 4.

is so vast; the world is so wicked; Jesus lived and died two thousand years ago; modern people have evolved past the need for God. Today, we know better.

In *Forming Intentional Disciples: The Path to Knowing and Following Jesus*, Sherry Weddell identifies a second obstacle to embracing Catholicism in a life-changing manner. Some Catholics believe in God, but only in a distant God, a sort of cosmic force behind the universe. Weddell writes, "When Pew researchers asked American adults a series of questions about the kind of God they believed in, a startling pattern emerged: *Nearly a third of self-identified Catholics believe in an impersonal God.*"[4] It's hard to imagine how someone who believes in such an impersonal God would continue to attend Mass regularly for an extended length of time. There is little meaning or comfort in knowing and loving a God who doesn't know and love us in return.

Even those who affirm the existence of a personal God slip at times into unhelpful beliefs about God, such as the idea that the God of Christianity will make everything work out in this life. Fr. Josh Johnson tells the story of a Christian woman whose faith began to flag as she suffered tremendous difficulties in her family. She told the priest, "If God cared about me, then I wouldn't be suffering so much." Fr. Johnson responded by speaking to the woman about Mary and the Apostles. They were chosen by God, yet they suffered greatly. God accomplished his purposes through their faithfulness in the midst of difficulties. And in their faithfulness, they were imitating Christ, who himself won the victory over the power of sin not by escaping suffering but through his own faithful suffering. This woman would not have called herself an atheist or an agnostic. She went to church and was part of a Christian community. Yet, as Fr. Johnson notes,

---

4. Sherry A. Weddell, *Forming Intentional Disciples: The Path to Knowing and Following Jesus* (Huntington, IN: Our Sunday Visitor Publishing, 2012), 43.

"the lies she learned and ultimately came to believe about God crippled her from really getting to know him. She never saw God as he has revealed himself in the Scriptures and the Church."[5]

This chapter explores the biblical teaching about God and Jesus Christ. How can we learn what the Bible has to teach about who God is and what Jesus Christ has done for us? The Bible not only teaches that God exists but also claims that we can come to know his existence when we contemplate the mysteries and order within the universe. The Bible also knows, however, that our human conceptions of God are often confused. We are invited to discover answers to questions that science can't answer on its own.[6] Thus, God reveals his true nature to the people of Israel over centuries. The God who created the universe and created us out of his love is the same God who seeks us out in our brokenness and reveals himself and his ways to us out of his mercy. In the New Testament, God reveals himself fully in Jesus of Nazareth, the Son of God, and offers us forgiveness of sins, the removal of shame, and eternal life.

Fulton Sheen once said that the religions and philosophies throughout history display the best—and at times the worst—of the human search for God. He observed that what makes Christianity unique can be seen in the mystery of Christmas, when the God of the universe became a small infant in arms of Mary. In this dramatic moment, God reverses the usual order: the Bible does not tell of our search for God; the Bible tells of God's search for us.[7] The goal of this chapter is to consider how God's search for us fulfills and elevates

---

5. Johnson, *Broken and Blessed*, 56, 58.

6. *Pace* such books as Stephen Hawking and Leonard Mlodinow, *The Grand Design* (New York: Bantam Books, 2010).

7. See Fulton Sheen, *The True Meaning of Christmas* (New York: McGraw-Hill, 1955), 7. Sheen makes clear that the theme of God's search for us likewise characterizes the Old Testament (and Judaism). See also Abraham Joshua Heschel, *God in Search of Man: A Philosophy of Judaism* (New York: Farrar, Straus, and Giroux, 1955).

our search for God in ways we could have never imagined. We will come to see why believing that God exists and that his Son, Jesus Christ, rose from the dead is not only central to the Catholic faith, but also in accord with our intelligence and our deepest desires to find meaning in our lives.

Seeking the Face of God

The words of the Psalmist proclaim: "'Come,' my heart says, 'seek his face!' Your face, Lord, do I seek. Do not hide your face from me" (Ps. 27:8–9).[8] Another Psalm likewise expresses this desire to see God, "As a deer longs for flowing streams, so longs my soul for you, O God. My soul thirsts for God, for the living God. When shall I come and behold the face of God?" (Ps. 42:1–2).

To see someone's face is to see the truth of that person, to know the other person without anything masking or hiding the person's identity. What does it mean to come to see the true face of God? One thing we can be sure of: on our own, there is nothing we can do to make God's face visible to us. He is not a statue covered in cloth that we can simply unmask. If we are to see his face, he has to take the initiative to reveal himself to us.

The word for "revelation" in the New Testament is *apo-kalypsis*, which means an "un-veiling." The word "revelation" is the title of the last book of the Bible, in which the heavenly worship of God is unveiled before our earthly eyes. The entire biblical narrative tells how God enters into our human story over time and slowly leads us out of darkness to come to see his truth, goodness, and beauty.[9]

---

8. Biblical quotations are taken from the New Revised Standard Version Catholic Edition with occasional modifications, unless otherwise noted.

9. Note that biblical passages can be taken out of canonical context in order to paint a different picture of God, especially by focusing on the portrayal of God in some of the Old Testament's passages as commanding the Israelites to put to death the entire populace of conquered cities (sadly, a relatively common practice in the ancient Near East). Some authors also highlight anthropomorphic depictions of God, such as passages where God is portrayed

Not everyone can be Enoch, who is described as having "walked with God" all his life (Gen 5:22). Indeed, many people over the millennia have paid little or no attention to the divine, other than perhaps occasionally to consult, as King Saul did, "the mediums and the wizards" in moments of stress (1 Sam. 28:3). Many people today have given up the quest for God. The message of the Bible is that God has not given up the quest for us.

In Israelite history, people found it difficult to worship God as the Creator and Savior—for some of the same cultural reasons that cause people to turn away from God today. In the ancient Near East, there were plenty of other gods to be worshipped, and they sometimes seemed to do better at protecting their people than God did at protecting his people. Israel's God, moreover, was demanding of upright living. The people were not averse to assimilation to the prevailing ways of the contemporary culture, as when in the second century BC some of the people urged, "Let us go and make a covenant with the Gentiles around us, for since we separated from them many disasters have come upon us" (1 Macc. 1:11). Our generation is not the first to find worshiping the revealed God of Israel off-putting.

---

as changing his mind or as jealous. See, for example, Dan Barker, *God: The Most Unpleasant Character in All Fiction* (New York: Sterling, 2016). In the present book, we will focus on the main lines of the Bible's portrait of God, allowing—as Jewish and Christian interpreters have done throughout the centuries—for the troubling passages to be understood in light of the full canonical and ecclesial witness to the truth about God. Readers seeking further insight into these issues should see such studies as Mark Sheridan, OSB, *Language for God in the Patristic Tradition: Wrestling with Biblical Anthropomorphism* (Downers Grove, IL: IVP Academic, 2014); Reinhard Feldmeier and Hermann Spieckermann, *God of the Living: A Biblical Theology*, trans. Mark E. Biddle (Waco, TX: Baylor University Press, 2018); R.W.L. Moberly, *The God of the Old Testament: Encountering the Divine in Christian Scripture* (Grand Rapids, MI: Baker Academic, 2020); Matthew J. Ramage, *Dark Passages of the Bible: Engaging Scripture with Benedict XVI and St. Thomas Aquinas* (Washington, DC: The Catholic University of America Press, 2013); Mary E. Mills, *Images of God in the Old Testament* (London: Cassell, 1998); Jon D. Levenson, *The Love of God: Divine Gift, Human Gratitude, and Mutual Faithfulness in Judaism* (Princeton, NJ: Princeton University Press, 2016). See also Steven Lewis, "Dan Barker and the Immoral God of the Bible," in *Answering the Music Man: Dan Barker's Arguments against Christianity*, ed. B. Kyle Keltz and Tricia Scribner (Eugene, OR: Wipf and Stock, 2020), 109–31.

In revealing himself, God therefore had to show both his reality and his love, without compromising the need for people to live in a new way, so as to be able to participate in divine life and love. In ancient Israel, one of the most common forms of idolatry was the worship of Baal, a male god who was thought to have the power to make lands and families fertile. Baal-worship did not require interior conversion or the practice of righteousness; it was simply an attempt to gain earthly abundance and control by appeasing an imagined god. Those who practiced such idolatrous worship at times engaged in sexual intercourse with cult-prostitutes, and some even practiced child sacrifice, killing infants for the purpose of supposed temporal gain.

For a moment, let us consider Baal-worship not as sinful disobedience, but rather as the enshrinement of a false image of God, false images still around today and indeed worthy of rejection. The people manufactured a god in their own image, as a representation of their own lust, greed, violence, and thirst for power. They failed to see the authentic face of God. The story of the Bible is the story of God correcting false human images of himself and progressively unveiling his true image by means of a dialogue with his people who come to know and express his name and his ways more and more over time.

The Prophet Hosea powerfully depicts God's efforts to correct our distorted understanding of his true nature as our merciful Creator and Redeemer. In a prophetic sign, God commands Hosea to marry a prostitute who will be unfaithful to the prophet. By directing Hosea to carry out this difficult and painful command, God offers a concrete image and unmistakable sign of his own love for Israel, since God is constantly faithful to an unfaithful and adulterous people.

God promises Hosea that idolatrous Israel, which God has espoused to himself, will one day be restored in fidelity: "On that day, says the LORD, you will call me, 'My husband,' and no longer will you call me, 'My Baal'" (Hosea 2:16).[10] In Hebrew, the word *baal* indicated a dominating master-slave relationship.[11] The biblical view of marriage, in contrast, is one in which the woman is an equal partner with her husband, "bone of my bones and flesh of my flesh" (Gen. 2:23). Isaiah likewise unveils God's relation to Israel not as a domineering master, but as a beloved husband: "Your Maker is your husband. . . . For the LORD has called you like a wife forsaken and grieved in spirit" (Isa. 54:5–6).

How hard it can be for us to imagine God as a merciful and loving husband who knows the truth about our infidelity and yet desires to call us apart and "speak tenderly" to us (Hosea 2:14)! Our images of God tend to reduce this tension in one of several false directions: either we imagine a perfect and distant god who despises and rejects our imperfections, a god who leaves us alone to suffer in this world; or we imagine a nice god who simply ignores and overlooks our sins and failings. If we are truthful with ourselves, we often do not even have a consistent false view of God. Instead, we have a confusion of false images about him from which we select, depending on our given moods from one day to the next.

The Bible reveals two great desires that are otherwise often hidden from our experience. First is God's desire for us. Rather than an indifferent or hostile God, the biblical God loves his creatures, desiring to see us and be seen by us. He chooses us not because of our good qualities or because he has any need for us but only out of his love for us (Deut. 7:7; cf. Eph. 1:4). Second is our desire for God. The

---

10. See Brant Pitre, *Jesus the Bridegroom: The Greatest Love Story Ever Told* (New York: Doubleday, 2014).

11. See Bergsma and Pitre, *A Catholic Introduction to the Bible*, 911.

Bible reveals that our deepest desires for life, security, and happiness are realized not through our obsessions with merely earthly security and pleasures, but rather in our coming to love and to see God as he is, in his awe-inspiring holiness and majestic humility.

The Old Testament figures of Moses and Elijah are united by their common desire to see God and by God's showing himself to them, if only imperfectly. Moses on Mount Horeb asks God, "Show me your glory." The Lord answers, "I will make all my goodness pass before you, and will proclaim before you the name, 'The LORD.' . . . 'But,' he said, 'you cannot see my face; for no one shall see me and live'" (Exod. 33:18–20). The language of God's "passing before" Moses is used in the Bible to indicate a theophany, a unique experience and manifestation of God's tremendous presence.

God shows himself to Moses and Elijah so they might come to know more clearly who he is. The Lord says to Moses, "I will be gracious to whom I will be gracious, and will show mercy on whom I will show mercy" (Exod. 33:19). In choosing the people of Israel, God reveals his true character as the God of mercy, although the full truth about the extent of God's mercy awaits the coming of Jesus Christ. When the prophet Elijah is on the same Mount Horeb (also known as Mount Sinai), the Lord instructed Elijah, "Go out and stand on the mountain before the LORD." The Lord then "passed by" Elijah, and he heard the Lord in "a still small voice" (1 Kings 19:11–13, RSV-CE).[12] Through this episode, we see that the power of God in working salvation is not only seen in great deeds visible to all. God also comes among us in humility because only thus can the humble God of love be rightly known.

Moses leads Israel away from the worship of the false image of God in the golden calf (Exod. 32). It is through him that the Lord

---

12. For a sharp critique of Elijah (which seems a stretch to us) while recognizing the parallel to Moses, see Jerome T. Walsh, *1 Kings* (Collegeville, MN: Liturgical Press, 1996), 288–89.

gives Israel its great prayer, "Hear, O Israel: The LORD is our God, the LORD alone" (Deut. 6:4). Elijah likewise promotes the worship of the one true God. He confronts the king and his people about the false prophets of Baal who had entered the northern kingdom of Israel: "How long will you go limping with two different opinions? If the LORD is God, follow him; but if Baal, then follow him" (1 Kings 18:21).

The question Elijah poses is intended for us as well. Who is God? What images and ideas come to our minds when we speak of God? Because we live within a fallen history, we must reject false images of God in order to see the one God in a faithful manner. God's revelation tells us the truth that there is one true Creator God who knows us, who loves us, and who offers us mercy. In revealing himself, God prepares his people not only to believe that God exists but to trust the God who has reached out to us.

The Old Testament, therefore, does more than present a vision of God as the Creator of the universe. God reveals himself as a Father of Israel, a loving husband, a Savior and Redeemer, one who never gives up on his beloved people. Furthermore, the Old Testament, in its gradual and partial revelation of God, consistently bears within itself a promise of a greater revelation to come. Deuteronomy speaks of a prophet like Moses who will come (Deut. 18:15–22). Toward the end of the Old Testament, Malachi promises that God will send Elijah to his people (Mal. 4:5). The desire of Moses and Elijah to see the face of God will be fulfilled in Jesus Christ in an even-greater mode of infinite love, mercy, and humility toward sinners.

Knowing God as Creator

To think correctly of God is to distinguish God from all of the things of creation. But more than that, to think correctly of God as *one* is to recognize God as the continual source of the whole of creation, the superabundant fount of all finite being, whose contingent existence is entirely his gift. The Creator is distinct from the creation in such a way that the creation depends upon the Creator, whereas the Creator does not depend upon the creation.[13] Let us consider these truths as they are presented in certain paradigmatic biblical instances.

We have seen that Moses is the great teacher of the oneness of God. Moses received his call to lead the people of Israel out of Egypt when he was shepherding a flock near the foot of Mount Horeb. It is here that he encounters the Lord in a burning bush. This bush, burning without being consumed, forms an earthly image of the perpetual actuality of God, whose fiery existence and love never burn out.

Moses hears the words, "I am the God of your father, the God of Abraham, the God of Isaac, and the God of Jacob" (Exod. 3:6). He hides his face in awe and reverence and receives the promise that the Lord will use him as an instrument to rescue the Lord's people Israel from their slavery in Egypt. But Moses wants more: he asks the Lord for his name.

So God speaks to Moses and reveals his name, "I AM WHO I AM." Moses is to speak to the people of Israel and say "I AM has sent me to you" (Exod. 3:14).[14] What could it mean to say "I AM" or "I AM WHO I AM"? Earlier God had revealed himself, saying, "I am the God of Abraham, the God of Isaac, and the God of Jacob" (Exod. 3:6). In that way, God was describing his relation to the people of Israel. Now he simply stops after saying "I AM."

To grasp the significance of the Lord's words, we might compare them to the ways in which we are used to conversing. When we meet another person, we often introduce ourselves by describing specific

---

13. For discussion, see Reinhard Feldmeier and Hermann Spieckermann, *God of the Living: A Biblical Theology*, trans. Mark E. Biddle (Waco, TX: Baylor University Press, 2011), 251–70.

14. For further discussion of "I AM WHO I AM," see Thomas Joseph White, OP, *Exodus* (Grand Rapids, MI: Brazos Press, 2016), 39–44, 292–304.

relationships or work. I might say, "I am his father," "I am her husband," or "I am a university professor." If I were speaking more generally, I might begin by saying, "I am a citizen of the United States." If I wanted to speak as generally as possible—perhaps addressing someone from Mars who has never met an earthling before—I could begin by saying, "I am a *homo sapiens*, a rational animal." In that way, I would reveal something fundamental not only about who I am or what I am, but also in what *way* I am; I exist in the mode or form of human-ness.

By the same token, when the Lord reveals his name as "I AM WHO I AM," he is making a statement about his very mode of being. He is saying that his existence is so perfect that it makes sense to say God is *is-ness*. God is existence itself, the perfect, unfathomably superabundant fullness of actuality or existence, both causing and transcending all finite beings, even the being of the entire universe.

Names given within creation distinguish creatures from one another. God does not exist as merely the greatest creature alongside the rest of creation. Thus, he cannot have a name in the same way as do created realities. His name is unlike other names: he is "I AM." To speak of God in this manner unveils profound truths. God is unlike all creatures since all creatures have a finite existence. They exist as particular kinds of things, as only parts of the larger whole. God, however, does not exist as a particular kind of thing or as part of the larger whole. God does not fall in a category of "divine beings" or even as the highest being within the universe. Thus, in revealing his name as "I AM," God reveals himself to exist not as one created thing alongside other created things, nor even as the highest created thing among all created things (see Isa. 45). His infinite existence—the source of all finite existence, but radically unlike any limited, contingent mode of existence—contains within itself all the perfections that we might imagine: infinite and indescribable goodness, love, wisdom, and beauty. Again, when God says "I *AM*," he is saying that there is no act of finite "*am*-ness" within the created world that does not depend upon his infinite "*am*-ness." To call God "He who *is*" is to say that there is no "*is*" within the created world that does not depend contingently for its being upon his perfect "*is*."

In a real sense, then, God claims the entire verb "to be" for himself! All created existence comes from—or shares or participates in—God's transcendent infinite existence.[15] Were God separated from creation, as in deism, then God would be separated from us, and we from him. Were God identified with creation, as in pantheism or contemporary forms of seeing the universe as divine, then he would be trapped within the universe. What the Bible reveals is neither a separation of God from the world nor an identification between God and the world. Instead, it reveals a powerful *distinction* in which God, in his infinite plenitude, lovingly, freely, and continually causes all creaturely existence as the Creator.

Knowing God as Creator and Redeemer

Because God is the Creator, he can also be the Redeemer, supremely loving and caring, able to unite his creatures to his own infinite blessedness. Let us consider several instances in which Scripture attests to the interplay of God's revelation of himself as the Creator and the Redeemer. We can first see it in the revelation to Moses just discussed. When God reveals his name as "I *AM*"—namely, the Creator or source of all being—he also reveals his plan to redeem and rescue Israel from slavery in Egypt. Similarly, in 2 Maccabees, a mother tells her son: "I beg you, my child, to look at the heaven and the earth and

---

15. For further discussion of what we mean here, see Andrew Davison, *Participation in God: A Study in Christian Doctrine and Metaphysics* (Cambridge: Cambridge University Press, 2019).

see everything that is in them, and recognize that God did not make them out of things that existed. And in the same way the human race came into being. Do not fear this butcher [the tyrannical king], but prove worthy of your brothers. Accept death, so that in God's mercy I may get you back again along with your brothers" (2 Macc. 7:28–29). God acts as the Redeemer because he is first the Creator.

Yet, how do we come to the knowledge of God as the Creator? The Psalmist affirms, "The fool says in his heart, 'There is no God'" (Ps. 14:1). For the Psalmist, to fail to recognize God indicates a lack of wisdom. Wisdom refers to a judgment about the whole of reality. Proverbs teaches that "the fear of [or respect for] the LORD is the beginning of wisdom" (Prov. 9:10). Our decision whether or not to affirm God as the Creator is a judgment that commits our entire self, both head and heart. Whatever we decide on that question comes down to either a true or a false judgment about the whole of reality.

Humans have the ability to reach the very foundations of reality through the power of reason that differentiates us from other earthly creatures. In fact, the Bible teaches that humans have the ability to come to know God as Creator by reflecting on creation. Specifically, the order, goodness, and existence of created things manifest the intelligence and goodness of a Creator (Rom. 1:20).[16] Human reason's abilities receive tribute from the author of the book of Wisdom, who writes, "From the greatness and beauty of created things comes a corresponding perception of their Creator" (Wis. 13:5).

Why then does the existence of God seem doubtful to people? For one reason, people see the evil and suffering in the world and in their own lives and draw the wrong conclusions. As the Wisdom

---

16. See N.T. Wright, "The Letter to the Romans," in *The New Interpreter's Bible: Volume X*, ed. Leander E. Keck (Nashville, TN: Abingdon, 1994), 393–770, at 432; also N.T. Wright, *Paul and the Faithfulness of God: Book II, Parts III and IV* (Minneapolis, MN: Fortress Press, 2013), 766–67. For the contrary position, see Douglas A. Campbell, *The Deliverance of God: An Apocalyptic Rereading of Justification in Paul* (Grand Rapids, MI: Eerdmans, 2013).

of Solomon's author also notes, our reason does not always take us where it should. The Wisdom of Solomon explains that this error is not God's fault but ours. "For all people who were ignorant of God were foolish by nature; and they were unable from the good things that are seen to know the one who exists, nor did they recognize the artisan while paying heed to his works" (Wis. 13:1). Our folly consists in impatience: we often end our search for goodness once we have found creatures—or creature comforts—that enrapture us. Wisdom 13 makes this point explicitly: "If through delight in the beauty of these things people assumed them to be gods, let them know how much better than these is their Lord, for the author of beauty created them" (Wis. 13:3). The Wisdom of Solomon sadly observes about people who are extraordinarily learned but who remain unseeing when it comes to God, "If they had the power to know so much that they could investigate the world, how did they fail to find sooner the Lord of these things?" (Wis. 13:9).

There are consequences to failing to pursue the quest to know God. After all, only the true God may be worshiped above all created things for only the true God ultimately satisfies the full drama of human longing. We cannot be happy without God. When human beings center their lives around created goods, there inevitably follows competition and strife over these necessarily limited goods. In a verse that might sound overly simplistic at first, the book of Wisdom states, "The worship of idols . . . is the beginning and cause and end of every evil" (Wis. 14:27). Recall that idols refer to created things that become the highest goals or values in our lives. Paul echoes this teaching against idolatry when he writes that "the love of money is the root of all kinds of evil" (1 Tim. 6:10). Without God, our hearts pursue the wrong goods in the wrong ways, seeking happiness where it cannot be found.

Drawing upon the teaching of Wisdom 13, Paul writes in Romans 1:20, "Ever since the creation of the world his eternal power and divine nature, invisible though they are, have been understood and seen through the things that he has made." The order and organization of visible creation manifest the ordering and organizing power of the Creator. Unlike nonrational creatures, humans may discern the order and physical laws of the universe and so discover the Creator's power and wisdom. Moreover, the very being of the universe, finite as it is, requires a Maker.[17]

Paul has more to say than merely to praise the ability of human reason to know God's eternal power and deity. In a similar manner to the book of Wisdom's author, he argues sadly that those who do not recognize God are "without excuse" (Rom. 1:20). Once the highest good of the Creator is ignored, then created goods are necessarily loved in a disordered way, since only God is worthy of being loved with all of our heart, soul, and strength. The pull of this disordered love darkens our mind, and our desires become confused. Paul thus observes that those who knew God but did not honor him "exchanged the truth about God for a lie and worshiped and served the creature rather than the Creator" (Rom. 1:25; cf. Rom. 1:21, Matt. 6:24; Eph. 4:17–19). Paul states that all people have sinned, all have fallen short.

All of us are without excuse, but we are not without a future. The light of reason is good, but it is not enough. God has given the world the light of Christ.

Knowing the One God as Father, Son, and Holy Spirit

Knowing the truth about the Creator's existence and goodness is wonderful and meaningful, but it is not enough to heal our wounds

---

17. For further discussion, see Matthew Levering, *Proofs of God: Classical Arguments from Tertullian to Barth* (Grand Rapids, MI: Baker Academic, 2016).

and disorders, to remove our sins and injustices. More is necessary. At the heart of the New Testament revelation is the startling claim that Jesus Christ shares in the oneness of God.[18] God has "so loved the world that he gave his only Son" (John 3:16) to bear our sins and to reveal his infinite divine love for us. The Gospels present the Son's intimate relationship to the Father as the foundation of Jesus' identity and mission. Let's unfold this relationship by examining some pivotal moments in the life of Jesus.

Matthew, Mark, and Luke each depict Jesus' baptism as the starting point of his public ministry. In terse and powerful language, Matthew writes, "When Jesus had been baptized, just as he came up from the water, suddenly the heavens were opened to him and he saw the Spirit of God descending like a dove and alighting on him. And a voice from heaven said, 'This is my Son, the Beloved, with whom I am well pleased'" (Matt. 3:16–17; cf. Ps. 2:7; Isa. 42:1). Right at the start of his earthly ministry, Jesus is revealed as the one on whom the Spirit dwells and the beloved Son of God.

It was not unheard of in ancient Israel for a human being to receive the Spirit of God or even to be called a son of God. Israel's prophets were often filled with the Spirit, and Israel's kings would be called sons of God at their coronations; these experiences are always presented as new states that come upon the recipients (1 Sam. 16:13; Ps. 2:7). At Jesus' baptism, however, he does not enter into a new state of being adopted by the Father. Rather, he manifests his identity as the Spirit-filled Son of the Father.

Jesus' own prayers to the Father show forth the power and intimacy of the Father-Son relationship. Just before Jesus enters into his

---

18. For further discussion, see Richard Bauckham, *Jesus and the God of Israel: God Crucified and Other Studies on the New Testament's Christology of Divine Identity* (Grand Rapids, MI: Eerdmans, 2008); Bauckham, *Gospel of Glory: Major Themes in Johannine Theology* (Grand Rapids, MI: Baker Academic, 2015).

suffering and death, John 17 transmits an intimate prayer of Jesus to the Father. Jesus expresses in words his unique relationship to the Father: "Father, glorify me in your own presence with the glory that I had in your presence before the world existed. . . . Father, protect them in your name that you have given me, so that they may be one, as we are one" (John 17:5, 11).

When Jesus speaks of being one with the Father, this unity is more than a unity of a creature in love with the Creator. Jesus shares in the Creator's own glory; as the divine Son or Word, he is with the Father from all eternity (John 1:1–2). What is more, it is the Father's will that the unity and glory of the Father and the Son become, through the Son's mediation, the source of the disciples' own unity and glory (see also Matt. 11:25–27).

Luke presents another prayer of Jesus to the Father. This prayer has a richly Trinitarian dimension, depicting the actions of the Holy Spirit, the Son, and the Father as distinct yet unified. Jesus rejoices in the Holy Spirit as he reveals to his disciples the uniqueness of his relationship with the Father: "I thank you, Father, Lord of heaven and earth, because you have hidden these things from the wise and the intelligent and have revealed them to infants. . . . No one knows who the Son is except the Father, or who the Father is except the Son and anyone to whom the Son chooses to reveal him" (Luke 10:21–22). As we saw in John 17, the mission of the Son is to reveal the Father to others. Elsewhere in Luke, Jesus will say that the Father will give the Holy Spirit to anyone who asks (Luke 11:13). The Spirit is thus to be given to us, and the Son is to reveal the Father to us. We are called to enter the intimate communion of the Father, the Son, and the Spirit.

This truth explains an otherwise puzzling aspect of Jesus' words from Luke cited above: if the Father is the Lord of heaven and earth, and if human beings may know God as Creator by reflecting on creation, why then does Jesus say that no one knows the Father except the Son and those to whom the Son reveals him? To know God as the Creator is a fulfillment of the intellectual and loving capacities of the human creature. Nonetheless, to know God properly as Father signifies a higher perfection.

To know God as Father means that, in some way, we share in his nature as his adopted sons and daughters in the Son. The depths of this teaching are made further apparent when we recall Peter's response when Jesus asked, "Who do you say that I am?" Peter responded, "You are the Messiah [Christ], the Son of the living God," to which Jesus said, "Blessed are you, Simon son of Jonah! For flesh and blood has not revealed this to you, but my Father in heaven" (Matt. 16:15–17). The Father, not human reason or "flesh and blood," revealed to Peter the uniqueness of Jesus' divine Sonship. In Christ, we are caught up into the wondrous eternal communion of Father and Son in the Spirit.

If Jesus is truly the Son of the living God, then he shares God's nature not merely as a creature but as a divine Son. Most importantly for us, Jesus's unique Sonship becomes the pattern for our adoptive sonship. The same Peter who confesses Jesus as "the Son of the living God" teaches that all Christians are "participants of the divine nature" (2 Pet. 1:4).[19] To be a participant of the divine nature is to share intimately in the life of the Father, Son, and Holy Spirit as adopted children, beloved and cared for eternally.[20]

In this way, God reveals himself to be both one and three not only in himself but also for us. God the Father reveals his love for us

---

19. For helpful discussions of the complicated question of Petrine authorship—given that the letter could faithfully reflect Peter's testimony without having been actually written by Peter—see Richard J. Bauckham, *Jude, 2 Peter* (Nashville, TN: Thomas Nelson, 1996), 131–47; and Keating, *First and Second Peter, Jude*, 127–29.

20. See Daniel A. Keating, *First and Second Peter, Jude* (Grand Rapids, MI: Baker Academic, 2011), 139–42.

in sending his Son and his Spirit; Jesus reveals himself as the Son of God so that others may become sons and daughters of God; and the Holy Spirit's presence in Jesus is ordered to the Holy Spirit's presence in us as sons and daughters of God.

Let us look to Paul's summary of this teaching in Galatians: "But when the fullness of time had come, God sent his Son, born of a woman, born under the law, in order to redeem those who were under the law, so that we might receive adoption as children. And because you are children, God has sent the Spirit of his Son into our hearts, crying, 'Abba! Father!'" (Gal. 4:4–6). Note the language of *sending*: "God *sent* his Son" and "God has *sent* the Spirit of his Son." These two sendings, or (in theological terms) missions, anchor the whole of our reality, allowing us to enter into a new relationship with God. Because of them, not only may we come to know and love him as our Creator, but we also may cry out to him, "Abba! Father!" (Rom. 8:15). God sent his Son and sent his Holy Spirit so that we might become sons and daughters, sharing in the Son's own intimate relationship with the Father and using the very language to address God that Jesus used when he prayed: "Abba, Father" (Mark 14:36).

But if the revelation of God as both one and three is central to the Christian faith, why is the doctrine of the Trinity not more explicitly stated in the New Testament? In response, we must bear in mind that the New Testament was written as part of the apostolic proclamation of the Good News that God had established a New Covenant by the death and Resurrection of Jesus Christ. Thus, the Bible does not explicitly ask or answer all theological questions. The Bible does not stand alone; rather, it always lives within the ongoing Spirit-filled community of the Church. With that said, it can be shown that the inner logic of the New Testament is fundamentally Trinitarian.

John presents the Trinitarian mystery in Jesus' discourse during the Last Supper. Jesus tells his disciples that, when he goes away, the Father and he will send the Holy Spirit to dwell with them. And he repeats that same point at least three different times during the discourse: "I will ask the Father, and he will give you another Advocate, to be with you forever. This is the Spirit of truth, whom the world cannot receive" (John 14:16–17); "When the Advocate comes, whom I will send to you from the Father, the Spirit of truth who comes from the Father, he will testify on my behalf" (John 15:26); and, "When the Spirit of truth comes, he will guide you into all the truth" (John 16:13). In this way, Jesus amplifies his teaching that the Father and the Son are one, and that this oneness of the Father and the Son is also shared by the promised Spirit of truth.

Paul displays a similar Trinitarian logic in his Letter to Titus through his Trinitarian use of the title of the Savior.[21] After Paul introduces himself as a "servant of God and an apostle of Jesus Christ," he speaks of the command he has received from "God *our Savior*" (Titus 1:1, 3; emphasis added). To confess God as the Savior is language that has been hammered out in the Old Testament. When the Lord delivers Israel out of Egypt, Moses and the people exclaim, "The Lord is my strength and my might, and he has become *my salvation*" (Exod. 15:2; emphasis added). The prophet Isaiah rejected the claims of idols and proclaimed that God alone is the Savior, "I am the LORD your *God*, the Holy One of Israel, *your Savior*" (Isa. 43:3; emphasis added). Immediately after calling God the Savior, Paul writes, "Grace and peace from God the Father and *Christ Jesus our Savior*" (Titus 1:4; emphasis added). Jesus shares in God the Father's identity as Savior.

---

21. For authorship questions regarding Titus (often considered to have not been written by Paul) in favor of Pauline authorship, see George T. Montague, SM, *First and Second Timothy, Titus* (Grand Rapids, MI: Baker Academic, 2008), 16–21.

Paul further shows that the Holy Spirit likewise shares in the divine work of salvation. In Titus 3, as he reiterates that both God and Jesus Christ are our Savior, he also identifies the Holy Spirit as the one by whom our salvation is accomplished: "When the goodness and loving kindness of *God our Savior* appeared, *he saved us*, not because of any works of righteousness that we had done, but according to his mercy, through the water of rebirth and *renewal by the Holy Spirit*. This Spirit he poured out upon us richly through *Jesus Christ our Savior*" (Titus 3:4–6; emphasis added). Who then is our Savior? God the Father *is* our Savior, who acts *through* Jesus Christ, and *in* the Holy Spirit. All three share the one divine identity while maintaining their distinctiveness. They carry out the divine, saving action in an ordered relationship—from the Father, through the Son, in the Holy Spirit.

Paul likewise appeals to the unified but distinct relations of the Spirit, the Son, and the Father when he calls the faithful to live in peace and unity.[22] In Ephesians 4, he writes, "There is one body and *one Spirit*, just as you were called to the one hope of your calling, *one Lord*, one faith, one baptism, *one God and Father* of all, who is above all and through all and in all" (Eph. 4:4–6; emphasis added). The title "Lord" designates Jesus Christ since Paul also writes in the same letter, "the Lord Jesus Christ" (Eph. 1:2), and since Paul interchanges "a prisoner for Christ Jesus" (Eph. 3:1) with a "prisoner in the Lord" (Eph. 4:1). This passage speaks of one Spirit, one Lord Jesus Christ, and one God and Father. Recall that Paul here is exhorting the church in Ephesus to live in unity. The logic of Paul's appeal depends upon the prior unity of God to serve as the foundation for the unity of the Church. When Paul speaks of the "one Spirit," the "one Son,"

---

22. For further discussion, see Wesley Hill, *Paul and the Trinity: Persons, Relations, and the Pauline Letters* (Grand Rapids, MI: Eerdmans, 2015).

and the "one God and Father," he does not speak of three entities but of one God, a unity now revealed to include the Son and the Spirit.

The announcement of the Trinitarian identity of God is a truth that saves. Paul summarizes this ordered Trinitarian agency earlier when he affirms that "for through [Christ] both of us have access in one Spirit to the Father" (Eph. 2:18). To affirm a unity of saving action *through* the Son, *in* the Spirit, *to* the Father is to see that one has been brought from sin and separation from God to forgiveness and intimacy. We now have access to the Father in the Spirit through the Son; the fullness of God's life has been opened to us and we have been called to enter.

The Incarnation and Resurrection of Jesus Christ

At Christmas, the Church's liturgy offers three different sets of Mass readings, each one assigned to a different time of day when Mass is celebrated. Taken together, these readings include not only the stories from Matthew and Luke concerning Jesus' birth but also the prologue of John. That is because Christmas is not merely the feast of the Nativity but also the feast of the Incarnation.

What does the Incarnation really mean and what is its importance in the Christian faith? Let us examine some key passages from the beginning of John to answer this question. Echoing Genesis' "In the beginning God created the heavens and the earth" (Genesis 1:1), John begins, "*In the beginning* was the Word, and the Word was with God, and the Word was God" (1:1; emphasis added).[23] John thus announces a new creation story, the story of our salvation. In telling this story of the new creation, the Evangelist introduces the Word—or *Logos* in Greek—of God. John continues, "He was in the beginning with God. All things came into being through him, and

---

23. See the illuminating discussion in Craig S. Keener, *The Gospel of John: A Commentary*, vol. 1 (Grand Rapids, MI: Baker Academic, 2003), 291–310, 339–381.

without him not one thing came into being" (1:2–3). The Word is the one through whom all things were made and the one through whom all things will be re-made.

John then presents the Word as the life of the world and the light of the human race. There is a straightforward logic to this role of the Word. In all of our experience and understanding of the world, we see life begotten by living things. So also, the light of reason is begotten by reasoning beings. Thus, if we see living and intelligent beings in the world, then it is reasonable to assume a living and intelligent Creator.

The divine Word in John's Gospel is identified with life and light: "In him was life, and the life was the light of all people" (John 1:4). We saw earlier that all created things participate in limited modes in God's own perfect existence. Through John's insight, we can now see that human beings also participate, in a unique way, in God's own intelligence and life. Human reason or "word" (in Greek, both are called *logos*) shares in the divine Word (*Logos*).

In addition to the presence of the Word in all creation and especially in human beings, the Word takes on a previously unheard-of presence by becoming a fellow human being in our history. John summarizes this fundamental reality of the New Creation and the New Covenant: "The Word became flesh and lived among us, and we have seen his glory, the glory of a father's only son, full of grace and truth" (John 1:14). The Word that is the light and life of men now becomes a particular man. The term "flesh" is *sarx* in Greek, which is translated as *caro* in Latin, so the term "in-*carn*-ation" means becoming enfleshed. Thus to see the man Jesus Christ is to behold the glory of the only Son of God. God, who is transcendent of and present to his creation, can truly become man because God's infinite "to be" does not compete with or occupy the same ontological level

as a creature. God assumes a human nature to perfect union with
himself in the person of the Son.

Sacred Scripture situates the Incarnation within the human
person's desire to see God. John writes, "The law indeed was given
through Moses; grace and truth came through Jesus Christ. No one
has ever seen God. It is God the only Son, who is close to the Father's
heart, who has made him known" (John 1:18). The only Son, now
incarnate as Jesus of Nazareth, makes known the eternal Father.
Later in John's Gospel, a dramatic dialogue takes place at the Last
Supper. The Apostle Philip, echoing the desires of Moses and Elijah,
asks Jesus, "Lord, show us the Father, and we will be satisfied." Jesus
responds, "Whoever has seen me has seen the Father. . . . Believe me
that I am in the Father and the Father in me" (John 14:8–11). To see
the incarnate Son is to see the Father (cf. 1 John 3:2).

In Jesus Christ, God takes on a human face. As we saw earlier, Paul taught in Romans that the invisible God is knowable, in
his eternal power and deity, through the visible things of creation.
Through the Incarnation, God is no longer visible simply through
the grandeur of his creation; now he is visible as supreme mercy and
love in and through the man Jesus Christ. Likewise, in Colossians,
Paul describes Christ as "the image [or *icon*] of the invisible God"
(Col. 1:15). The invisible God is now visible. And Paul does not soften
this arresting claim by saying it is metaphorical. Instead, he intensifies the point when he writes a few verses later, "All the fullness of
God was pleased to dwell [in Christ]" (Col. 1:19).

But how can all the fullness of God dwell in a human? In the
Old Testament, we discover initial ways in which God chose to dwell
among his people Israel, especially in the tabernacle and temple.
When God comes to dwell in the majestic temple of Solomon, Solomon declares that "heaven and the highest heaven cannot contain

you, much less this house that I have built!" (1 Kings 8:27). It was understood that the Creator of the heavens and the earth dwelt in a mysterious way in the temple in order to enable Israel to worship him properly.

In contrast to the spiritual presence of God in the temple, the Incarnation is a more radical form of indwelling. This indwelling or incarnation means that God becomes substantially present in the world as a human being. No one would have said that God was the temple, but John teaches that the "Word became flesh." Let us again look at the great expression from John 1:14, which describes the reality of the Incarnation: "The Word became flesh and lived among us, and we have seen his glory, the glory as of a father's only son, full of grace and truth" (John 1:14). The Greek word translated here as "lived among us" could also be translated as "tabernacled among us" or even "templed" among us.[24]

The theme of indwelling in John's Gospel becomes even clearer when we recall the first tabernacle built by Moses, which was a large, portable, tent-like structure for divine worship. Upon completion, "the cloud settled upon it, and the glory of the LORD filled the tabernacle" (Exod. 40:35). In the first tabernacle, the cloud, which signifies the presence of the Lord, fills the tabernacle, and then the glory of the Lord fills the tabernacle. This same pattern is fulfilled in Jesus Christ. In the new tabernacle, the new temple, of God, the Word becomes flesh, and he is filled with the glory of the Lord. Those who see Jesus as the Lord behold his glory, "glory as of the only Son from the Father" (John 1:14 RSV-CE).

In addition to the glory of Jesus revealed to those with the eyes of faith, there was also one time before the Resurrection when his glory became visible to earthly eyes. Shortly before Jesus' final entry

---

24. See *The Word on Fire Bible*, vol. 1, *The Gospels* (Park Ridge, IL: Word on Fire, 2020), 463.

into Jerusalem, Peter, James, and John went up with Jesus on the mountain to pray. As Jesus was praying, "the appearance of his face changed, and his clothes became dazzling white.... Now Peter and his companions were weighed down with sleep; but since they had stayed awake, they saw his glory" (Luke 9:29, 32).[25] The Gospel accounts of the Transfiguration (in Matthew, Mark, and Luke) depict Moses and Elijah conversing with the glorified Jesus. Moses and Elijah represent the Law and the prophets, all of which point to Jesus Christ (see Luke 24:26–27). But there is more. Earlier we observed how Moses and Elijah encountered God in dramatic and powerful experiences in which God somehow appeared to them. Yet remember that, in their experiences, God's face was not visible to them. This all changes when Moses and Elijah appear at the Transfiguration. For the first time, they behold the face of God.[26]

The Gospels continue to disclose Jesus' divine identity in other episodes. Matthew, Mark, and John all tell the story of Jesus walking on water near the disciples' boat on the Sea of Galilee. Mark presents an apparently odd detail when he says that Jesus was walking toward them on the sea and that "he intended to pass them by" but that they saw him and became afraid (Mark 6:48). Was Jesus merely playing tricks on his disciples? It is helpful here to recall that the verb "to pass by" is a specific phrase for divine appearance and was used when God appeared to Moses and to Elijah.[27] With this in mind, Jesus was not intending to trick his disciples but meant "to pass by" his disciples walking on the water and so reveal his divine glory specifically to them.

---

25. For historical-critical discussion, see Michael Wolter, *The Gospel According to Luke: Volume I (Luke 1—9:50)*, trans. Wayne Coppins and Christopher Heilig (Waco, TX: Baylor University Press, 2016), 391–96.

26. See Brant Pitre, *The Case for Jesus: The Biblical and Historical Evidence for Christ* (New York, NY: Image, 2016).

27. See Richard B. Hays, *Reading Backwards: Figural Christology and the Fourfold Gospel Witness* (Waco, TX: Baylor University Press, 2014).

One more way in which Jesus is presented as the incarnate Word is when he takes upon himself the name of God revealed to Moses: "he who is" or "I AM." In John and in Revelation, the lips of Jesus frequently reverberate with the expression "I am"—*ego eimi* in Greek. In one of his arguments with the Jewish authorities, Jesus makes a striking claim: "Truly, truly, I say to you, before Abraham was, *I am*" (John 8:58; emphasis added). The narrative makes it clear that his audience recognized he was intentionally taking up the divine name; the authorities condemned him for blasphemy and "took up stones to throw at him." Later in John, when Jesus is arrested in the garden, the Jewish soldiers and leaders ask for Jesus of Nazareth. Jesus replies "'I am' . . . [and] they drew back and fell to the ground" (John 18:6).

In the book of Revelation, Jesus says, "I am the Alpha and the Omega, the first and the last, the beginning and the end" (Rev. 22:13). Alpha and Omega are the first and last letters of the Greek alphabet, the beginning and the end. The book of Revelation uses this same language not only to speak of Jesus but also to speak of God, "'I am the Alpha and the Omega,' says the Lord God, who is and who was and who is to come, the Almighty" (Rev. 1:8) The prophet Isaiah uses these same expressions to identify the God of Israel: "I am the first and I am the last; besides me there is no God" (Isaiah 44:6; 45:5). Jesus is associated both with the divine name, "I am," and with attributes that only belong to God: to be the living one, to be alive forever, to be the first and the last.

The Resurrection of Jesus and Life's Purpose

The Incarnation culminates in the death and Resurrection of Jesus Christ, by which the whole world is redeemed. God's Son becomes a man, lives among us, suffers a horrific death, rises to glorified life on earth, manifests himself to his Apostles, and then ascends to reign with the Father. It is a dramatic rescue mission in which God enters the territory of sin and death in order to free the human race from our tyrannous enslavement to sin and the devil and to restore us to full communion with himself. In a later chapter, we will consider the way in which the death of Jesus reconciles us with God. Here we wish to focus on the Good News that Christ has risen from the dead.[28]

The preaching of the Apostles focuses on one announcement: Jesus has risen from the dead and forgiveness of sins and eternal life are now possible through him. Paul describes the pivotal role of the Resurrection to the Corinthians: "For I handed on to you as of first importance what I in turn had received: that Christ died for our sins in accordance with the scriptures, and that he was buried, and that he was raised on the third day in accordance with the scriptures, and that he appeared to Cephas [Peter], then to the twelve" (1 Cor. 15:3–5). Let us unpack this key testimony to Christ's death and Resurrection.

Paul uses highly precise and formulaic language in two ways. First, he begins by showing that this is not something that he invented on his own but something that he received and then handed on. The word for "I delivered to you" is *tradere* in Latin, from which we get our word "tradition," meaning what is handed on from one person and received by another. In this way, Paul provides a witness to one of the foundational elements of the apostolic tradition. The Apostles received and then handed on the Good News of the death and Resurrection of Christ.

Second, Paul repeats the phrase "in accordance with the scriptures" twice within one sentence (1 Cor. 15:3–4). The first usage refers to Christ's death for our sins; the second refers to Christ's Resurrection. Christ's death and Resurrection are God's startling fulfillment of the covenants and promises of the Old Testament. The language

---

28. For further discussion, see Matthew Levering, *Did Jesus Rise from the Dead? Historical and Theological Reflections* (Oxford: Oxford University Press, 2019).

of "according to the scriptures" not only is foundational in Paul's preaching but also is recorded in the Gospels. When the risen Jesus appeared to the two disciples on the way to Emmaus, he explained to them that it was "necessary that the Messiah [Christ] should suffer these things and then enter into his glory" (Luke 24:26). Then Luke writes, "Beginning with Moses and all the prophets, he interpreted to them the things about himself in all the scriptures" (Luke 24:27).[29] The Apostles consistently preached that Christ's death and Resurrection were not isolated or accidental events but rather were the primary way in which God brought to fulfillment his promises to Abraham and Israel and through them brought salvation to all the other nations of the world.

At Pentecost, when the Holy Spirit descends upon the Apostles, Peter proclaims to the crowd of amazed onlookers that Jesus of Nazareth who was crucified has now been "raised up" and "made both Lord and Messiah [Christ]" (Acts 2:24, 36).[30] Later Peter will preach that his listeners had unwittingly "killed the Author of life, whom God raised from the dead" (Acts 3:15). The early preaching of the Resurrection includes the reality that Jesus had such a unique sharing in the divine power that he could be called "the Author of life." Only someone who shared in our human nature could suffer death and then rise again; only someone who shared in the divine nature would be able to become the author of new life through his death and Resurrection.

The Resurrection of the Son of God is the Good News. Paul summarizes the Gospel: "If you confess with your lips that Jesus is Lord

---

29. For discussion of the encounter of the two disciples with the risen Jesus on the road to Emmaus, see Robert Barron, *The Priority of Christ: Toward a Postliberal Catholicism* (Grand Rapids, MI: Brazos Press, 2007), 118–123.

30. For an historical-critical evaluation of the speeches in Acts, see Craig S. Keener, *Acts: An Exegetical Commentary*, vol. 1, *Introduction and 1:1–2:47* (Grand Rapids, MI: Baker Academic, 2012), 258–319; see also 862–990 on this particular speech of Peter (Acts 2:14–40).

and believe in your heart that God raised him from the dead, you will be saved" (Rom. 10:9). And Peter, when asked how he and John were able to perform miracles, responded by showing how salvation is in the name of Jesus: "Let it be known to all of you, and to all the people of Israel, that this man is standing before you in good health by the name of Jesus Christ of Nazareth, whom you crucified, whom God raised from the dead. . . . There is salvation in no one else, for there is no other name under heaven given among mortals by which we must be saved" (Acts 4:10, 12). God alone can save—and he has done so through Jesus Christ.

Paul encourages the faithful to think about the meaning of their lives in light of the Resurrection. As a kind of thought experiment, he invites his readers (or rather listeners, since his letters were often read aloud at church gatherings) to ask what would be different if this earthly life were all there is. And he boldly answers, "If for this life only we hoped in Christ, we are of all people most to be pitied" (1 Cor. 15:19). Likewise, he adds, "If the dead are not raised, 'Let us eat and drink, for tomorrow we die'" (1 Cor. 15:32). In this way, the Apostle challenges a this-worldly view of Christianity that treats the faith as though it were merely a self-help manual promising earthly peace and prosperity. The author of Hebrews summarizes the mindset to be adopted by the faithful: "For here we have no lasting city, but we are looking for the city that is to come" (Heb. 13:14). Just as the center of all reality is revealed to be the Trinitarian, Creator God, so our earthly life is shown to be a pilgrimage to God the Father, through the crucified and risen Son, in the Spirit.

The fundamental disposition of the Christian is thus one of hope and trust in God. Hope expresses confidence in attaining the goal of eternal life with God not due to our own efforts but due to his mercy. Paul holds firmly to the hope of the glory to come. He writes, "I consider that the sufferings of this present time are not worth comparing with the glory about to be revealed to us" (Rom. 8:18). This heavenly glory gives Paul's life direction and purpose. "But this one thing I do," he says, "forgetting what lies behind and straining forward to what lies ahead, I press on toward the goal for the prize of the heavenly call of God in Christ Jesus" (Phil. 3:13–14). All people are likewise called to have the same hope in the glory that is to come.

This hope for glory helps Christians discover the true meaning of their lives. No matter how much we suffer either from our own faults or those of others, Paul invites us to remember we too are called to rise with Christ and to experience the fruits of his Resurrection in our lives today.

Jesus risen—and ascended—gives his followers a new mission and purpose. In the Holy Spirit and through the Son, who now sits at the right hand of the Father, we are called to become united to the Father for eternity. His followers are to proclaim the Trinitarian life they have received so that others may enter that union with God. Jesus gives the Great Commission: "All authority in heaven and on earth has been given to me. Go therefore and make disciples of all nations, baptizing them in the name of the Father and of the Son and of the Holy Spirit, and teaching them to obey everything that I have commanded you. And remember, I am with you always, to the end of the age" (Matt. 28:18–20).

Conclusion

Does God exist? Yes, God is the Creator of the universe. According to Scripture, human reason can know the truth about the existence of God who is the source of all that is good, true, and beautiful in the universe. The capacity of human reason to come to know God, however, also reveals just how much we have failed to know and love him with all of our heart, mind, and strength. Human history should be a story of men and women returning the love of their Maker. Instead it is the story of our pridefully loving ourselves and the created things of this world more than the Creator and so forming a distorted image of God as either spiteful and unfair or indifferent and untrustworthy.

Thankfully, God did not leave us in our sinful condition with these false conceptions of God and the meaning of our lives. In his revelation to Israel, he already began to show who he truly is and how we truly yearn to know his life-giving love. God reveals to Moses his perfect existence as the "I AM," the Creator of everything that is. And God likewise shows himself to Moses as the merciful and powerful Redeemer of Israel.

In the Incarnation of the Word and the sending of the Holy Spirit, God revealed that in his one divine nature, supremely humble and merciful, he is Father, Son, and Spirit. Through Christ, this God has acted decisively to allow us to enter a new relationship with him as adopted sons and daughters in the Spirit. This relationship is sealed by the Resurrection and Ascension of Christ.

The apostolic testimony is clear. The Good News is not just that some man has been raised from the dead. Rather the Good News is that the living God, who already began to reveal himself and his goodness by forming his people Israel, has revealed himself in Israel's Messiah as the one who enters into the very depths of our sorrow and meaninglessness. In Jesus, we have redemption. In Jesus, we see the true face of God. It is he who, having proclaimed his identity and inaugurated his kingdom by calling his disciples and teaching them, reconciles all things on the cross. It is this man who is raised from the dead to glorious life. These are truths worth believing—and worth living—united to "the Author of life, whom God raised from the dead" (Acts 3:15).

CHAPTER 2

Why Listen to the Church?

"The obedience of faith" (Romans 1:5)

How do Catholics who drift away from the faith think about the Catholic Church? Even if we believe at some level that God exists and loves us, why should the Church's claims about God be privileged above other views? Isn't it enough—and perhaps even better—for each of us to find our own personal God and determine our own beliefs? One contemporary lapsed Catholic, Mary, offers some insight based on her observations of her Catholic friends, most of whom are lapsed like her: "If you ask them, they'll say they are Catholics. They go to church maybe once a year. . . . Their attitude is, either they can identify something that they really like about the Catholic Church, such as family life, or its social justice side. . . . Or, [their faith is] something they don't think about."[1]

Many people who were baptized Catholic have an attitude similar to Mary's friends. Faith is, at most, a personal thing that involves one's own beliefs about God and the purpose of life. Often such Catholics, as they begin to doubt their faith, come to think that faith in God and Christ is opposed to reason and facts. They may assume that faith is now impossible since modern science has gone so much further than the ancient world of the Bible. To them, faith seems to be, at best, something people invented long ago to help understand the mysteries of life. They might admit that Catholicism points

---

1. Dean R. Hoge, William D. Dinges, Mary Johnson, SND de N, and Juan L. Gonzales, Jr., *Young Adult Catholics: Religion in the Culture of Choice* (Notre Dame: University of Notre Dame Press, 2001), 111.

toward the unknowable divine mysteries that every religion seeks to express. But the Church's claim to speak on God's behalf and to invite people to follow its specific teachings on faith and morals seem rigid or simply unintelligible to them.

On the other hand, a Catholic who, in faith, tries to hear God speaking through the Church might well be discouraged by the Church's sheer messiness over the course of history. The Bible itself reveals many arguments and divisions among the people of Israel over many centuries as well as serious disagreements among the Apostles during Jesus' life and soon thereafter. The Church in each century seems filled with arguments and divisions.

If both the Bible and the Church contain tensions, then why should we suppose that they have the authority or ability to hand on faithfully the authoritative content of a divine revelation? Should anyone really listen to the Bible and the Church as though God speaks authoritatively through them or as though their solemn teachings should command our belief?

According to the Bible, faith is not merely a love of particular Catholic things—be they liturgical vestments, hymns, church buildings, or the Christmas season. Faith is not like supporting a political party or a favorite sports team. Instead, faith says to God, "Yes, I believe in you." It is a hearing that draws us to the God who loves us and who has spoken in order to free us from our slavery to sin and death. Hearing Jesus Christ leads us to union with him. His path is one of obedience to God's will, because God's will is perfect love. We too are invited into this obedience—an obedience founded not upon subjection but rather upon love.

Understood in this way, faith is a willing assent to the God who reveals himself through his word and who thereby frees us for the fullness of life. Hence it is a unique and deeply personal encounter with our Creator, beyond any encounter that could take place by means of human powers alone. God's Word, however, does not come to us in individualistic isolation but through the Church he founded on Peter and the Apostles and their successors down to this day. The Church is the living community that receives and shares the saving life and redeeming words of Jesus Christ. Of course, salvation history shows that human beings, within the process of becoming and being God's people, have often failed to respond fully to God. The Bible does not hide this reality. But the Bible also shows that God does not wait for us to fix ourselves. Rather, he comes to us and offers us hope in his power and mercy. Despite our human weaknesses, Christ does not fail in speaking his saving truth to us through his Scripture and his Church.

Hearing the God Who Speaks

Not surprisingly, many modern societies bristle at the word "obedience." This word is often reserved for children's obedience to parents, or for dogs who attend obedience school. The image that comes to mind is often that of one person having control over another. Such an understanding misses the key element of the obedience of faith. God has no wish to control us. The English word obedience comes from the Latin *obedire*, meaning "to listen to." Obedience freely says, "Yes, I will listen. I will trust you."

God has the power to reveal himself. But divine revelation must be heard to be received. The pre-eminent daily prayer of the Jewish people, known as the *Shema*, begins, "Hear [*Shema*], O Israel: The LORD is our God, the LORD alone is one LORD. You shall love the LORD your God will all your heart, and with all your soul, and with all your might" (Deut. 6:4–5). Jesus quotes this prayer in answer to the question, "Which is the greatest commandment?"

We tend to focus on the call to love God (Matt. 22:37). Before the call to love God, however, is the command to hear God. We cannot love someone to whom we do not listen. Jesus categorically affirms the necessity of hearing God: "He who has ears to hear, let him hear" (Matt. 11:15 RSV-CE). Hearing makes possible a two-sided relationship. Jesus says, "My sheep hear my voice. I know them, and they follow me" (John 10:27). Just as God created the world by his mysterious "speaking" in Genesis 1, so he truly has spoken in history.[2] God's speech has a purpose not merely to gratify human curiosity about God but to unite a people in communion with the divine life and love.

Faith, at its heart, is listening to the truth about God's plan. As such, the story of the prophet Samuel is the story of each person before God. The young man, upon hearing the Lord's call, responds as he was instructed by Eli the priest—"Speak, for your servant is listening" (1 Sam. 3:10). And so Samuel sits before the Lord, listening. The Psalms echo this disposition of faithful hearing: "Let me hear what God the Lord will speak, for he will speak peace to his people" (Ps. 85:8).

Paul likewise emphasizes the need to hear what God has communicated. He writes, "Faith comes from what is heard" (Rom. 10:17), and the unique provenance of God's own word forms the basis for all of his preaching: "We also constantly give thanks to God for this, that when you received the word of God that you heard from us, you accepted it not as a human word but as what it really is, God's word, which is also at work in you believers" (1 Thess. 2:13). Paul does not preach his own word but the word he has received from God.

---

2. For further discussion, see Mats Wahlberg, *Revelation as Testimony: A Philosophical-Theological Study* (Grand Rapids, MI: Eerdmans, 2014); Nicholas Wolterstorff, *Divine Discourse: Philosophical Reflections on the Claim that God Speaks* (Cambridge: Cambridge University Press, 1995).

This Word of God is the word of salvation and Good News. Hebrews summarizes the power of God's message: "The word of God is living and active, sharper than any two-edged sword" (Heb. 4:12). What then has God spoken in the Bible? Above all, the Bible speaks of God's love for his creatures and how this love drives his actions across history to restore us to himself. "For God so loved the world . . ." (John 3:16). When we listen to God's revelation, we know that we are not alone in this universe, not without love, not without hope.

A Covenantal Relationship

God's healing and renewal takes the form of covenant.[3] The making of the covenant in Exodus includes several stages, but we will focus on the aspect of hearing and obedience.

In Exodus 19, the Lord summarizes this history of his faithfulness to Israel and his intention for them in this covenantal relationship: "You have seen what I did to the Egyptians, and how I bore you on eagles' wings and brought you to myself. Now therefore, if you obey my voice and keep my covenant, you shall be my treasured possession out of all the peoples" (Exod. 19:4–5). With these words, the Lord showed that he is not merely a more powerful version of the Egyptian Pharaoh; he does not capture his people into a new slavery.[4] Instead, God grants his people the dignity of choice: "*If* you obey my voice."

By inviting his people to obedience, God does not conquer by force but allows the people freely to enter into a new relationship with him. "You shall be my treasured possession," he tells the Israelites (Exod. 19:5), letting them know that they shall be a people

---

3. For background, see Scott W. Hahn, *Kinship by Covenant: A Canonical Approach to the Fulfillment of God's Saving Promises* (New Haven, CT: Yale University Press, 2009).

4. See Jonathan Sacks, *Covenant and Conversation: A Weekly Reading of the Jewish Bible. Exodus: The Book of Redemption* (Jerusalem: Maggid Books, 2010).

beloved and cared for by the living God. The people then respond by freely giving their consent: "Everything that the LORD has spoken we will do" (Exod. 19:8). As we witness throughout the biblical story, our freedom is never an end in itself. It finds its perfection in our gift of ourselves to God and to one another in love.

Beyond the need for us to say "yes" to God as the Israelites did to enter into the covenant, the Bible also describes what we must do to remain in this new relationship with God. The Ten Commandments in Exodus 20 have pride of place, as God's instruction to Israel attempts to straighten out our wounded human nature.

Through the commandments, God first leads us to have no other gods, to worship his holy name, and to set aside the Sabbath in his honor. God then invites us to be further transformed in our relationships with one another in accord with our better selves: "Honor your father and your mother," "you shall not murder . . . not commit adultery . . . not steal." He calls for a renewal not only of our actions but even of our words and desires: "You shall not bear false witness against your neighbor . . . not covet your neighbor's wife . . . not covet your neighbor's house . . . or anything that belongs to your neighbor."

The biblical witness confirms that God initiates the gift of his Law and that this Law is recognizable as a good and holy gift from God. We become more fully human and more truly free when we love God our Creator above all created goods and love our neighbor as ourselves. Indeed, the Bible presents the commandments not as a burden but as a way to freedom, "the path of life" (Ps. 16:11).

Following the giving of the Ten Commandments, Exodus 21–23 presents a number of more particular laws concerning justice toward one another and toward God. These apply the foundational laws of the Decalogue to the specific circumstances of the people of Israel. Although the specifications of the Law may change over time, the foundational laws do not since they are rooted in what all humans owe to God and one another in justice.

The prophet Jeremiah later summarizes God's calling of his people: "For in the day that I brought your ancestors out of the land of Egypt, . . . this command I gave them: 'Obey my voice, and I will be your God, and you shall be my people; and walk only in the way that I command you, so that it may be well with you'" (Jer. 7:22–23). Here we see the same precise order: first, listening to God's word; then, becoming his people; and finally, walking in his ways. We respond by listening to him, by becoming his, and by living according to his ways. The commandments are not a path by which we earn God's loving mercy; God always takes the initiative in grace.

After the declaration of consent and the gift of the commandments, the stage is set for the "making" of the covenant itself. Exodus 24 presents the making of the covenant in a cultic form: the sacrifice of the animals and the sealing of the covenant through the sprinkling of blood. The covenant binds God to the people and establishes bonds that are at once political and familial. God will be a king and a father to them. After Moses reminds the people once more of the Law, the people respond, "All that the LORD has spoken we will do, and we will be obedient" (Exod. 24:7). The promise of obedience is a promise to hear and to remember all that has been said and to live according to God's word.

The people's disastrous disobedience comes all too quickly after such a promise. Saying "yes" to God means saying "no" to other gods. And yet the people, lacking firmness in their faith, are quick to embrace an idol. Less than forty days after the covenant ceremony, the people of Israel engage in worship of the golden calf and they revel in immorality (Exod. 32). Although it is unusual today to find someone worshiping a golden calf, people continue to preoccupy themselves in an idolatrous manner with objects that are not God, but that deliver temporary pleasure or false security. Thankfully, God understands his people's weakness and has a plan for helping his people turn toward him, first through his subsequent covenants with Israel and ultimately through the New Covenant of Jesus Christ.

At this point, let us consider how God makes himself known to his people. First of all, the Bible is adamant that God speaks. The unique character of his speech, and the presence of human mediation, mean that we cannot grasp directly the ways in which God makes himself known. Nonetheless, he, as the living God, has the power to make himself known and does in fact do so. Second, when God speaks, he invites the people into a new relationship with him.

The people of Israel handed on God's revelation in a fully historical way, in accord with the ups and downs of the community over the centuries. There is a revealing incident in the story of Josiah, one of the last kings of Judah. As his high priest was cleaning out the temple after years of idolatrous worship, Josiah came across the "book of the law" (2 Kings 22:3–22). The king responded with great faithfulness to the Lord. He read the entire "book of the covenant" before all of the assembled people, renewed the covenant, restored faithful worship in the temple, and even celebrated the first Passover in generations (2 Kings 3).

Thus, the Bible does not hide the fact that parts of Sacred Scripture that gave knowledge of the great covenant were lost for generations! Human unfaithfulness does not overcome God's faithfulness. Isaiah addresses the same truth when he says that as the rain always waters the land and brings forth fruit when it falls, so also will it be with God's word: "So shall my word be that goes out from my mouth; it shall not return to me empty, but it shall accomplish that which I purpose" (Isa. 55:10–11). God's word is not stopped by human failure.

Amid the complexities and confusions that are part of the history of God's people, the Old Testament directs our focus to the goodness of the commandments and the way in which they address the fundamental situation of human existence. The commandments reveal the way of life and the way of death, the way of goodness and the way of evil. When Moses presents the Law a second time in Deuteronomy, he says, "This commandment that I am commanding you today is not too hard for you, nor is it too far away. . . . See, I have set before you today life and prosperity, death and adversity" (Deut. 30:11, 15).

The Psalms present the commandments as evidence of God's special love and care for his people. Psalm 147 sees the commandments as an occasion for praise: "He declares his word to Jacob, his statues and ordinances to Israel. He has not dealt thus with any other nation; they do not know his ordinances. Praise the LORD!" (Ps. 147:19–20). What would it mean for us to embrace this Psalm and to praise the Lord because we know his commandments? Perhaps the clue is within the Psalm itself. The commandments are the means through which we enter into our vocation of giving praise to God.

Psalm 19 shows us the path for the restoration of creation before the Creator. Let us look at the threefold division of this Psalm. The first part discusses the heavens and the sun (1–6); the second part presents the perfection of the Law (7–10); and the third part discusses sin and conversion (11–14). At the beginning of the Psalm is a beautiful invocation: "The heavens are telling the glory of God; and the firmament proclaims his handiwork" (Ps. 19:1). In a silent manner, the physical creation speaks of God by acting in accordance with its internal laws. The orbits of the planets, the paths of the stars, sunrises and sunsets—each in its own way bears witness to the grandeur of the Creator.

But if we consider the actions of rational creatures, we discover that not all of creation gives such ready witness to God. Due to the corruption of sin, human beings fail in so many ways "to tell the glory of God" and "to proclaim his handiwork" (see Ps. 19:1). Instead, we want to tell of our own glory and so end up telling a story of shame. The long history of human suffering, bloodshed, and familial hurts and wounds, is tragic. God speaks into this history and offers a different path: "The law of the LORD is perfect, reviving the soul. . . . The commandment of the LORD is pure, enlightening the eyes" (Ps. 19:7–8). Through the divine commandments, the human soul is renewed and the eyes enlightened, giving cause for rejoicing.

But the final part of Psalm 19 declares that our obedience to God's commands is not enough, since we fail to keep them perfectly. The Psalmist thus prays, "Who can detect their errors? Clear me from hidden faults. Keep back your servant also from proud thoughts" (Ps. 19:11–13 RSV-CE). The commandments and the Law of God are only the beginning of our restoration to a right order of creation. More will be needed.

Nevertheless, the Psalm concludes in a hopeful key: "Let the words of my mouth and the meditation of my heart be acceptable to you, O LORD, my rock and redeemer" (Ps. 19:14). Reading it through the lens of the entire canon of Sacred Scripture, we know that the Lord will accomplish the redemption of Israel and all humanity through Jesus Christ.

Jesus Christ

Jesus Christ radically fulfills God's plan for all people by establishing the New Covenant. "Do not think that I have come to abolish the law or the prophets," he says in the Sermon on the Mount. "I have come not to abolish but to fulfill" (Matt. 5:17). Paul complements this teaching when he speaks of Christ as "the *telos*"—the purpose and goal—"of the law . . . that there may be righteousness for everyone who believes" (Rom. 10:4).[5] In this way, Sacred Scripture shows us that Christ fulfills and brings the Law to its completion, and we enter Christ's fulfillment through faith.

Faith, by uniting us to Christ through our free assent to him as our Savior and Lord, gives us a share in Christ's justice before God. In Christ, the commandments first given to Moses are perfectly fulfilled, for Christ loves God above all created things and his neighbor as himself.

Paul, in his Letter to the Galatians, shows that Christ not only fulfills the Law but also establishes the new Law. By the power of "faith working through love" (Gal. 5:6), we are able to "bear one another's burdens," he writes, "and in this way you will fulfill the law of Christ" (Gal. 6:2). We do not fulfill the law of Christ by our own strength but by faith in what Jesus has done and promises to do in us.

We began this section with the prayer of Israel, "*Hear*, O Israel: The LORD is our God, the LORD alone. You shall love the LORD your God with all your heart, and with all your soul, and with all your might" (Deut. 6:4–5). We are called first to listen to God's words challenging us to love him as the Creator above all created realities. As the Word of God incarnate, Jesus claims this obedience for himself: "He who has ears to hear, let him *hear*" (Matt. 11:15; emphasis added). Hearing Jesus' word opens up a new way of living since he is "the way, and the truth, and the life" (John 14:6). We need to be freed from the distortions of our own thinking and that of our histories and cultures. Human cultures contain some truths and wisdom, but they are manifestly incomplete, unable to address fully the deep wounds of sin and evil, of suffering and death.

---

5. For further discussion, see Brant Pitre, Michael P. Barber, and John A. Kincaid, *Paul, a New Covenant Jew: Rethinking Pauline Theology* (Grand Rapids, MI: Eerdmans, 2019).

Paul highlights the contrast between our prior way of thinking and the new way that Christ puts before us: "We destroy arguments and every proud obstacle raised up against the knowledge of God, and we take every thought captive to obey Christ" (2 Cor. 10:4–5). To accomplish this, we must receive revelation attentively. Christ conquers our merely human modes of thinking, our human attempts to fulfill the Law and reshape the people around us in our own image. His humility overcomes our pride. When we listen to him, receiving his words obediently, we allow our thoughts and efforts to be captured by Christ, not so they might be enslaved but so they might be set free and restored to the proper order of creation. Again, the message of the Bible is that obedient listening leads to freedom. Paul summarizes this dynamic: "For freedom Christ has set us free" (Gal. 5:1).

How might we learn to listen to Jesus and find such freedom? Let us consider three biblical images of Jesus: Jesus as shepherd, Jesus transfigured, and Jesus at prayer. The image of the shepherd is used in the Old Testament to establish proper leadership. David was taken from his own flocks of sheep to become the shepherd of Israel. Yet the earthly kings of Israel and Judah typically abused their role as shepherds. The prophet Ezekiel spoke of a time in which God would remove these unfaithful shepherds and would himself shepherd his people. In a moving passage of Ezekiel's prophecy, God promises, "I myself will search for my sheep, and will seek them out. . . . I myself will be the shepherd of my sheep, and I will make them lie down, says the Lord God" (Ezek. 34:11, 15). Those words are the voice of the same Spirit that moved King David to write, "The Lord is my shepherd, I shall not want. He makes me lie down in green pastures; he leads me beside still waters; he restores my soul" (Ps. 23:1–3). To call the Lord our shepherd is to listen to him and to let him lead us.

Jesus claims these images of the divine shepherd for himself. He says that he is the shepherd and that his sheep "hear his voice" and "follow him because they know his voice" (John 10:3–4). And he exposes the exploitation of Israel by corrupt shepherds when he declares, "I am the good shepherd. The good shepherd lays down his life for the sheep" (John 10:11). God himself is the good shepherd shepherding his people through his Son, the Word become flesh.

The shepherd's voice leads the sheep to safety and freedom. Sheep must trust in the shepherd to do for them what they cannot do for themselves. When we choose to listen to Jesus, to trust in his words and teachings, then each of us can say with the Psalmist: "He leads me beside still waters; he restores my soul" (Ps. 23:2–3).

The story of the Transfiguration is a pivotal moment in which the Bible presents Jesus as the central figure in the drama of revelation and faith. In this story, Peter, James, and John, Jesus' three closest Apostles, accompany him up a mountain. As Jesus prays, his physical body shines with a radiant splendor that reveals his hidden glory.

A cloud then overshadows Jesus and his disciples, in the same way that a cloud overshadowed the tabernacle in Exodus 40 and the temple in 1 Kings 8. In the tabernacle and the temple, the cloud was a visible manifestation of God's invisible presence with his people Israel. But at the Transfiguration, the cloud's overshadowing Jesus means that God's presence is now fully realized in Jesus Christ.

Then a voice speaks: "This is my Son, the Beloved; with him I am well pleased; listen to him!" (Matt. 17:5). Through this utterance, the Father fulfills a dual purpose: to reveal who Jesus is ("my Son, the Beloved") and how we are to be in relationship to him ("listen to him"). By listening to him, placing our faith in him and his word, we likewise become beloved sons and beloved daughters with whom the Father is well pleased.

Let us turn then to another time when Jesus was in prayer, this time when no splendor was revealed. What happens when the path of listening and obedience is filled with suffering? Are we still to accept God's will and trust in his word? If we examine Jesus's prayer at Gethsemane, we will find that we are invited to affirm three points simultaneously: God wills only goodness; God permits evil; and God brings goodness out of evil. In fact, God brings the greatest good of eternal life out of the greatest evil of the Crucifixion of his innocent Son. When we turn our wills over to God in imitation of Jesus during his agony, we trust in him to bring goodness out of our evil and suffering.

Yet if we had to rely on our own strength, we would be simply too fearful and insecure to trust God with our entire being and to surrender ourselves entirely to his care. So Jesus Christ makes possible for us what we could never do for ourselves. On the night before his Crucifixion, Jesus leaves the walls of the city of Jerusalem for the Mount of Olives, where he stops at the Garden of Gethsemane. There he invites Peter, James, and John to accompany him in prayer. He is sorrowful and prays with great intensity—kneeling down, falling on the ground, and saying, "My Father, if it is possible, let this cup pass from me; yet not what I want but what you want" (Matt. 26:39).

Matthew records that Jesus repeats this sequence of going away a little and praying to the Father three separate times. In this way, we are made to witness how Jesus, like us in all things but sin, asks for this cup of suffering to pass from him. He asks his Father to take away his imminent torture and death, the rejection of the crowd and the leaders of Israel, and the fleeing of so many of his disciples. But Jesus does not stop there. In the midst of his suffering and rejection, Jesus pledges himself to the will of his Father in heaven.

Jesus' agony is not the only Gospel example of resignation to God's will amid challenging circumstances. When Mary was at the wedding at Cana and noticed that the wine was running low, she did not merely accept it as God's will. No, first, she informed her son, "They have no wine"; and then she told the servants, "Do whatever he tells you" (John 2:3, 5). Here is a powerful model of attentive listening and active obedience. When we face difficulties that arise from our faith or when we witness injustice and tremendous suffering, we might begin by following Mary's example and telling Jesus, "They have no wine," while telling others, "Do whatever he tells you." We may ask Jesus to repeat in us his own words, "Father, if it is possible, let this cup pass from me; yet not what I want but what you want" (Matt. 26:39).

Faith as Hearing the Word of God

In an almost embarrassing story from the Gospel of Mark, Jesus' disciples were unable to perform a miracle.[6] The father of the tormented son asks Jesus if Jesus himself can do anything. Jesus responds, "All things can be done for the one who believes" (Mark 9:23). The father, knowing that his faith is imperfect and recognizing that Jesus is asking for more, responds with the desperate cry, "I believe; help my unbelief!" (Mark 9:24). Here we witness a concrete example of how faith takes root. The father in this story exemplifies the situation of one who knows he lacks the fullness of faith—and responds to this lack by asking that his faith be made perfect. As Jesus heals the son from his torment, so he also heals the father of his unbelief.

We perceive a similar powerful lesson about faith, as it grows and then shrinks, in the experience of Peter when he boldly steps out

---

6. For contrasting ways of understanding miracles, see Craig S. Keener, *Miracles: The Credibility of the Gospel Accounts*, 2 vols. (Grand Rapids, MI: Baker Academic, 2011); Luke Timothy Johnson, *Miracles: God's Presence and Power in Creation* (Louisville, KY: Westminster John Knox, 2018).

in obedient faith to walk to Jesus on the waters of the Sea of Galilee. As he reaches Jesus, he becomes afraid and begins to sink, calling out for the Lord's help. Jesus catches his hand but also rebukes him: "You of little faith, why did you doubt?" (Matt. 14:31). On another occasion, the disciples will likewise ask Jesus for the strengthening of their faith when they exclaim, "Increase our faith!" (Luke 17:5). God delights in our faith and wants us to ask him for more of it. Doing so is part of the process by which we grow in faith.

To put all this another way, as the Bible presents it, human history involves an odd twist: Even though God created us and we belong to him, he often asks permission before bringing his grace to bear upon our lives. Rather than overwhelming us with his power and truncating our free will, he presents his word for us to respond. "Ask, and it will be given you; search, and you will find; knock, and it will be opened to you" (Matt. 7:7). The Creator of the universe, who has made us and could unmake us in a moment, wants our freedom to have center stage. We are to ask, to search, and to knock.

Jesus emphasizes this dynamic of asking and receiving. He teaches that if even sinful human fathers give good gifts to their children, "how much more then will your Father in heaven give good things to those who ask him!" (Matt. 7:11). James, taking Jesus' lead, likewise encourages his readers to ask for wisdom from God, while at the same time qualifying his instruction: "But ask in faith, never doubting, for the one who doubts is like a wave of the sea, driven and tossed by the wind" (James 1:6).

If growth in faith were entirely dependent upon our own efforts, we would be left in a bind. But in fact we are not stuck in our doubts or our struggles to live in perfect faith, for God is the origin of all good gifts. As Paul exhorts, "What do you have that you did not receive?" (1 Cor. 4:7).[7] God is the one who gives the gifts of faith and

---

7. See John M.G. Barclay, *Paul and the Gift* (Grand Rapids, MI: Eerdmans, 2017).

obedience, and yet he calls for our response and cooperation in the reception of those gifts. James, like Paul, emphasizes the priority of God in all giving: "Every generous act of giving, with every perfect gift, is from above" (James 1:17). God's gifts are the source of our gifts—not only our gifts to one another but especially to God. This truth helps to correct a misunderstanding of many who think they need to earn God's love. God does not love us because we are good but because *he* is good.

God thus takes the initiative in the drama of faith. The truths necessary for our salvation are above the capacity of unassisted human intelligence. We see this in the Gospel episode where Jesus asks Simon Peter, "Who do you say that I am?" Peter responds, "You are the Messiah [Christ], the Son of the living God" (Matt. 16:15–16). Jesus then announces, "Blessed are you, Simon Son of Jonah! For flesh and blood has not revealed this to you, but my Father in heaven" (Matt. 16:17). With those words, Jesus teaches us two important points regarding the priority of the divine initiative. First he teaches that Peter is "blessed" for his faith, for faith is the blessing that opens us up to receive further gifts of grace. Second, he teaches that such faith is never the result of human ingenuity and discovery; it follows upon divine inspiration and the human person's free response.

For Jesus, the necessity of God's initiative is cause for celebration:

> At that same hour Jesus rejoiced in the Holy Spirit and said, "I thank you, Father, Lord of heaven and earth, because you have hidden these things from the wise and the intelligent and have revealed them to infants; yes, Father, for such was your gracious will. All things have been handed over to me by my Father; and no one knows who the Son is except the Father, or who the Father is except the Son and any one to whom the Son chooses to reveal him." (Luke 10:21–22)

Those words are humbling—especially for those of us who pride ourselves on our wisdom and learning. Although learning can prepare us for belief and help us in our life of faith, our knowledge of God does not depend upon our intellectual ability. In fact, there is not even a necessary link between the two. The Son reveals God the Father to those who are humble enough to listen to him.

Paul likewise presents the priority of divine revelation in our acts of faith. He summarizes his teaching in a memorable and succinct remark: "No one can say that Jesus is Lord except by the Holy Spirit" (1 Cor. 12:3). "Jesus is Lord" functions as a condensed creed, another updated version of "Hear, O Israel: The LORD our God is one LORD." Now Jesus Christ is the Lord. To affirm Jesus as Lord orients us to God and moves us away from idolatry. When the early Christians called Jesus "Lord" (*Kyrios*), they were affirming that Jesus shares in the divine identity.[8] Paul emphasizes the activity of the Holy Spirit in enabling us to make this declaration (1 Cor. 12:3). To see Jesus as a man is something we may do by human reason alone; to see Jesus as the Son of the living God, as Lord, is the fruit of God's action in us.

At the same time, God's inspiration allows us, in trusting him, to make a truly free and personal act of faith. Even in the sudden and dramatic conversion of Paul on his way to Damascus, God does not overwhelm Paul or crush his free will. Instead he invites Paul to listen, to respond, and to obey. Paul sees a light from heaven, falls to the ground, and then hears a voice, saying, "Saul, Saul, why do you persecute me?" The shocked young zealot replies, "Who are you, Lord?" Then the voice replies, "I am Jesus, whom you are persecuting. But get up and enter the city, and you will be told what you are to do" (Acts 9:4–6).

---

8. See C. Kavin Rowe, *Early Narrative Christology: The Lord in the Gospel of Luke* (Grand Rapids, MI: Baker Academic, 2009).

Call and Response

The Lord's call invites a decisive response, such as that given by Abraham. God's many promises to Abraham began with a call: "Go from your country and your kindred and your father's house to the land that I will show you" (Gen. 12:1). Abraham "went, as the Lord had told him" (Gen. 12:4). Paul even speaks of Abraham as "the father of all who believe" (Rom. 4:11 RSV-CE). Abraham lived out this faithful obedience to God at many points in his life. After he left his home country, he believed that God would fulfill his promise to grant him many descendants and make him a blessing to others even though he and Sarah were already old and still childless. Indeed, throughout Abraham's story, his "yes" to God is both efficacious and exemplary. He receives God's promises in faithful obedience. He listens to the Word of God and does it.

Mary's "yes" to God in the New Testament is likewise both efficacious and exemplary. Her response to the angel Gabriel's promise that she would bear the Messiah is to say, "Here am I, the servant of the Lord; let it be with me according to your word" (Luke 1:38). Let us focus on a particular line from her cousin Elizabeth, who exclaimed to Mary, "Blessed is she who believed that there would be a fulfillment of what was spoken to her by the Lord" (Luke 1:45). Among Mary's many excellences, Elizabeth singles out her faith—"Blessed is she who believed." What does belief mean in this context?

Notice that belief is something that makes Mary blessed, which is the same language that Jesus will use in his Beatitudes, as when he declares, "Blessed are the poor in spirit." Earlier we saw that Jesus declared Peter "blessed" for his act of faith in Jesus as the Son of the living God. For both Peter and Mary, to believe means recognizing the truth of God's words and actions. To assent to such truth involves the entire being of the person—all one's heart and mind.

When Elizabeth says to Mary, "Blessed is she who believed that there would be a fulfillment of what was spoken to her by the Lord," she shows that human beings are happiest when we trust completely in the wisdom of God's plans and his power to carry them out. Later in Luke, Jesus will clarify that Mary's spiritual motherhood is greater than her physical motherhood: "Blessed rather are those who hear the word of God and obey it!" (Luke 11:28). In Mary's blessedness, we find the model of a good life: unconditional trust in the Lord.

The Bible discloses a regular pattern in which God gives direction without over-prescribing detail. Much depends on the exercise of human freedom in responding to God. In the Old Testament, God works through Abraham, Moses, and David in decisive ways, bringing different stages of his covenantal relationship with his people to fulfillment through them, but he also leaves much in their own hands. In the New Testament, Jesus continues his ministry through his Apostles but, having imparted to them the gift of the Holy Spirit, again leaves much of the governance of the Church to their judgment. For instance, in his earthly ministry, Jesus did not settle how to handle the entrance of the Gentiles into the covenant. Instead, at the first council in Jerusalem (described in Acts 15) the Apostles, freely cooperating with the Holy Spirit, definitively decided that Gentile converts would not be bound by the full Jewish Law.

Obedience thus entails a great paradox. When we choose to hear the Word of God in its fullness, we do not become enslaved but free. When we refuse to listen to the Word of God, we do not become free but remain enslaved. The unreserved "yes" to God does not truncate our human freedom or intelligence but rather liberates us to use them to the fullest without their being distorted by our pride or ignorance. Listening to God frees us and elevates us to participate in the realization of God's plan for creation.

The Word of God as Mediated by the Church

At this point, you may be wondering what exactly it means to hear the voice of God or the voice of Jesus. At least in theory, it appears it would be easier to obey if I personally heard God's voice thundering from the sky. Some of us live with the illusion that we are not accountable to God's revelation since we were not a contemporary of Jesus or did not see him risen gloriously from the dead.

One startling thing about the Gospels, however, is that they not only describe Jesus' successes as a preacher but also his apparent failures. On various occasions, crowds gathered to him in the thousands and remained with him apparently for entire days to listen to his teachings. Yet when he spoke in Capernaum of the bread of life as his flesh, not only did the crowds disperse, but many of his own disciples left him (John 6:66). When he returned to his hometown of Nazareth, those who had known him as the carpenter's son refused to believe in him (Mark 6:1–6).

Even the Resurrection appearances include references to doubting. In Mark, Jesus rebukes the disciples for having doubted the stories of his Resurrection (Mark 16:14). Matthew records a final appearance of Jesus to his eleven disciples, according to which "when they saw him, they worshiped him; but some doubted" (Matt. 28:17). John includes a long story about the Apostle Thomas, who, having been away when Jesus first appeared to the Apostles after his Resurrection, refused to believe unless he could see and touch the risen Jesus.

Great doubting, however, sometimes gives way to great faith. The same doubting Thomas subsequently makes the greatest confession of faith in Jesus recorded in any of the Gospels: "My Lord and my God!" (John 20:28).

A few verses after John records Thomas' confession, the evangelist makes clear that faith in God has a content; indeed, it has a human face. To communicate this faith in the person of Jesus is the very reason why John wrote his Gospel: "These [words] are written so that you may come to believe that Jesus is the Messiah [Christ], the Son of God, and that through believing you may have life in his name" (John 20:31).[9] Belief in Jesus is the condition for true blessedness. In God's plan, the Gospels are written so we might hear the voice of Jesus speaking across the ages and thereby find faith and life.

Just as John wrote his Gospel so "that you may come to believe . . . and have life in his name," Christ established the Church to spread belief and life in him. We see in the New Testament this understanding of the Church as the ongoing communication of God's message of salvation; it presents the Church and its human members as sharers in a divine mission.

A favorite theme for Paul is that the power of God is revealed in the midst of human weakness. The Church, although divinely constituted as the Body of Christ, remains a human community, as befits Christ's real entrance into our personal histories. In the New Testament, we see that at times there were serious disagreements between the Apostles. Paul corrected Peter when the latter, as a Jewish Christian, had stopped eating with Gentile converts (see Gal. 2:11–21). In Acts, we read that Paul and Barnabas separated after many years of preaching together, their partnership torn apart by a painful disagreement about whether to bring Mark on their next journey (Acts 15:36–40).

Paul acknowledges the human weakness characteristic of himself and the other Apostles: "But we have this treasure in clay jars, so that it may be made clear that this extraordinary power belongs to

---

9. See Richard Bauckham, *Jesus and the Eyewitnesses: The Gospels as Eyewitness Testimony* (Grand Rapids, MI: Eerdmans, 2017).

God and does not come from us" (2 Cor. 4:7). He tells of how the Lord said to him, "My grace is sufficient for you, for power is made perfect in weakness" (2 Cor. 12:9). God's power can work through even the human weakness of the Church, since the Church is the community founded by the reception of God's word—the word that was spoken in the Old Testament and that is now incarnate in the New.

Paul's favorite image of the Church as the Body of Christ shows forth the dependence of every member upon Jesus. The image of being members of one Body is not always understood in its full significance. To be in the Body of Christ means that we are members of one another and so ought to seek unity and peace (Rom. 12 and 1 Cor. 12). This horizontal unity of the members of the Church, however, follows upon its unity with its Head. The unity with the Head is primary.

Just as the body cannot live without the head, the Church cannot live without Christ. Were we to imagine the Body of Christ merely as a call to unity with each other, we would unwittingly be severing the body from the head. Thus when we affirm that the Church is the Body of Christ, we likewise affirm that the Head is Christ and that he acts through all of the members of the Body (Col. 1:18). To see the Church as the Body of Christ means that the Church does not speak with her own voice; it is Christ who speaks and acts through his Church.

Paul learned firsthand about the doctrine of the Body of Christ. When Jesus appeared to him on his way to Damascus, the voice Paul heard said, "I am Jesus, whom you are persecuting" (Acts 9.5). In other words, when Paul was persecuting the followers of Jesus, he was persecuting Jesus. This is the deep reality of the Body of Christ. Conversely, and what is more important in the context of this chapter, as the head acts through the body, so also Christ acts through his members. Christ continues to teach and to heal through the preaching and sacramental ministry of his Church.

Hearing Christ in the Church

The Gospels invite us to listen to Christ speaking and acting through his Church. We can recognize this invitation through the accounts of Jesus' preaching, his forgiveness of sins, and his shepherding of his flock. Let us consider how Christ uses each of these acts to tell us something about how his words and actions reach us in and through the Church he founded.

Jesus' preaching. During his earthly life, Jesus commissioned his followers to announce the Good News. This was not simply effective delegation; instead, Christ shared his personal authority with them. Luke records how Jesus appointed seventy disciples and sent them out two by two. When the disciples entered a house and said "Peace to this house," their words were efficacious, and peace would indeed rest on the household unless the household's members rejected it (Luke 10:5). One of the options for the beginning of the Catholic Mass has the priest extend this same peace to us: "Grace to you and peace from God our Father and the Lord Jesus Christ." The New Testament word for "peace" comes from the Hebrew understanding of *shalom*, which may be translated as peace as well as completeness, soundness, and welfare. In Jeremiah, the prophet announces, "I know the plans I have for you, says the LORD, plans for your welfare [*shalom*] and not for harm, to give you a future with hope" (Jer. 29:11). Thus, in preaching peace or *shalom*, Jesus announces a restoration of God's good creation in self-surrendering love, a restoration that gives us a future and a hope of life with God.

When we read the phrase "the kingdom of God" in light of this holistic and all-encompassing peace, it becomes clear that the kingdom is not about an individualistic relationship with God. God will indeed bring individuals into his restored creation, but he will do so by bringing them into new relationships with one another and with him. Moreover, God brings about his kingdom through Jesus Christ and through his Apostles. Jesus describes this real, ordered unity as existing among the Apostles, himself, and the Father: "Whoever listens to you listens to me, and whoever rejects you rejects me, and whoever rejects me rejects the one who sent me" (Luke 10:16). Founded by Christ, the Church enables us to listen to God speaking to us about his love for us and his plan for our salvation.

This explains the hierarchical structure of the Church, which carries forward the apostolic leadership of Peter and the other Apostles. Amidst the messiness and sinfulness of the Church's members, this truth about the Church may sometimes be hard to see. And yet Christians must seek to listen to the voice of Christ speaking through the Church. His voice calls us at each Mass in the proclamation of the Bible and particularly the Gospel. We also hear his voice in the proclamation of the Creed at each Sunday Mass, which summarizes in a trustworthy manner what Jesus speaks to us. It is in and through the Church that we hear the living Christ.

Jesus' forgiveness of sins. The unity of Christ and his Church is unmistakable when we look at the message of forgiveness in the New Testament. In Jesus' public ministry, besides his healing many with diseases, he shocked people by claiming to forgive sins, which only God can do (Luke 5:21). He boldly claims this power of forgiveness, "that you may know that the Son of man has authority on earth to forgive sins" (Luke 5:24). Yet what is perhaps less frequently noticed is that he passes on this remarkable authority to his Apostles. They also are to forgive sins!

One might even go so far to say that Jesus constitutes the Church by sharing with it his power to forgive sins. In Matthew 16, Jesus gives

Peter the keys of the kingdom and explains that whatever he binds or looses on earth will be bound or loosed in heaven, an expression that signifies teaching authority, authority over the community's membership, and spiritual authority to forgive sins.[10] In John 20, the resurrected Jesus breathes on the Apostles and says, "Receive the Holy Spirit. If you forgive the sins of any, they are forgiven them; if you retain the sins of any, they are retained" (John 20:22–23). In Luke 24, Jesus' final commission to his disciples includes this same power, "that repentance and forgiveness of sins is to be proclaimed in [Christ's] name to all nations" (Luke 24:47). Yes, God alone can forgive sins. God does so in Christ, and indeed it is Christ himself who forgives sins through his Apostles and their successors. This is an astonishing fact. God's voice of forgiveness and mercy comes to us in the written word of the Bible and the sacramental word of the priest.

Jesus' shepherding of his flock. We saw earlier how Jesus is the divine shepherd now present within human history. His is the voice of the good shepherd that his faithful will listen to and hear. In his shepherding, just as with his preaching and his forgiving of sins, Jesus first claims for himself divine authority and then, secondly, shares it with his followers, without ceasing to be their Head. He shares his ministry as shepherd with his Apostles, beginning with Peter. After Peter denies Jesus three times on the night leading to the Crucifixion, the Apostle is asked three times by the resurrected Jesus, "Simon son of John, do you love me?" Three times, Peter responds, "Yes, Lord; you know that I love you." And, three times, Jesus responds, "Feed my lambs. . . . Tend my sheep. . . . Feed my sheep" (John 21:15–17). In this way, Jesus not only reconciles Peter to himself but also commissions him to act as the Church's chief shepherd on earth.

---

10. See Curtis Mitch and Edward Sri, *The Gospel of Matthew* (Grand Rapids, MI: Baker Academic, 2010), 210.

Jesus shepherds his flock through Peter. First, Jesus establishes Peter as the shepherd, "Feed . . . tend . . . feed"; and second, he establishes that the sheep Peter will shepherd remain Christ's possession: "*my* lambs . . . *my* sheep . . . *my* sheep." The Church's shepherds and pastors are not independent agents who pass along a message to us; rather, they are vehicles of Christ's ongoing activity of announcing peace, communicating forgiveness, and teaching the paths of right living. When the faithful hear the Church proclaiming the Gospel, they do not merely hear human beings; rather, through these human beings, they hear the voice of Christ, the good shepherd, speaking. In this way, Jesus extends to us the same personal and intimate friendship he extended to his disciples.

Jesus' farewell discourse in the Gospel of John reveals the intimacy of divine communion that he is establishing: "I do not call you servants any longer, because the servant does not know what the master is doing; but I have called you friends, because I have made know to you everything that I have heard from my Father" (John 15:15). In our friendship with Jesus, we also discover new bonds of friendship with one another in his Church.

The voice of Christ speaks through both written and unwritten tradition. Paul often introduces himself in his letters as "an apostle of Christ Jesus" (1 Cor. 1:1) who speaks in the name of Christ. He exhorts the Thessalonians to "stand firm and hold fast to the traditions that were taught by us, either by word of mouth or by letter" (2 Thess. 2:15; cf. 1 Thess. 2:13). The Gospel he preaches is not his own but that which comes from God. As such, the Gospel is to be received and listened to wholly as the infallible Word of God, not rejected or taken partially as the fallible word of men. Scripture is a primary witness to the Good News of the Gospel.

Paul speaks of the Bible's inestimable worth: "All scripture is inspired by God and is useful for teaching, for reproof, for correction, and for training in righteousness, so that everyone who belongs to God may be proficient, equipped for every good work" (2 Tim. 3:16). This passage affirms the inspiration of the Bible. The Greek word for "inspired by God" is *theo-pneustos*, literally "God-breathed." Recall that the human voice requires breath. The breath, spirit, and voice of God come to us through the Bible. Because the Bible is the Word of God, we are to listen to the Bible so that we may be taught, corrected, trained, and equipped to assist in God's plan of salvation. How often do we approach the Bible with this understanding in mind, that we are meant to let the words of the Bible train and equip us?

The Bible teaches that its own word is meant to stand with—and not be separated from—Christ's living voice in the Church. Its human authors, under the inspiration of the Holy Spirit, are fully aware that the human members of the Church will often disagree with one another and fall short of their calling in significant ways. Paul speaks of "false apostles, deceitful workers, disguising themselves as apostles of Christ" (2 Cor. 11:13) and of leaders who will be "treacherous, reckless, swollen with conceit, lovers of pleasure rather than lovers of God" (2 Tim. 3:4).

It is a painful reality that the leaders of the Church often fail to live out their calling to holiness. The sins of sexual abuse and abuse of power by Christ's representatives, both today and down through the ages, are shocking to consider. Jesus himself warns his followers of false prophets who will come "in sheep's clothing but inwardly are ravenous wolves" (Matt. 7:15), thereby condemning leaders who fail to shepherd but rather devour the flock. Addressing his disciples before he ascends to heaven, he does not promise that the Church will always have holy leaders or perfect people. Instead he offers us the promise of his faithful presence: "I am with you always, to the end of the age" (Matt. 28:20).

Jesus' presence in the Church enables Paul to identify the Church, the living apostolic tradition, as "the pillar and bulwark of the truth" (1 Tim. 3:15). Through the Incarnation, through the Bible and the Church, God's truth and goodness enter into our sordid human history. Just as the soul gives life and unity to the body, so Christ and his Holy Spirit give life and unity to the Church. Just as we encounter the soul of the other person through bodily words and actions, so too we encounter Christ and his Spirit through the solemn words and actions of the living, historical Church. It is by Christ's power, and not by mere human power, that we have assurance that the Church's proclamation of the truth of faith is trustworthy, just as we know that Scripture, canonized by the Church under the Spirit's guidance, is trustworthy.

The Word of God as Spoken Once and For All

Christianity seeks to remain ever connected with God's definitive speaking into human history, which took place when "the Word became flesh," as John so powerfully describes the Incarnation (John 1:14). The author of Hebrews summarizes the same truth in a memorable phrase: "Jesus Christ is the same yesterday and today and forever" (Heb. 13:8). To put it another way, Christian revelation possess an unchanging reality—Jesus himself who liberates us from sin and death. The word preached by the Apostles in their lifetimes is the same word preached today by their successors, for there is no other Word of God to be preached. To preach a different word—or for the faithful to listen to a different word—would be to depart from the fullness of Christ and his revelation.

Paul emphasizes how important it is that the Gospel be received faithfully. He writes to the Galatians, "I am astonished that you are so quickly deserting the one who called you in the grace of Christ and turning to a different gospel—not that there is another gospel, but there are some who are confusing you and want to pervert the gospel of Christ" (Gal. 1:6–7). There is only one Gospel, the new and eternal covenant into which we have been called. Because the faith is given once and for all, it must be received once and for all. Paul affirms this directly, "Timothy, guard what has been entrusted to you" (1 Tim. 6:20). A central Christian task is to guard what has been entrusted to us.

With that said, the Word of God once spoken always invites its hearers to a greater understanding. Paul describes the faith in another place as "this mystery . . . [that] has now been revealed to his holy apostles and prophets by the Spirit" (Eph. 3:5). This mystery is revealed in its fullness in Christ. When we come to know this mystery, the reality of what is known begins to dwell in us and transform us. Because the mystery is God's revelation of himself, it always exceeds our understanding. Paul exhorts the faithful to grow in faith and love and so "to comprehend, with all the saints, what is the breadth and length and height and depth, and to know the love of Christ that surpasses knowledge, that you may be filled with all the fullness of God" (Eph. 3:18–19; emphasis added). What does it mean to know that which surpasses knowledge? It means to know God, *to know the love of Christ*, so that the infinite and almighty Creator of the universe might dwell in our hearts.

Conclusion

Why should anyone listen to the Church's teachings? The reason is that God has spoken first to his people Israel and pre-eminently through Israel's Messiah, Jesus the Son of God. Through his Son and by his Spirit, God has called us into a covenantal relationship with him. The embrace of God's word is called "faith." To say "yes" to

God's word is to enter into the loving embrace of God, who wants our everlasting good. Without hearing God's revelation, we would not know that the Creator of the universe knows and loves us personally and has a plan for our forgiveness and salvation.

The voice of God addresses us personally and calls us out from isolation and brokenness. God speaks to us definitively through the person of Jesus Christ, who speaks to us through the words and actions of his Apostles. The Bible and the living tradition of the Church mediate this divine speech. We are called into Christ's new covenant as members of his Body.

In this light, we come to see that listening to the Church does not limit us or our relationship with God. Rather, it allows us to find true *freedom from* our sins and many wounds and *freedom to* discover the meaning and purpose of our lives as children of God, both now and for eternity.

In the Sermon on the Mount, Christ explains that whoever follows the commandments and teaches others to do so "shall be called great in the kingdom of heaven" (Matt. 5:19). The greatness of Christ's followers corresponds to the extent of their willingness to hear—and to help others hear—God's voice. Christ invites us to hear his voice through the most imperfect of instruments, our fellow human beings. Yet what other voice could we hear and read other than human words spoken and written, bound up in the community founded and guided by Christ and his Spirit, sharing with us God's wondrous plan of creation and redemption? Our greatest calling is to listen to this divinely given word of salvation, to obey it in faith, and to share it with others so that all of us together, filled with the Spirit, may come to reign in self-sacrificial love with Christ in the glory of God the Father, through the "obedience of faith" (Rom. 1:5).

Does the Holy Spirit Actually Transform Christians?

"You shall receive power when the Holy Spirit has come upon you" (Acts 1:8)

Who are we to talk about the transformative power of the Holy Spirit? After all, the countless sins of believers over the centuries appear to disprove Jesus' promise to send his Spirit and void Paul's claim that the Spirit has indeed been poured out. For many baptized Catholics today, the notion that the sacraments communicate grace or that believers are filled with the grace of the Spirit is pious nonsense. There is no doubt that we humans, and we Catholics, are often irresponsible and untrustworthy, and even just plain wicked. It would be great if the Spirit would transform people, but believers hardly seem to be noticeably transformed.

At the center of the Gospel is the Spirit's power to liberate us from our sinful inclinations and to enable us to love and forgive each other. Nevertheless, it seems all too common for many people, even devout believers, not to forgive but rather to harbor grudges. And why do even fervent Catholics report regular struggles with sinful desires (such as lust, greed, envy, and so on) that one might have expected the Spirit to have driven out?

No doubt, this is one reason people turn away from prayer and faith. After all, if being a Catholic does not appear to deliver you from the power of sin, why bother? In *Faith with Benefits: Hookup Culture on Catholic Campuses*, Jason King quotes an undergraduate named

"Cole" who attends a Catholic college. Cole observes, "My college is about 45 percent Catholic but most of those are Catholic in name only. On Sunday nights, the chapel is almost empty. . . . Hookup culture is very present, but the Catholic culture not so much."[1]

We believe that one reason people lose faith in the power of the Holy Spirit to transform their lives is that many Catholics and ex-Catholics have not yet experienced any kind of transforming encounter with God. Moreover, they do not appear to be seeking one. Mark Hart, recalling his youthful ideas about faith, describes a common experience: "I knew I was a Catholic, but when I got to college, I began to wonder what difference it really made, and I wondered if I even wanted to remain one."[2]

Certainly there are a number of faithful Catholic colleges and institutions in which young people may receive an inspiring instruction in Catholic faith and life. But as King shows, the majority of young Catholics fail to experience an authentic and vibrant Catholic culture. Understandably, they may come to feel that being Catholic does not make much of a difference. They may still identify as "spiritual," but their experiences convince them that Catholics are not distinctive from the world around them. From this perspective, if the Holy Spirit has been sent by Jesus Christ, he seems to have gotten lost in the mail.

In fact, the Holy Spirit truly has been sent by Christ, and the Church continues to be filled by the Spirit and to mediate the grace of the Spirit through word and sacrament. The Bible speaks to us about who the Spirit is and what it means to receive the Spirit's

---

1. Jason King, *Faith with Benefits: Hookup Culture on Catholic Campuses* (Oxford: Oxford University Press, 2017), 128–129.

2. Mark Hart, *Blessed are the Bored in Spirit: A Young Catholic's Search for Meaning* (Cincinnati, OH: Servant Books, 2006), 1.

power. Above all, it means a new relationship with God and with one another in truth and love—a relationship rooted in Christ.

We yearn for connection. To be Catholic means to be friends of Christ and friends of each other, sharing in his Spirit of self-giving love. These are the true, humble, loving friendships that inspire and encourage us to find hope and grow in our faith. Such transformative relationships are even now available to us through the power of the Holy Spirit, whom Jesus promises his disciples he will send to them from the Father (see John 15:26).

Of course, the authors of the New Testament are aware that people may resist the Spirit. Likewise, they are highly conscious that even the power of the Holy Spirit does not transform us into perfect people. Just as Christ comes with a mission of mercy, so does the Holy Spirit. As long as we remain open to God's invitation, the Spirit constantly renews our love of God and neighbor, even after we fall. The sacraments communicate the Spirit's grace, and heal and elevate us into a deeper friendship with God and neighbor.

This chapter explores how the Bible testifies both to our need for the gift of the Holy Spirit and to the reality of the Spirit's grace. It might seem that we should begin this chapter with the story of Pentecost when the Holy Spirit descended upon the Apostles. But in fact, in order to consider more fully how the Spirit creates us anew, we need first to consider the Spirit's role in God's original creation.

Creation and Fall: Our Need for the Spirit's Grace

The biblical story opens with God's extraordinary work of creating the heavens and the earth.[3] The first chapter of Genesis presents the whole of creation as a cosmic temple in which human beings dwell

---

3. See William P. Brown, *The Seven Pillars of Creation: The Bible, Science, and the Ecology of Wonder* (Oxford: Oxford University Press, 2010).

with God and worship him.[4] God created Adam and Eve "in the image of God" (Gen. 1:27) in order to rule over this cosmic temple for the glory of God. Their role in the cosmic temple was priestly: they were to govern creation in such a way as to maintain its status as sacred space, offering holy worship to God.

Adam and Eve were also charged by God with reigning over the temple of creation. The Bible speaks of them as being made in the image of God and possessing "dominion" over the rest of creation, not in any exploitative sense, but as caring for creation (Gen. 1:27–28; 2:12). Their royal reign as God's representatives, however, depended upon their first accepting God's order of creation. In other words, they could only be *over* the plants, the animals, and the earth because they were *under* God. What is more, their priestly and kingly role also had a familial dimension, for they were created in God's image and likeness and were therefore children of God (Gen. 1:28; Gen. 5:3). Human beings were not under God as slaves but as sons and daughters sharing in his dominion.

Genesis describes the creation of Adam: "The Lord God formed man from the dust of the ground, and breathed into his nostrils *the breath of life*; and the man became a living being" (Gen. 2:7; emphasis added). The word for breath of life here is from *ruach* in Hebrew or *pneuma* in Greek, and could also be translated as the "Spirit of life." Human beings were not only created to live with God, but to live and breathe with the very breath or Spirit of God.[5] The gift of the Holy Spirit constituted the original creation of human beings in grace, in the image and likeness of God.

---

4. See John H. Walton, *The Lost World of Genesis One: Ancient Cosmology and the Origins Debate* (Downers Grove, IL: IVP Academic, 2009).

5. This is emphasized by R.R. Reno, *Genesis* (Grand Rapids, MI: Brazos Press, 2010), 67. For the argument that the "breath of life" is a natural (not divine) reality, see Bill T. Arnold, *Genesis* (Cambridge: Cambridge University Press, 2009), 57.

Thus, humans were created to praise God, to love and care for each other and all creation, and to share in the Trinitarian life. Yet the first humans rebelled against God's love. Tempted by the serpent, they chose to believe that God was trying to dominate them and to impose his own arbitrary rules. They sought to "be like God" (Gen. 3:5) without God and on their own terms, imagining that God wished to dominate and control them. As a result, they lost the abundant life for which they had been created, and came to experience suffering and death as a punishment and something to be feared.

Amidst the poetic language of the first humans' eating of the forbidden fruit, the Genesis story teaches us something fundamental about human nature and how human beings have abused their God-given power of free will. When the amazing reality of rational human consciousness first manifested itself, the first humans, cared for by God, fell into pride.[6] They did not want the kingdom of love; they wanted self-sufficient power.

The consequence was the fracturing of the kingdom of love, the kingdom of communion with God and one other—a kingdom that could not exist without the interior holiness of the first humans. Henceforth humans were enslaved to their disordered desires, disordered fears, and disordered angers. They were soon to become enslaved to one another, not to mention to the evil powers of the world. No wonder the author of Hebrews announces that Jesus Christ delivered "those who all their lives were held in slavery by the fear of death" (Heb. 2:15). By sinning against their spiritual and

---

6. The *Catechism of the Catholic Church* teaches, "The account of the fall in Genesis 3 uses figurative language, but affirms a primeval event, a deed that took place at the beginning of the history of man. Revelation gives us the certainty of faith that the whole of human history is marked by the original fault freely committed by our first parents" (no. 390). For a defense of the truth of the historical fall, see Matthew Levering, *Engaging the Doctrine of Creation: Cosmos, Creatures, and the Wise and Good Creator* (Grand Rapids, MI: Baker Academic, 2017), chapter 6. For the contrary view, see Peter Enns, *The Evolution of Adam: What the Bible Does and Doesn't Say about Human Origins* (Grand Rapids, MI: Brazos Press, 2012).

bodily integrity, human persons handed themselves over to the terror of death.

Sobering realism colors the Bible's presentation of the difficult truth of the human historical situation, filled as it is with suffering, injustice, and death. Jealousy, rage, murder, pride, vengeance, war, and so forth become commonplace, and love for the Creator God becomes rare.

God, however, initiates a new story in the midst of our fallen history. The Bible tells again and again of how God offers himself in love to us in increasingly personal ways through the covenants with Israel, culminating in Jesus Christ. Believers receive an opportunity to begin afresh in Christ and by the grace of the Holy Spirit, in communion with God as priests and kings in the "new creation" (2 Cor. 5:17; Gal. 6:15). God has begun a new story characterized above all by the self-sacrificial love of Christ communicated to us in the Holy Spirit. In God's new creation, his new true story, he offers our wounded free wills the healing power of his own Spirit so that, through love, we might freely enter the kingdom and family of his love.

The Spirit in the People of Israel and the Promise of Restoration

In order to understand the role of the Holy Spirit in the life of the Church, it is helpful to consider the presence and promise of the Spirit in the story of Israel. The Bible offers consistent testimony that the people of Israel received a unique calling and a covenantal relationship with God, which unfolded over many centuries.

Many styles of writing are included in the Old Testament—poetry, prophecy, wisdom literature, and historical narratives—and these writings were composed by members of a people living in many different historical and political settings. Yet this people consistently bears witness that God is shaping their history and their Scriptures through the unique presence of his word and Spirit in their midst. The people of Israel are the first witnesses to God's Spirit and his purposes and actions in their lives.

According to the Bible, David's own kingship was in the Spirit. When the prophet Samuel proclaimed David as King, "Samuel took the horn of oil, and anointed him; . . . the spirit of the LORD came mightily upon David from that day forward" (1 Sam. 16:13).[7] David was the Lord's anointed, filled with God's Spirit to lead the people of Israel into right relationship with God. But David failed to live up to his full calling, as did his many descendants who ruled from his throne over a kingdom that became divided just two generations after his death.

The prophets had a particularly important role in teaching about the Spirit. Filled with the Spirit, the prophets spoke truthfully about the sins of the kings and, often with great sorrow and suffering, repeatedly warned the people to turn from their rebellions against the good. Even more importantly, they foretold the Spirit's coming restoration of Israel and the transformation of the whole world.

For example, in the midst of warning the people of Judah about their dire situation in the sixth century BC, the prophet Ezekiel identified the presence of the Spirit as the source of his preaching: "The Spirit of the Lord fell upon me, and he said to me, 'Say, Thus says the LORD'" (Ezek. 11:5). Guided by the Spirit, Ezekiel presents a portrait of terrible idolatry and corruption even within the temple itself (Ezek. 8–10). In a particularly dramatic chapter of his prophetic book, he depicts the glory of the Lord mounting up on a chariot of fire and abandoning the temple. The idea that God's presence or

---

7. See P. Kyle McCarter, Jr., *1 Samuel: A New Translation with Introduction, Notes and Commentary* (Garden City, NY: Doubleday, 1980), 276.

Spirit would depart from the temple was unheard of in ancient Israel, and yet this is the reality that God reveals through Ezekiel.

God's Spirit led the people of Israel along the paths of their eventual restoration. Through Ezekiel, God promises that, on the day of restoration, he will give his people a new spirit so that they will freely choose to obey his holy Law: "I will remove from your body the heart of stone and give you a heart of flesh" (Ezek. 36:26).

It can be hard for us to hear this Good News in its fullness, given that we often think of law as merely an external set of rules. But God's Law is not something extrinsic to believers. It is more akin to the law of gravity—a principle of motion—for it is a participation in the movements of God's Spirit. Ezekiel reveals that the fruit of this promised obedience is the realization of God's promise that "they shall be my people, and I will be their God" (Ezek. 11:20). Just as God previously dwelt in the temple in Jerusalem, so now his Spirit will dwell in the renewed spiritual hearts of God's people who will become a new temple in Christ.

When Ezekiel describes the rebuilding of the temple, he does not describe a building like the first temple, or even an ordinary building at all. In Ezekiel 40–48, the restored temple appears in highly symbolic and idealized terms. For example, Ezekiel 47 sets forth a vision of water pouring out in an eastward direction from the restored temple. The water begins as a small flow and then gradually becomes a larger and larger river. It has miraculous powers: it makes salt water fresh, and on its banks wondrous trees grow, whose healing leaves never fall off and whose branches "bear fresh fruit every month" (Ezek. 47:12; see Rev. 22:2). This river is a paradisal river streaming forth from the temple to restore the conditions of Eden.

The symbolic connection between water and the Spirit is made clear when God promises, "I will sprinkle clean water upon you, and you shall be clean from all your uncleannesses, and from all your idols I will cleanse you. A new heart I will give you, and a new spirit I will put within you. . . . I will put my spirit within you" (Ezek. 36:25–27). In a parallel to the imagery of fresh water flowing from the temple and refreshing salt water, God will send his Spirit into our broken and stubborn spirits and refresh and renew them to be in relationship with God.

Ezekiel prophesies that, in the restored and renewed people of Israel, God himself will be Israel's king. In the prophecy, God condemns the wicked rulers of Israel as worthless kings, worthless shepherds. God promises, "I myself will be the shepherd of my sheep. . . . I will feed them with justice" (Ezek. 34:15–16). God also promises that a descendant of David who will be obedient to God will rule Israel under God. Under this "everlasting covenant" of peace between God and his people Israel, "they shall all have one shepherd" (Ezek. 37:24, 26). In a way that will only be fulfilled in Jesus Christ, God and the Davidic king will be the one shepherd.

God promises to restore his kingdom in such a way that it accomplishes the purpose of Eden—namely, to be the dwelling place of God with his people (Ezek. 37:27). Ezekiel depicts this kingdom with the miraculous imagery of a valley of dry bones restored to living human beings. What is even more amazing is that Ezekiel promises that the dry bones will be breathed into and so live once more: "Come . . . O breath, and breathe upon these slain, that they may live" (Ezek. 37:9). Ezekiel echoes here the original story of creation in which God breathed "the breath of life" into the first human beings (Gen. 2:7). That intimate union and harmony with God and his Spirit is exactly what the human race lost through sin. The promised coming of the Spirit will be a new creation of God's people.

The kingdom of God will come about *when God pours out his transformative Spirit*. This image of the kingdom is not meant to conjure up the idea of a remote or despotic king but rather the intimate presence of a loving God who draws all of the people in his kingdom into his own family. Ezekiel summarizes many of his prophecies of restoration when he writes, "I will never again hide my face from them, when I pour out my Spirit upon the house of Israel, says the Lord GOD" (Ezek. 39:29). The restoration of the kingdom, the giving of the Spirit, God's revealing his face—all of these express renewed intimacy and restored access to God.

In addition to the profound promises of the book of Ezekiel, the Bible presents us with the writings of the prophet Isaiah, who likewise discloses the unique role of God's Spirit in the restoration of Israel and the renewal of all humanity. In a striking passage, God first identifies himself as the Creator, the first and the last, the one and only God, and then promises, "I will pour my spirit upon your descendants" (Isa. 44:3). We see here that the Spirit of God somehow shares in the divine identity and power. God alone is the Creator, but he does not abandon his creation. Instead, he will accomplish the restoration of Israel and of his creation, through his Spirit. In the restored Israel, all will know the Lord and worship him.

The restoration of creation, however, will involve suffering and sacrificial love. God promises that he will do "a new thing" (Isa. 43:19), something unheard of before. This will be the "day of salvation," the day on which God finally establishes his covenant with Israel, a covenant embodied and enacted by his servant (Isa. 49:8). God's servant is the "man of suffering" who will be "wounded for our transgressions" so that "by his bruises we are healed" (Isa. 53:3, 5).[8]

---

8. See Hans-Jürgen Hermisson, "The Fourth Servant Song in the Context of Second Isaiah," in *The Suffering Servant: Isaiah 53 in Jewish and Christian Sources*, ed. Bernd Janowski and Peter Stuhlmacher, trans. Daniel P. Bailey (Grand Rapids, MI: Eerdmans, 2004), 16–47.

The promise of a suffering leader, a wounded servant of God, means that we cannot interpret this restoration as the temporal renewal of the kingdom of Israel in a geopolitical sense. Isaiah pledges a greater, spiritual restoration of creation in right relationship with its Creator by means of God's servant and God's Spirit.

In arresting imagery, Isaiah speaks of how God's splendor will overflow into creation even more than physical light presently shines from the sun and the moon. "The sun shall no longer be your light by day, nor for brightness shall the moon give light to you by night; but the Lord will be your everlasting light, and your God will be your glory" (Isa. 60:19). Such a promise depicts an extraordinary spiritual renewal of God's people, enabling them finally to be God's kingdom. Just as the sun makes the earth warm and golden with its rays, so God's light and glory will illumine and transform his people. Isaiah concludes this segment of his prophecy in this way: "Your people shall all be righteous; they shall possess the land for ever" (Isa. 60:21). Thus, in the story told by Israel's prophets, a central place is given to the outpouring of God's Spirit by which God's kingdom of love and justice will be established.

Another significant passage comes from the prophet Joel, which is cited by the Apostle Peter in his famous Pentecost sermon in the book of Acts. God promises that on his day of victory—the day when God fully judges sin and unites his people—"I will pour out my spirit on all flesh; your sons and your daughters shall prophesy, your old men shall dream dreams, and your young men shall see visions" (Joel 2:28).[9] Similarly, the prophet Zechariah describes the day of the Lord's victory as accompanied by the outpouring of the Spirit: "I will pour out a spirit of compassion and supplication on the house of David and the inhabitants of Jerusalem" (Zech. 12:10). Throughout

---

9. For background, see Christopher R. Seitz, *Joel* (London: Bloomsbury, 2016), 191–199.

many different times and distinct prophets, a common and decisive promise emerges: God will give his Spirit to his people and make possible a truly restored relationship with God and with neighbor.

The Inaugurated Kingdom of the Spirit

The New Testament is nothing other than the proclamation that these promises have been fulfilled. Jesus Christ has poured forth God's Spirit and inaugurated God's kingdom of love. The Gospel of John describes the risen Christ bestowing his Spirit upon his Apostles, just as he had promised to do. Christ enters their midst in the upper room, gives them his peace, commissions them for their mission, and then breathes on them, saying, "Receive the Holy Spirit" (John 20:22). Here Christ renews our fallen creation by restoring God's breath or Spirit of life that enlivened Adam, created in grace, at the dawn of the human race (Gen. 2:7).

Christ fulfills not only the Old Testament's prophecies about the inauguration of God's kingdom, but also his own prophecies during his Farewell Discourse. He promised his disciples at the Last Supper that "when the Advocate comes, whom I will send to you from the Father, the Spirit of truth who comes from the Father, he will testify on my behalf" (John 15:26). At the very outset of the Gospel, John the Baptist prophesied that Christ, filled with the Spirit, would be known as the one "who baptizes with the Holy Spirit" (John 1:33). The Gospel of John emphasizes that this prophecy came true in Jesus Christ, the incarnate Son "who takes away the sin of the world" (John 1:29). In the upper room, Jesus' words enact what they announce: "Receive the Holy Spirit. If you forgive the sins of any, they are forgiven them; if you retain the sins of any, they are retained" (John 20:22–23). The Spirit, given by Jesus and through his Apostles, takes away sins and restores life.

The book of Acts shows that the outpouring of the Spirit is the beginning of the restoration of God's people. Before Jesus ascends into heaven, the disciples ask whether the kingdom will now be restored to Israel (Acts 1:5). Jesus responds that, although they are not to know the time of the final consummation of the kingdom, they will receive the promised outpouring of the Spirit that inaugurates the kingdom. And he promises them, "You will be baptized with the Holy Spirit not many days from now" (Acts 1:5). "You will receive power when the Holy Spirit has come upon you," Jesus adds. "And you will be my witnesses in Jerusalem, in all Judea and Samaria, and to the ends of the earth" (Acts 1:8). The gift of the Spirit will empower the Apostles to be witnesses to Jesus' Resurrection.

Little more than a week after the Ascension, Jesus fulfills his promise to the Apostles on the day of the Jewish feast of Pentecost. When the disciples are gathered together in the upper room on Pentecost, the Spirit is poured forth upon them so that "all of them were filled with the Holy Spirit" (Acts 2:4). Suddenly they could speak in languages that they had not previously known, for the purpose of prophetically proclaiming the Gospel.[10]

At the Pentecost gathering in Jerusalem, Peter teaches that the outpouring of the Spirit on the Apostles is the fulfillment of "what was spoken through the prophet Joel" (Acts 2:16). Again, the gift of the Spirit is connected to the forgiveness of sins and the renewal of humanity's relationship with God.

Those who hear the preaching of the Apostles ask them what they should do. Peter answers, "Repent, and be baptized every one of you in the name of Jesus Christ so that your sins may be forgiven; and you will receive the gift of the Holy Spirit. For the promise is for you, for your children, and for all who are far away, everyone whom

---

10. See Craig S. Keener, *Acts: An Exegetical Commentary*, vol. 1, *Introduction and 1:1–2:47* (Grand Rapids, MI: Baker Academic, 2012), 794–816.

the Lord our God calls to him" (Acts 2:38–39). The gift of the Spirit is the fulfillment of God's promise, his promise to bring all who are far off near to him. What happens when we repent, are baptized, and receive the gift of the Holy Spirit? We become part of God's story and his plan for salvation.

Filled with the Spirit, Peter and the other Apostles courageously evangelize and even perform miracles in Christ's name (Acts 4:8–9). According to Acts, the experience of the first Christians was tremendous: "they were all filled with the Holy Spirit and spoke the word of God with boldness" (Acts 4:31). Not only Jewish converts and Apostles such as Paul, but also Gentile converts received the Spirit (Acts 10:44–48). Peter and the Apostles go so far as to celebrate their persecution, rejoicing that "they were considered worthy to suffer dishonor for the sake of the name [of Jesus]" (Acts 5:41). In a similar vein, Paul later exhorts Christians in Rome to have a strong hope amidst sufferings because of the gift of the Spirit: "Hope does not disappoint us, because God's love has been poured into our hearts through the Holy Spirit who has been given to us" (Rom. 5:5).

At the heart of the Holy Spirit's work is to enable believers, in word and deed, to profess and follow Christ. The Spirit testifies interiorly to the truth of Christ, because "the Spirit is the one that testifies, for the Spirit is the truth" (1 John 5:6). As we will see, the Spirit thereby builds up the "hierarchical" Church led by the Apostles and their successors in the bishops. God knows that in our prideful tendencies, we like to decide everything for ourselves. For that reason, he sends his Spirit to enable believers to learn how to depend upon and be receptive to God's gifts rather than relying upon our own resources. One way the Spirit does this is through the structure of the Church, through which we receive Christ through the hands and voices of sinners such as ourselves. We are humbled by the Spirit so that we can receive our humble Lord's grace and truth in union with others.

The Spirit amidst Weakness

Although Christ *inaugurated* his kingdom with the gift of his Spirit, Christ has not yet *consummated* his kingdom.[11] This truth adds a layer of complexity to the New Testament message. Although the Spirit has been given, Christians may resist the Spirit. Catholics may receive the sacraments exteriorly, but interiorly may refuse to hear the transformative word of Christ's love and victory over sin. We may fall into lives of grievous sin, usually beginning with small sins and building from there. Even those who seek to conform themselves to the Holy Spirit will still struggle against temptations and stumble at times.

The authors of the New Testament are visibly aware of two realities: the Spirit has been poured out; and the Spirit does not transform us magically. We must receive it, and this requires a disciplined effort and regular repentance. Repeatedly, Jesus says, "He who has ears to hear, let him hear" (Matt. 11:15 RSV-CE). In the well-known parable of the seeds and the different kinds of soils, Jesus warns that it will be all too easy for us to be like the seed that grows up among weeds and dies without bearing fruit. Such a disciple is one "who hears the word, but the cares of the world and the lure of wealth choke the word, and it yields nothing" (Matt. 13:22). Soon after Pentecost, Acts symbolically depicts the fate of professed Christians who choose to deceive the Apostles and thus "lie to the Holy Spirit" (Acts 5:3).

The dual reality of creation-in-renewal alongside that of creation-in-rebellion is present in the members of the Church. Having received the Holy Spirit, the Church is perfectly holy in the gifts Christ has

---

11. For discussion, see Joseph Ratzinger, *The Spirit of the Liturgy*, trans. John Saward (San Francisco: Ignatius Press, 2000), 53–54.

given it, in the truth of her teachings and the power of her sacraments. These are the cornerstone of the power of the Spirit to grant us new beginnings. But clearly the Church is not yet perfectly holy in its earthly members—with one notable exception.

The exception is Mary.[12] Other than Christ, who as the head of the Body was like us in all things but sin, Mary is the only member of the Church who is "full of grace" (Luke 1:28 RSV-CE). Mary still "rejoices in God my *Savior*" (Luke 1:47; emphasis added) since she too needed redemption in Christ, a redemption provided in her very conception without sin. Contrary to human expectations, Mary's conformity to the Spirit does not remove suffering from her life. Her unique calling leads her to a deep sharing in her Son's cross (John 19:25). Thus the prophecy of Simeon to Mary comes true: "A sword will pierce your own soul too" (Luke 2:35). Exhibiting the true meaning of human configuration to God's merciful love, Mary freely chooses to suffer with Jesus in love for all those whom Jesus loves.

Christ knew we would need to begin again each day. He thus instructed us to pray, "Give us this day our daily bread. And forgive us our debts [i.e., sins]" (Matt. 6:11–12). We need to ask God each day for our daily bread of physical food, of spiritual wisdom, and of sacramental life in the Eucharist. We cannot live on our own resources but rather must pray each day that God bestow his Spirit upon us.

Asking God for this bread of the Spirit enables us to admit our inadequacies in the face of the world's troubles and our own weaknesses. We may feel powerless in the face of challenges, but we are not helpless. When we ask for the Spirit, God gives his Spirit generously and abundantly. Paul encourages us to turn "to him who by the power at work within us is able to accomplish abundantly far more than all we can ask or imagine" (Eph. 3:20). This powerful grace is

12. For further discussion, see Matthew Levering, "Mary and Grace," in *The Oxford Handbook of Mary*, ed. Chris Maunder (Oxford: Oxford University Press, 2019), 289–302.

what gives us the confidence to face our sinful tendencies without fear. Yet, our sinful tendencies remain. Paul tells the Romans "the Spirit helps us in our weakness" (Rom. 8:26). We Christians continue to live amidst the reality of our own sinful inclinations and disordered reactions. To recognize our imperfections and weaknesses, however, ought not discourage us but rather encourage us to turn more to the Spirit and ask for his help and strength.

In Jesus' inaugurated-but-not-yet-consummated kingdom, there is joy alongside despair, obedience alongside disobedience, "weeds among the wheat" (Matt. 13:25). The "weeds" represent persons who are visibly members of the Church but interiorly lack the faith and love that following Christ requires. In another sense, however, "weeds" are present in all persons who are united to Jesus by faith and love but still lack perfection. When the servants in the parable suggest they pull out all of the weeds to purify the harvest, the master— representing Jesus—commands them instead to wait until the harvest when the weeds and the wheat will be separated. This harvest represents the Last Judgment. God knows there will be evil among his people; but he is more interested in the wheat's growth than in prematurely and destructively demanding immediate perfection.

Jesus describes the kingdom of God as first being "sowed," or "planted," and then "harvested." The planting and growing is the present activity of God's Spirit in the Church. The harvesting will come at the consummation of the kingdom, its full perfection.[13]

When the kingdom is finally perfected, there will be no more sin, suffering, and hatred but only peace, joy, and love. The book of Revelation powerfully depicts this promised kingdom to come: "[God] will dwell with them; they will be his peoples, and God himself will be with them; he will wipe away every tear from their eyes. Death will

---

13. On the kingdom according to the Gospel of Matthew, see Edward Sri, *God with Us: Encountering Jesus in the Gospel of Matthew*, 2nd ed. (Steubenville, OH: Emmaus Road, 2019).

be no more; mourning and crying and pain will be no more, for the first things have passed away" (Rev. 21:3–4). Death, mourning, crying, and pain all belong to this present age; they will themselves pass away in the new age to come. In the age to come, all sin and suffering will be overcome, and, healed and united, we will fully and entirely dwell with God.

The Power of the Holy Spirit in the Inaugurated Kingdom

In the period between the inauguration and the consummation of the kingdom, Catholics are called to follow Jesus the King on a new exodus—to the true promised land of the final kingdom.[14] We share in the glory of our King's self-sacrificial cross so as to share in his glorious Resurrection, a participation made possible by the power of the Holy Spirit within us. This sharing configures us to Christ—including to his brokenness.

The power that comes from the Holy Spirit is unlike fallen human power. It is the opposite of the power of Babel (Gen. 11) that represents all human desire to build our own kingdoms by our own strength. The desire of Alexander the Great, Genghis Khan, or Napoleon to conquer the whole world is reflected in Babel (and in us in smaller ways). So is the division and pain caused by their violence. Babel's founders say to each other, "Come, let us build ourselves a city, and a tower with its top in the heavens, and let us make a name for ourselves; otherwise we shall be scattered abroad upon the face of the whole earth" (Gen. 11:4). We want our name to be great, our kingdom to come, and our will to be done; but the result of our selfish power-grabbing is inevitably further division and misunderstanding. By contrast, Jesus teaches us to ask our Father for his

---

14. For discussion, see L. Michael Morales, *Exodus Old and New: A Biblical Theology of Redemption* (Downers Grove, IL: IVP Academic, 2020).

name to be made holy, his kingdom to come, and his will to be done (Matt. 6:9–10).

After Babel, humans were divided and scattered, unable to understand each other. Pentecost reverses this division by enabling the Apostles to speak and be understood in all the languages of the world. The source of this new unity is not human power, but rather is divine self-surrendering love. The Holy Spirit frees us to cooperate with God by beginning to align our wills with God's plan and love. Paul shares with us how he learned to rely entirely on the Lord, who promised him, "My grace is sufficient for you, for power is made perfect in weakness" (2 Cor. 12:9).

The Spirit of God helps us to no longer be mastered by a spirit of pride. In a beautiful section in Philippians 2, Paul describes the new power unveiled by Christ. There Paul instructs the Christians to "do nothing from selfish ambition or conceit, but in humility regard others as better than yourselves" (Phil. 2:3). To see what humility means, Paul turns our attention to Jesus Christ. Humility is not a call to think poorly of ourselves but to surrender ourselves fully to God and then let him act through us. We are to let Christ live in us; Christ, who "emptied himself, taking the form of a slave . . . and became obedient unto death—even death on a cross" (Phil. 2:7–8).

Again, Christ wins his kingdom not through pride and violence but through obedience and service.[15] As he says in the Gospel of John, "My kingship is not from this world. If my kingdom were from this world, my followers would be fighting to keep me from being handed over to the Jews. But as it is, my kingdom is not from here" (John 18:36). Jesus' kingdom is one in which worldly power has been turned upside down and replaced with the love and power of the Spirit. In this way, it is both a *king*-dom and a *kin*-dom, a kingdom of

---

15. This is a favorite theme of Augustine's.

restored kinships, a family in which Jesus the first-born son leads his adopted brothers and sisters into a renewed relationship with God the Father.[16]

Christ thereby overcomes the twisted and wounded legacy of Adam and Eve's desire to have power on their own apart from their Spirit-filled relationship with God. With that in mind, we can now look afresh at another aspect of Paul's hymn in Philippians: "Christ Jesus, who, though he was in the form of God, did not count equality with God a thing to be grasped, but emptied himself, taking the form of a servant" (Phil. 2:4–7 RSV-CE). Adam and Eve sought to be like God by grasping for divinity and for security through an act of aggressive and rebellious power. By comparison, Christ, who is already divine, showed his power not by grasping or dominating but by humbly loving.

Jesus reveals God's power to love—we might even say to *be* love. This power is manifested not only in the way of the cross but also in the way of the Resurrection. Paul will teach that "the Spirit of him who raised Jesus from the dead dwells in you" (Rom. 8:11). This same Spirit, the one who had the power to raise the human body of Jesus from the dead and unto eternal life, is given to us to raise us from sin in this life and then from death in the next.

God's kingdom is nothing other than a sharing in this all-powerful love through the gift of his Spirit. The kingdom that God aims to build—the cosmic temple that will be the restored and perfected creation—is not a kingdom of self-seeking power, as we (as fallen creatures) often think kingship should mean, but rather a kingdom of self-sacrificial love. Inasmuch as it is a kingdom of power, it is empowered by God's own love, his own Holy Spirit, shared with us. Paul teaches this truth to the early Christians in Rome when he

---

16. See Scott W. Hahn, *Kinship by Covenant: A Canonical Approach to the Fulfillment of God's Saving Promises* (New Haven, CT: Yale University Press, 2009).

writes, "God's love has been poured into our hearts through the Holy Spirit that has been given to us" (Rom. 5:5). God has no other love to give than his own love, no other Spirit than his own Spirit. The Holy Spirit imparts the power to love God and to love our neighbor as ourselves—with God's own love. There is no competition here, for God is our Creator and thus makes us truly free when his Spirit dwells in us.

Loving God and neighbor fully can only be done through the grace of the Holy Spirit. In our desire to be masters of our own fate, we may fear that the priority of God's powerful grace threatens our free will. But, in fact, holiness involves active receptivity to God working through us. Every day, we are confronted with choices. Should we look at something inappropriate on our phones or computers? Should we be silent rather than talk behind our friend's back? Should we take a moment to pray and ask for God's light to see our part in a situation? To speak of the priority of God's grace, then, means that throughout our discernment we can count on God to renew, sustain, and strengthen us in Christ through his Spirit. The message of the Gospel is that "God, who is rich in mercy, out of the great love with which he loved us even when we were dead through our trespasses, made us alive together with Christ" (Eph. 2:4–5). Through this powerful grace, this movement from death in sin to life in Christ, a life of self-surrendering love, becomes actually possible.

Against the power of grace, Paul contrasts the desires of the rebellious self. The mark of losing touch with God is an increasing tendency to live "in the passions of our flesh, following the desires of flesh and senses" (Eph. 2:3). The book of Judges, in which the people of Israel are repeatedly overcome by all kinds of sin, describes the chaos of sin with its observation, "In those days there was no king in Israel; all the people did what was right in their own eyes"

(Judg. 21:25). The profusion of sexual violence, exploitation, murder, and so on in our societies likewise exhibits the chaos of sin. Paul puts the contrast sharply and simply between the two ways of life: "Live by the Spirit, I say, and do not gratify the desires of the flesh" (Gal. 5:16).

The Bible treats sin on both personal and communal levels. It shows us that we sin personally when we treat God as a tool to serve our own wishes. Likewise, it describes how we sin when we neglect, dominate, or harm our neighbor. But the Bible also provides accounts of sinful societal structures. Empires such as Egypt and Babylon comprise sinful structures that promote idolatry and self-seeking. Since humans are fallen, all human societies promote sin to some degree. Yet living in a sinful society does not condemn us to sin. The New Testament proclaims that Jesus "knew no sin" (2 Cor. 5:21) and was "without sin" (Heb. 4:15; cf. 1 John 3:5). No doubt, this made Jesus a unique—and at times unwelcome—member of his society. In both what he did and what he refused to do, Jesus was perceived as a threat by those bent on using earthly power to serve themselves.

Paul goes so far as to ask us turn from "the flesh" and live according to the "the Spirit" (see Rom. 8). Although human desires of the flesh are not in themselves evil since they were created by God, we do not experience these desires in their natural state: we are fallen creatures. But what if we are hungry? Should we not gratify our desire of the flesh and eat some food? Paul handles this potential misunderstanding by explaining what count as "works of the flesh": they are "fornication, impurity, licentiousness, idolatry, sorcery, enmities, strife, jealousy, anger, quarrels, dissensions, factions, envy, drunkenness, carousing, and things like these" (Gal. 5:19–21). These are not bodily desires simply speaking but desires of a prideful and rebellious spirit that has not yet been healed by God's Spirit. It is in this sense that "those who belong to Christ Jesus have crucified the flesh with its passions and desires" (Gal. 5:24).

On a positive level, Paul explains that to "live by the Spirit" means to live in "love, joy, peace, patience, kindness, generosity, faithfulness, gentleness, and self-control" (Gal. 5:22–23). The Spirit shows its power in granting us new habitual ways of seeing and responding to reality. By it, we are freed from the interior drive to control and exploit others. Now we may find joy and peace, faithfulness and self-control and do what is genuinely good for ourselves and for others. Paul describes this new life in a succinct manner: "It is no longer I who live, but it is Christ who lives in me" (Gal. 2:20).

Presumption and Despair, Power and Weakness

The power to live a new life comes from the Spirit. When we read of the descent of the Holy Spirit and the words of the Father at Jesus' baptism—"This is my Son, the Beloved, with whom I am well pleased" (Matt. 3:17; cf. Rom. 8:14 17; Gal. 4:5–7)—we should also understand them as being spoken to us with regard to our identity as baptized Christians who have been adopted as sons and daughters in the Son.[17] But we also should ask ourselves whether we have truly given over control of our lives to the Holy Spirit and asked him to fill us with his gifts (Isa. 11:2–3).

So many Christians fail to realize the power of the Holy Spirit. Paul asks the Corinthians to reflect on the reality of the Holy Spirit: "Do you not know that you are God's temple and that God's Spirit dwells in you?" (1 Cor. 3:16). This is the heart of the Good News of Christianity. God's Spirit dwells in us, the Spirit of the forgiveness of sins, the Spirit of sacrificial love, the Spirit of Jesus.

---

17. Here we are reading Matthew 3:17 through the lens of Pauline theology of adoptive sonship. On the latter, see Trevor J. Burke, *Adopted into God's Family: Exploring a Pauline Metaphor* (Downers Grove, IL: InterVarsity, 2006).

But how can the Spirit dwell in us if we still struggle with so many temptations and habits that hurt ourselves and others? Often we find ourselves in one of two spots, neither of which reflects the Spirit. First, we may imagine ourselves to be among God's favorites, to be a spiritual elite. This is not a Christian sensibility. After all, if we are indeed filled with love, we give thanks to the Giver, knowing ourselves to be "unworthy servants" since "we have only done what was our duty" (Luke 17:10 RSV-CE) and have hardly done even that. Paul instructs the Ephesians that "by grace you have been saved through faith, and this is not your own doing; it is the gift of God—not the result of works, so that no one may boast" (Eph. 2:8–9). If we have faith and love, then this is God's gift. Besides, neither with regard to ourselves nor with regard to others may we "pronounce judgment before the time, before the Lord comes" (1 Cor. 4:5).

If the first temptation is to become "puffed up" (1 Cor. 4:6) with pride, thereby falling away from real love, then the second temptation is to despair that the outpouring of the Holy Spirit can ever really heal or elevate us. Many Christians get used to living with the same old sins. It is not surprising that we find ourselves particularly afflicted by certain characteristic vices, since it reflects our fallenness as well as the scars left by past sins. Given how difficult it can be to overcome our characteristic defects, we Catholics may come to fear that, even if grace exists, it is weak and impotent in our own lives and in the Church of Christ.

Paul is well aware that there is a battle ongoing in the hearts of believers. He warns that sinful Christians, especially sinful Christian leaders, bring shame and disrepute upon Christ's inaugurated kingdom, making the whole thing look unreal. Grave sin must not be normalized and accepted in the Christian community. We must call each other to repentance, or else the whole community will break down. In this regard, Paul cites Deuteronomy 17:7, "Drive out the wicked person from among you" (1 Cor. 5:13). At the same time, he exhorts, "Let us therefore no longer pass judgment on one another, but resolve instead never to put a stumbling block or hindrance in the way of another" (Rom. 14:13). Only God has the full knowledge necessary to judge justly. We are called rather to judge our neighbor's actions only when necessary, and then to do so in a spirit of humility, since we cannot see into a person's heart.

Having warned against the dead ends of presumption and despair, we may now turn to the path of faith and trust in the power of God's merciful love to save us and heal us. To receive the power of the Holy Spirit, we must have faith in Jesus Christ—real faith in him as our Savior from sin and death.[18] In faith, we freely embrace "the redemption that is in Christ Jesus, whom God put forward as a sacrifice of atonement, effective through faith" (Rom. 3:24–25).[19] Faith involves recognizing that we human beings are sinners chained to death and that we need a Savior. Christ comes to us each day precisely as that Savior. When we have faith in him, we obtain "access to this grace in which we stand; and we boast in our hope of sharing the glory of God" (Rom. 5:2).

The good news is that we really can experience the Spirit's transformative power. The "bad" news—which in fact only *seems* bad—is that the Spirit's power configures us to the cruciform *weakness* of Jesus Christ. As we saw earlier, God tells Paul, "My grace is sufficient for you, for power is made perfect in weakness" (2 Cor. 12:9). Even more, Paul "boasts" about his weakness. Our weaknesses and suffer-

---

18. See Michael Patrick Barber, *Salvation: What Every Catholic Should Know* (Denver, CO: Augustine Institute, 2019).

19. On this theologically rich passage, see N.T. Wright, "The Letter to the Romans," in *The New Interpreter's Bible: Volume X*, ed. Leander E. Keck (Nashville, TN: Abingdon, 1994), 470–77.

ings destroy our illusions of self-sufficiency and invite us to surrender ourselves more fully to God.

Even as Jesus pours out his Spirit and enables his followers to share in his mission of self-sacrificial love for the salvation of the world, every follower of Jesus must also engage in interior spiritual warfare, striving against the temptations of pride, lust, greed, worldly ambition, and so on. Paul describes the state of the world as often one of "quarreling, jealousy, anger, selfishness, slander, gossip, conceit, and disorder" (2 Cor. 12:20). Such things are not of God but may be endured in the power of the Holy Spirit. Thus Paul exhorts the Ephesians to "be strong in the Lord and in the strength of his power. Put on the whole armor of God, that you may be able to stand against the wiles of the devil" (Eph. 6:10–11).[20]

The Spirit's power consists in a love that is patient even in the midst of our own repeated failings and those of others. Such love "bears all things, believes all things, hopes all things, endures all things" (1 Cor. 13:7). Since we need the power of the Spirit, we must be sustained by a relationship with Christ in prayer. Paul calls the Ephesians to "pray in the Spirit at all times" and to make "supplication for all the saints" (Eph. 6:18). In our willingness to depend upon God in prayer, we heed Jesus' word that "unless you change and become like children, you will never enter the kingdom of heaven. Whoever becomes humble like this child is the greatest in the kingdom of heaven" (Matt. 18:3–4). The Spirit does not turn us into super-Christians who no longer struggle and need forgiveness. Instead, in our awareness of our need of God's mercy, we let the Spirit of the Son cry out in our hearts, "Abba! Father!"

---

20. See Iain M. Duguid, *The Whole Armor of God: How Christ's Victory Strengthens Us for Spiritual Warfare* (Wheaton, IL: Crossway, 2019).

The Holy Spirit and the Hierarchical Church

The disciples "receive power when the Holy Spirit" comes upon them (Acts 1:8). Jesus worked during his earthly ministry to draw together twelve Apostles from among his much larger group of followers. On a symbolic level, the number twelve indicates that Jesus intended to reconstitute Israel around himself.

Jesus's title of "Messiah" means anointed king. But Christ cannot be the new king without forming a new kingdom. He chooses his twelve Apostles after spending a night in prayer and promises them that "at the renewal of all things, when the Son of Man is seated on the throne of his glory, you who have followed me will also sit on twelve thrones, judging the twelve tribes of Israel" (Matt. 19:28). The repetition of the number twelve presents a picture of the restored Israel, the new creation, and the Apostles sharing in Christ's royal reign. It is not intended to describe a physical throne room in heaven, but rather to affirm the unique roles (or offices) the Apostles will hold in Christ's kingdom.

We learn from the Bible that God wills to give his people a visible and hierarchical operating structure, founded upon the apostolic ministry and carried forward by their successors. That there is a hierarchy does not mean that the successors of the Apostles are greater than ordinary Christians—in fact, as we have seen, the only real measure of greatness in Christ is love. Instead, the structure of ordered authority in the Church is intended to teach us to be willing to receive from others, even from others whom we may consider at times to be lesser than us. In the people of God, hierarchy is an antidote to pride. It teaches receptivity and dependence upon others. It also provides a way of fostering and sustaining unity amid the centrifugal forces that make such unity so difficult and challenging as the Gospel spreads across time and space.

When leaders in the Church are behaving rightly, they behave with humble love in service to the truth of the Gospel. Jesus warns his disciples, "The kings of the Gentiles lord it over them; and those in authority over them are called benefactors. But not so with you; rather the greatest among you must become like the youngest, and the leader like one who serves" (Luke 22:25–26). No doubt, Catholics have often failed in this and still do today. Indeed, the disciples themselves, at the moment when Jesus issued that warning, were bickering about "which one of them was to be regarded as the greatest" (Luke 22:24). Since the Church depends not on the human spirit but on the Spirit of God, it continues to communicate God's loving presence despite its members' sins and failings.

As all the Gospels show, Jesus uniquely commissioned Peter to be the leader of the Apostles. Peter is the one who speaks for the Twelve. He is listed first in the lists of the Apostles (Matt. 10:2–4; Mark 3:16–29; Luke 6:14–16). Prior to Peter denying Jesus three times, Jesus tells him, "Satan demanded to have you, that he might sift you like wheat, but I have prayed for you that your faith may not fail; and when you have turned again, strengthen your brethren" (Luke 22:31–32 RSV-CE). Similarly, in Matthew 16, Jesus identifies Peter as the one upon whom Jesus will found his Church. It is Peter, Jesus says, who will be the royal steward who guides the inaugurated kingdom on earth and exercises the keys of the kingdom on behalf of the king: whatever Peter binds or looses on earth will be bound or loosed in heaven (Matt. 16:19; see Isa. 22:22). And in John 21, the risen Jesus gives Peter a threefold commission to tend his flock.

The commissioned authority of the Apostles is decisive for the earliest Church. In Acts 15, a controversy over whether Gentile converts must be circumcised in order to be saved is settled by means of a council of the Apostles and elders at Jerusalem. Peter and James speak authoritatively at this council as the living instruments of the Holy Spirit: "it has seemed good to the Holy Spirit and to us" (Acts 15:28). When the believer assents to authentic dogma, the believer is believing Jesus himself who speaks through the ministry of the Petrine office and the councils of the Church in their role of interpreting the Word of God. Jesus shows forth the instrumental role of Church authority at broader levels when he sends out seventy disciples, two by two, to proclaim his proclamation of the coming kingdom of God: "Whoever listens to you listens to me" (Luke 10:16).

With regard to the generations of Christians that come after the Apostles, the First Letter of Peter states, "Now as an elder myself and a witness of the sufferings of Christ, as well as one who shares in the glory to be revealed, I exhort the elders among you to tend the flock of God that is in your charge" (1 Pet. 5:1–2). Although we can recognize that offices in the Church have developed in certain ways over the centuries, the Spirit's outpouring is not in opposition to the hierarchy of authority in the Church. Hierarchy, however, is not a *carte blanche* to run over people simply by virtue of possessing rightful authority. Like all Christians, leaders must hearken to the words that Peter goes on to say: "Humble yourselves therefore under the mighty hand of God, so that he may exult you in due time. . . . Discipline yourselves, keep alert. Like a roaring lion your adversary the devil prowls around, looking for someone to devour. Resist him, steadfast in your faith" (1 Pet. 5:6, 8–9).

The authoritative role of leaders in the Church depends not on their individual holiness—thank God!—but upon the promise of Christ to have his Spirit dwell in the Church. Across history and up to the present, individual Catholic leaders too often have abused their office. Catholic laity, too, have frequently failed to trust in the power of the Holy Spirit, and instead have succumbed to "the desire

of the flesh, and the desire of the eyes, the pride in riches" (1 John
2:16). Jesus Christ knew that it would be so. In the Gospel of Luke,
Jesus even poses the question, "When the Son of man comes, will he
find faith on earth?" (Luke 18:8). In the book of Acts, Paul warns his
fellow Christians that "savage wolves will come in among you, not
sparing the flock. Some even of your own group will come distorting
the truth in order to entice the disciples to follow them" (Acts 20:29–
30). The sins of Catholics are a shameful thing, but the solution is not
to imagine that there is no Holy Spirit and no inaugurated kingdom.
On the contrary, the solution is precisely the opposite. We see it in
Paul's words when, having installed Timothy in a position of authority, he urges the young leader, "Rekindle the gift of God that is within
you through the laying on of my hands" (2 Tim. 1:6).

Renewal of the Church must always come from the Spirit's
power to renew through forgiveness and healing. The Bible antici-
pates the ongoing reality of sin among Christians: "If anyone does
sin, we have an advocate with the Father, Jesus Christ the righteous;
and he is the atoning sacrifice for our sins, and not for ours only but
also for the sins of the whole world" (1 John 2:1–2). Every human sin,
no matter how heinous and no matter how ingrained in our habits,
is absolutely forgivable by God if only we repent and appeal to Jesus
in sincerity of heart, seeking out the sacrament of Reconciliation.
This is the true power, the power that the "world" cannot recognize
because it is merciful love.

Let us return to the upper room when the risen Jesus appeared
to his fearful disciples. Jesus' first words to them address us as
well, "Peace be with you. As the Father has sent me, so I send you"
(John 20:21). We have received the peace of Jesus, not a peace established by our own effort, but the peace of him who overcame death
through obedient love. Moreover, we have received a mission and

purpose. The gift of the Holy Spirit is above all the gift of the forgiveness of sins. All the faithful are called to experience the power of the forgiveness of sins and to help others to do the same.

Conclusion

Paul writes to Timothy, "God did not give us a spirit of cowardice, but a spirit of power and of love and of self-discipline" (2 Tim. 1:7). The Holy Spirit promises us freedom from the bondage of fear and frustration no matter whether we are facing discouragement, hostility, or simply our own sinful inclinations. When we embrace faith in Jesus Christ, have our sins forgiven, and receive adoption as children of God, we allow God to breathe in us again "the Spirit of life." This new life is not the fruit of our own efforts but rather of God's power to remake and restore us in relationship with him. The Holy Spirit truly dwells in us and offers us continual mercy and assistance.

We must be patient with ourselves and with others since healing may be slow and gradual, especially insofar as we carry with us bad habits and tendencies toward particular failings. The Spirit's work of renewing creation will not be complete until we are fully alive with God in heaven. Yet even now, Christians may invite the Spirit more deeply into their lives, "a spirit of power and of love and of self-discipline." Since the Spirit is powerful, he will make us more powerful. Since he is love, he will make us more loving and more lovely. Since he is self-disciplined or, better, self-possessed, he will make us more self-possessed. The more we surrender our rebellious egos and turn our lives over to the Spirit indwelling our hearts, the more we find our true selves.[21] As Jesus promises, "Those who want to save their life will lose it, and those who lose their life for my sake will find it" (Matt. 16:25).

---

21. See G.K. Beale, *We Become What We Worship: A Biblical Theology of Idolatry* (Downers Grove, IL: IVP Academic, 2008).

Empowered by the Spirit of Christ, let us commit ourselves to living as God's people. May the members of the Catholic Church—clergy, consecrated religious, and laity—become what God has called us to be. Opening ourselves in faith to the power of Christ's love, let us live according to the Spirit rather than according to the flesh. With the Psalmist, let us cry out to God and ask him, "Send forth your Spirit and renew the face of the earth" (see Ps. 104:30). God will do this, and God has done this. For indeed, "the Holy Spirit has come upon you" (Acts 1:8).

CHAPTER 4

How Can Christ's Blood
Be Good News?

"A sharing in the blood of Christ"
(1 Corinthians 10:16)

On the face of things, Jesus Christ's death on a Roman cross is the worst event of human history. The killing of an innocent man, let alone the Son of God, stains the Roman empire, stains his disciples, stains the Jewish leaders, and stains the entirety of humanity. Jesus' death appears as well to discredit God the Father. As one of our students, some years ago, mistakenly said on an exam: "God saw that the world was a mess, so he decided to kill his Son." In fact, such a God would simply be a murderer, not a God worthy of worship and praise. The execution of an innocent person is a tragic crime, and the proper response appears obvious: we should protest it rather than celebrate it.

In a similar manner, the idea that the Eucharist received by Catholics is truly Christ's Body and Blood may appear disturbing. Not only do Catholics typically have crucifixes with the wounded body of Jesus rather than a simple cross, but Catholics also claim to consume the very Body and Blood of Jesus. Are Catholics cannibals? In the Bible, the consumption of animal blood is outlawed—let alone human blood!

Should Catholics therefore distance themselves from both the cross and the Eucharist? Some Catholics find it all unworthy of belief. A survey of modern American Catholics found that four out of ten agreed with the statement, "A person can be a good Catholic without believing that, in the Mass, the bread and wine really become the body and blood of Jesus."[1]

Can the Bible give us any help in this regard? It may be surprising at first to notice how often the New Testament refers to the Blood of Christ as central to the entire plan of salvation. Here are a handful of representative passages (emphasis added):

- "This cup that is poured out for you is the new covenant *in my blood*" (Luke 22:20).

- "Much more surely then, now that we have been justified *by his blood*, will we be saved through him from the wrath of God" (Rom. 5:9).

- "Through him God was pleased to reconcile to himself all things, whether on earth or in heaven, by making peace *through the blood of his cross*" (Col. 1:20).

- "In him we have redemption *through his blood*, the forgiveness of our trespasses, according to the riches of his grace that he lavished on us" (Eph. 1:7–8).

- "How much more will *the blood of Christ*, who through the eternal Spirit offered himself without blemish to God, purify our conscience from dead works to worship the living God!" (Heb. 9:11–14).

- "To him who loves us and freed us from our sins by *his blood*" (Rev. 1:5).

In fact, the favored manner of expressing the Good News of salvation in the New Testament is to say that it has happened "by his blood," "through his blood," or "in his blood." It is fair to say that,

---

1. William V. D'Antonio, Michele Dillon, and Mary L. Gautier, *American Catholics in Transition* (Lanham, MD: Rowman & Littlefield, 2013), 114.

if we do not understand that salvation took place through the Blood of Christ, then we likely do not understand the biblical message of salvation.

If we were to ask Joe or Jane Catholic why Jesus shed his Blood, we might receive the answer, "To save us from our sins." This answer is correct, but it does not go far enough. It does not confront the issue of why God would want the free sacrifice, in love, of his innocent Son. Why should there be bloodshed at all? Furthermore, even if the cross were somehow needed, now that Jesus is risen from the dead, why do we need to participate in his Blood through faith and the Eucharist?

This chapter will examine the realities of sacrifice, love, and salvation across the Old and New Testaments to see why we should rejoice in the Blood of Christ, given up for us on the cross in supreme love and shared with us in the Eucharist.

God's People Israel: Sin and Sacrifice

A central difficulty that we have in understanding the role of sacrifice stems from our failure to understand the significance of sin. How can we know what is needed to restore real communion with God when we do not experience genuine communion with ourselves or with one another? Far from being filled with love, we tend toward evil and distrust in our fallen condition. The need for sacrifice may never become perfectly clear before our eyes, but we must first understand the darkness of sin to begin to make any sense of it.

As the book of Genesis recognizes, the history of the emergence of the human race involves not only developments in tool-making, farming, city-building, and so on, but also ugly injustice and conflict. Soon after the fall of Adam and Eve, Cain is depicted as murdering his brother Abel. One of Cain's lineage, Lamech, is renowned for his violence and injustice. Lamech boasts, "I have killed a man for wounding me, a young man for striking me" (Gen. 4:23).

The stench of festering injustice continues to permeate human history as further events of Genesis unfold. Sinful human actions rooted in hate, greed, envy, ambition, lust, and pride cause deep wounds of pain and scars of oppression. In Genesis 6:5, God diagnoses humanity's illness: "The Lord saw that the wickedness of man was great in the earth, and that every imagination of the thoughts of his heart was only evil continually." Such injustice makes the earth "corrupt" and fills the earth "with violence" (Gen. 6:11).

Unfortunately, when we reflect upon the problem of sin, we cannot merely blame a few bad apples among the large number of good people. Rather, we all have wicked impulses. How many of us, in a bout of anger, have wished harm on a neighbor? Even Noah, who "was a righteous man, blameless in his generation" and who "walked with God" (Gen. 6:9), upon surviving the flood became drunk, and the chain of events led to him cursing his son Ham.

Sin likewise afflicts the divinely chosen family of Abraham. Consider the case of Jacob and his sons. After wrestling all night with an angel of God, Jacob receives a blessing and a new name, "Israel" (Gen. 32:28). Jacob fathered twelve sons, and their descendants constitute the twelve tribes of Israel. One might expect that Scripture would provide an idealized portrait of the heroic founding family of Jacob/Israel. But in fact the opposite is the case. Jacob steals his brother Esau's birthright. His wives fight enviously with each other. He plays favorites with his wives and his children, giving rise to envy that has deeply destructive consequences. His sons, in their jealousy, decide to kill their brother Joseph. After relenting, they instead sell him to foreign slave traders. And they deceive and slay all the men of the village Shechem in retaliation for the rape of their sister Dinah.

Once we understand the depths of sin, we can understand the desire that humans rightly have to make sacrificial offerings to God. In order to be worthy, such sacrifices would have to signify a genuine repentance and so, by symbolizing contrition and giving up something of value, invite God's forgiveness. Yet it is important to perceive that sin can afflict us even in this regard. In the ancient Near East, as throughout the world, child sacrifice was all too common. God condemns it as radically sinful: "Every abhorrent thing that the Lord hates they [the nations] have done for their gods. They would even burn their sons and their daughters in the fire to their gods" (Deut. 12:31).

The story of the near-offering of Isaac in Genesis 22 countermands child sacrifice. Though God commands Isaac to sacrifice his son, the purpose of this command is to reveal that the covenant depends not on Abraham's clinging to his self-interest but on Abraham's reliance upon the life-giving God. In fact, the story shows God overcoming the practice of child sacrifice by stopping Abraham's hand and providing a ram, which Abraham duly offers "as a burnt offering instead of his son" (Gen. 22:13).[2] Even this action, however, leads to further questions—namely, why would shedding the blood even of an animal be an appropriate part of a relationship with the Creator God who does not need blood to be reconciled to humans whom he already perfectly loves?

Answering this question requires attention to the developing history of Israel's relationship with God, in which the blood of animals takes on a symbolic role indicative of covenantal relationship. The role of animal sacrifice intensifies during Israel's exodus from Egyptian slavery. On the night of the Passover, God requires each

---

2. For the variety of interpretations of Genesis 22 over the centuries, see Edward Kessler, *Bound by the Bible: Jews, Christians, and the Sacrifice of Isaac* (Cambridge: Cambridge University Press, 2004).

Israelite family to sacrifice a lamb and put the lamb's blood on the doorpost of its home in order to spare the Israelites from the tenth plague, the death of all the firstborn in Egypt. After the Israelites have escaped from Egypt and received the Ten Commandments at Mount Sinai, Moses binds them in a sacred covenant with God. The covenant is ratified by sacrificial blood. The Israelites first "offered burnt offerings and sacrificed oxen as offerings of well-being to the LORD," and then "Moses took half the blood" and threw it against the altar (Exod. 24:5–6). He took the other half of the blood and threw it on the people, proclaiming, "See the blood of the covenant that the LORD has made with you" (Exod. 24:8).[3] In the book of Leviticus, too, sacrificial blood plays a central role in the cult. At the priestly ordination of Aaron and his sons, for example, Moses kills a ram and places the blood on Aaron's ears, hands, and feet before proceeding to throw "the blood against all sides of the altar" (Lev. 8:24). He then sprinkles the blood on Aaron and his sons. He concludes by taking part of an animal that he has sacrificed and presenting it as "an elevation offering before the LORD" (Lev. 8:29).

Perhaps the most notable sacrifice prescribed in Leviticus is that of the Day of Atonement. On that day each year, the high priest makes an offering to atone for his own sins and for those of the whole people. The high priest is to take "some of the blood of the bull, and sprinkle it with his finger on the front of the mercy seat" seven times (Lev. 16:14). He is also commanded to place ritually the sins of the people upon a chosen goat and then banish the goat into the wilderness.

The Day of Atonement shows that Israel's cultic worship was not sufficient to prevent the Israelites from sinning against God. Indeed, at Mount Sinai Israel turned away from God entirely, preferring to

---

3. For discussion of cultic sacrifice, see Thomas Joseph White, OP, *Exodus* (Grand Rapids, MI: Brazos Press, 2016), 211–214.

worship a god symbolized by a golden calf and linked to orgiastic sexual practices. After worshiping the golden calf, "the people sat down to eat and drink, and rose up to revel" (Exod. 32:6).[4] Moses returns and the people repent, but not before a deadly civil war.

Similarly, according to the book of Numbers, the people complain against God and concoct plans to "choose a [different] captain, and go back to Egypt" (Num. 14:4). In response, God decrees that none of that generation of Israelites on the exodus, except for Caleb and Joshua, will ever enter into the Promised Land. Shortly afterwards, Korah and his companions organize a rebellion against Moses and Aaron. God puts down the rebellion through a devastating plague. Then Moses, under the influence of pride, performs a miracle in a way that makes it appear as though he is acting by his own power. For this sin, God bans Moses from entering the Promised Land. Bringing matters to a head, idolatry takes over the whole people: "While Israel was staying at Shittim, the people began to have sexual relations with the women of Moab. These invited the people to the sacrifices of their gods, and the people ate and bowed down to their gods. Thus Israel yoked itself to Baal of Peor" (Num. 25:1–3).

The book of Numbers' account of the Israelites serves as a proxy for all of us in that it depicts them preferring disordered eating, drinking, and sexual activities rather than the restored relationship with the Creator patterned on justice and love.

It is within this context that Christians might begin to reflect upon animal sacrifice. To sacrifice an animal meant to give up something important for human existence. In offering an animal, one made reparation for one's acts of breaking the covenant with God. In a sin offering or purification offering, the blood was understood to remove the offending aspect of the sin and to reconcile with God; the

---

4. See Thomas B. Dozeman, *Exodus* (Grand Rapids, MI: Eerdmans, 2009), 682–683.

blood was therefore wiped or sprinkled on the altar. In a burnt offering, the ascending smoke symbolized a spiritual ascent in prayer to God's own dwelling-place.

We can see that the very breaking and wounding involved in the animal sacrifice corresponds in a mysterious way to the breaking and wounding caused by human sinfulness—united with the contrasting reality of human yearning for relationship with God. Jesus Christ will show forth the deeper meaning of sacrifice when he enters into our sinful alienation from God in order to establish perfectly that communion with God that we yearn for. Through his sinless and loving offering of himself as the incarnate Lord, he accomplishes what no animal sacrifice could accomplish. He heals our wound from within by replacing our injustice with his justice in cleaving to God rather than to bodily life.[5]

Sin and Sacrifice in the Psalms and Prophets

To sum up the above remarks: Israel's story oscillates between, on the one hand, its call to do right by God and neighbor, and on the other, its persistent and pervasive failure to do so, despite its sacrificially solemnized covenants with God. In witness of Israel's fighting this losing moral battle, Psalm 14 goes so far as to wonder whether anyone in the world is truly good. It depicts a terrible scene: "The Lord looks down from heaven on humankind, to see if there are any who are wise, who seek after God. They have all gone astray, they are all alike perverse; there is no one who does good, no, not one" (Ps. 14:2–3). The Psalmist begs God to accomplish his promise to restore Israel, "for God is with the company of the righteous" (Ps. 14:5). After praising the perfection of God's Law, the Psalmist

---

5. For further discussion, see Matthew Levering, *Engaging the Doctrine of Creation: Cosmos, Creatures, and the Wise and Good Creator* (Grand Rapids, MI: Baker Academic, 2017), chapter 7.

asks God to forgive the "hidden faults" of his servants and to keep his servants from "presumptuous sins" (Ps. 19:12–13 RSV-CE). In this way, Psalm 19 and other Psalms proclaim both the goodness of the Law and the reality that Israel awaits from the Lord some greater deliverance.

The Psalms also depict the incompleteness of the animal sacrifices in Israel's worship of God. In Psalm 69, the Psalmist calls upon the Lord to deliver him and promises that, in the midst of his afflictions, "I will praise the name of God with a song; I will magnify him with thanksgiving. This will please the LORD more than an ox or a bull with horns and hoofs" (Ps. 69:30–31). The Psalmist recognizes that it is love and justice that the Lord wants, not the blood of animals per se. Only the sacrifice of thanksgiving will truly please God. Psalm 50 employs the same sacrifice of thanksgiving to reject any false idea that God somehow directly desired the blood or flesh of animals: "If I [God] were hungry, I would not tell you, for the world and all that is in it is mine. Do I eat the flesh of bulls, or drink the blood of goats?" (Ps. 50:12–13). Israel offers plenty of animal sacrifices, but all animals in fact already belong to the Lord. What the Lord really wants is a holy heart, a heart filled with love and justice.

In the Psalmist's heart, inspired by the Holy Spirit, he hears God tell Israel, "Offer to God a sacrifice of thanksgiving, and pay your vows to the Most High. Call on me in the day of trouble; I will deliver you, and you shall glorify me" (Ps. 50:14–15). God sums up the message: "Those who brings thanksgiving as their sacrifice honor me" (Ps. 50:23). The proper stance of the human person before the Creator is to recognize everything as having been given by God and thus to give thanks to God in return. Once the human person is in covenantal relationship with God, he or she gives thanks to God as Redeemer who has responded to pleas for help.

Psalm 51 confesses "my sin is ever before me" and acknowledges that every sin against our neighbor is also against God (Ps. 51:3–4). Every serious sin, by rejecting God's Law and choosing to do the things forbidden by the Decalogue, breaks communion with God. The Psalmist therefore begs God, "Purge me with hyssop, and I shall be clean; wash me, and I shall be whiter than snow" (Ps. 51:7). He pleads that God may not only free him from guilt but also transform him so he can fully relate to God in holiness. "Create in me a clean heart, O God, and put a new and right spirit within me" (Ps. 51:10). God has "no delight in sacrifice" or in "a burnt offering" because what God truly wants is love and justice (Ps. 51:16). The Psalmist explains, "The sacrifice acceptable to God is a broken spirit; a broken and contrite heart" (Ps. 51:17). The ultimate thanksgiving that the Psalmist offers to God is for the deliverance from sin. In our broken-ness and contrition, we may begin to turn rightly to the Lord.

Despite the Psalmist's view that sacrifices of love and thanksgiv-ing are more important than those of animals, the Psalms should not be understood to reject animal sacrifice. Animal sacrifices remained part of Israel as long as there was a temple. The Psalms alert the Isra-elites that the animal sacrifices must be offered with a holy and just spirit, a spirit of gratitude to God and love of God. Although the sacrifices find their deeper value when they embody one's interior self-offering to God, nonetheless they remain an imperfect instru-ment of such self-offering.

The books of the prophets, as with the Psalms, emphasize the difficulty of living in communion with God and point forward to God's eventual action to bring about such communion. In the proph-ecy of Jeremiah, God condemns the entire people: "From the least to the greatest of them, everyone is greedy for unjust gain; and from prophet to priest, everyone deals falsely" (Jer. 6:13). The prophets help us to realize that disordered desires and false justifications are not merely present in other people; instead, this disorder and conflict describes each of us and so reveals the radical inadequacy and incompleteness of the visible order in our human society. Jeremiah teaches that Israel's inability to follow God's Law and establish true harmony among neighbors is the reason why their "burnt offerings" and "sacrifices" are "not acceptable" (Jer. 6:20). Not only have Israel's people failed to love their neighbors, they have not even obeyed the commandment against idolatry; on the contrary, they assiduously worship false gods.

Jeremiah does not reject the animal sacrifices in themselves but shows the need for a renewed heart for true worship. Indeed, through Jeremiah, God promises that if the people will obey his law and observe the Sabbath, then the sacrificial worship in the temple will again flourish (Jer. 17). At the same time, Jeremiah also points to a New Covenant to heal the broken covenant that God made with the people at Sinai. This New Covenant will transform the people interiorly. God promises, "I will put my law within them, and I will write it on their hearts" (Jer. 31:33). On this day of victory, God will heal Jerusalem and restore Israel and Judah. God states, "I will cleanse them from all the guilt of their sin against me, and I will forgive all the guilt of their sin and rebellion against me" (Jer. 33:8).

In light of this promise of restoration and renewal, it might seem that on such a day, animal sacrifice would come to an end, as no longer needed. On the contrary, God pledges through Jeremiah that the animal sacrifices will be renewed: "The levitical priests shall never lack a man in my presence to offer burnt offerings, to make grain offerings, and to make sacrifices for all time" (Jer. 33:18; cf. Ezek. 43: 27; Mal. 3:4). God's promise of a New Covenant includes perfecting Israel's sacrificial worship. How should we understand this?

Here we should remember that the exemplar of all temple sacrifices was that of the Passover lamb by whose blood the people were saved from Egyptian slavery. God commanded that the Passover be commemorated each year: as part of the annual ritual, each family was supposed to sacrifice a Passover lamb and to eat it without breaking any of its bones (Exod. 12:46).

As noted above, in addition to the Passover lamb, there was the ritual enactment of the Day of Atonement. The instructions regarding the Day of Atonement describe how Aaron as the high priest is to "lay both his hands upon the head of the live goat, and confess over him all the iniquities of the people of Israel, and all their transgressions, all their sins, putting them on the head of the goat, and sending it away into the wilderness" (Lev. 16:21).[6] The sacrifices are inextricably connected to sin. Sin is not something external to us that may be easily removed. Much like cancerous cells, it grows among each of our hearts and among our societies.

Isaiah 53 powerfully describes a suffering servant who will bear the people's sins. The vicarious suffering of the servant has resemblance to the sacrificial goat who takes on the punishment for the sins of Israel on the Day of Atonement. According to Isaiah's prophecy, the suffering servant is the one who "has borne our griefs and carried our sorrows" (Isa. 53:4 RSV-CE). Isaiah further specifies that the servant "was wounded for our transgressions, crushed for our iniquities; upon him was the punishment that made us whole, and by his bruises we are healed" (Isa. 53:5). The unwilling and unknowing sacrificial animals, therefore, point to a far greater sacrifice in love— one that will come about by the interior willingness and knowledge of God's suffering servant.

---

6. See Jacob Milgrom, *Leviticus: A Book of Ritual and Ethics* (Minneapolis, MN: Fortress Press, 2004), 162–172.

It will be God's servant, and not a mere animal, whose sacrificial death truly reconciles for sin. But the mystery runs even deeper, since God's servant will be the Lord himself. In Isaiah 59, the Lord is depicted as looking upon the whole of humanity and seeing that none of us are just and none of us can restore the human race to justice. In response, the Lord himself promises to come "to Zion as Redeemer," and to "put on righteousness like a breastplate, and a helmet of salvation on his head" (Isa. 59:16–17, 20). The suffering servant will be none other than the Lord himself. As the Lord, full of righteousness and salvation, he will be the first "offering for sin" that finally has the power of redemption for the sins of all people, and he will undergo the suffering "that made us whole" (Isa. 53:5, 10; cf. 53:12).

In our fallen condition, which is marked by a deadly pride, the offering of blood remains important because it involves giving back God's gift of life rather than clinging to human self-sufficiency. Sacrificing animals means offering creatures that sustain human life. How much greater will be the sacrifice of God's servant—the incarnate Lord—who sacrifices his own life freely out of love for our sake, bearing the very death that is the farthest point of our sinful alienation.

When the servant prophesied by Isaiah freely wills to give back to God his very life, then the human race will be no longer caught up in the serpent's false promise that sinful rebellion can secure human life—"You will not die" but rather "you will be like God" (Gen. 3:4–5). Pride has so completely inserted itself into our human history that removing such pride admits of no easy solution. In fact, the solution God proposes of the holy sacrificial offering made in love for God and neighbor hardly makes sense to us as long as we view things from our earthly perspective. It makes sense only when, in faith, hope, and love, we perceive God's love for and solidarity with sinners, entering into our woundedness and alienation—manifested most fully in our dying—to heal us from within by his divine power, restoring the justice and love that creatures owe to the Creator.

The Sacrifice of Jesus Christ

When Jesus suffered on the cross, he fulfilled and revealed the deepest meaning of the animal sacrifices of the covenants and Law of Israel. Their meaning comes ultimately from Christ rather than the other way around. He is the true "mercy seat," and his death is the true Day of Atonement for the whole world.

As the Messiah, the anointed king and divine Son, Jesus reconfigured the temple around himself. In Matthew 12:6, he proclaims—speaking about himself—that "something greater than the temple is here." In the Gospel of John, explaining his authority for cleansing the temple, he compares his own body to God's temple, indicating that his risen body will replace the temple (John 2:18–22).[7] Not only does Jesus reveal that he is the new temple, John the Baptist reveals that Jesus is the new sacrifice. When John the Baptist sees him, he says to his disciples, "Here is the Lamb of God who takes away the sin of the world!" (John 1:29). The connection between Jesus' Crucifixion and the sacrifice of the Passover lamb, by whose blood the people of God were spared, is manifest in all the Gospels. Jesus is both the new Temple of God and the new Lamb of God.

The theme of the lamb of God plays a significant role in the book of Revelation. There, Jesus appears as "a Lamb standing as if it had been slaughtered, having seven horns and seven eyes" (Rev. 5:6). To understand this imagery, it is helpful to remember that the number seven symbolizes perfection, the horn the king's strength,

---

7. See Paul M. Hoskins, *Jesus as the Fulfillment of the Temple in the Gospel of John* (Milton Keynes, UK: Paternoster, 2006).

and the eyes wisdom. Seven horns thus signify the perfection of power (omnipotence) and seven eyes the perfection of knowledge (omniscience). The slain Lamb is now standing—a sign of Christ's Resurrection and Ascension. This scene from Revelation shows us that Jesus Christ who was sacrificed is now the risen one who governs history and receives worship from all creatures.[8]

The saints in this scene from Revelation are those who have been configured to Christ and who "have washed their robes and made them white in the blood of the Lamb" (Rev. 7:14). To understand the imagery of robes made white by Christ's Blood, recall the language of Isaiah, "We have all become like one who is unclean, and all our righteous deeds are like a filthy cloth" (Isa. 64:6). Due to our sins and the sinful inheritance of the human race, we cannot overcome our separation from the all-holy God. What is needed is not our imperfect and self-seeking attempts at love, but the perfect sacrificial love of the Son of God now in human form. The Blood of Christ opens up a new path of purity, cleanliness, and union with God. In his love for us, Christ takes upon himself our disorder and its resulting penalty of death.

Jesus at the Last Supper shows how the shedding of his Blood for the sake of the salvation of God's people will inaugurate a new Passover, its destination being the perfect Promised Land of God's kingdom, the new creation. He celebrates the Last Supper as a Passover meal and goes to his death in deliberate connection with the celebration of Passover.[9] Luke's Gospel depicts him using a word that is translated as "passover"—but in this case refers to the paschal lamb that was central to the Passover ritual meal—as he tells his disciples, "I have earnestly desired to eat this Passover with you before I suffer"

---

8. See Scott Hahn, *The Lamb's Supper: The Mass as Heaven on Earth* (New York: Doubleday, 1999).

9. See Brant Pitre, *Jesus and the Last Supper* (Grand Rapids, MI: Eerdmans, 2015), chapter 5.

(Luke 22:15). In Mark's account, when passing around the ritual cup of wine, he says, "This is my blood of the covenant, which is poured out for many" (Mark 14:24). This statement echoes Moses' words, "See the blood of the covenant" (Exod. 24:8). Jesus' words here draw a connection between his actions at the meal and the cult of the sacrificial animals that, as we have seen, were used for covenant-making and covenant-renewal rituals. In this way, he inaugurates a New Covenant relationship with God—not through the blood of bulls and lambs, as in ages past, but in his own Blood.

Mark's account of the Crucifixion shows us spectators who mock Jesus by saying, "You who would destroy the temple and build it in three days, save yourself, and come down from the cross!" (Mark 15:29–30).[10] These spectators fail to realize the irony of their words. As the supreme sacrifice of the new Passover, Jesus' crucified and risen body will be the new Temple. The saving sacrifice of Christ will suffice once and for all for the forgiveness of sins and the reconciliation of the world to God. This point is highlighted in the Gospel of Matthew's rendering of Jesus' words over the cup at the Last Supper: "This is my blood of the covenant, which is poured out for many for the forgiveness of sins" (Matt. 26:28). Jeremiah's promise of a New Covenant has been fulfilled; our hearts are now renewed through the perfection of sacrifice and the forgiveness of sins.

Jesus' Blood makes possible a newfound forgiveness of sins. Since our culture has been affected in so many ways by the Christian story, we often overlook the radical nature of this saving act. We often even replace the true and costly forgiveness bought with Jesus' Blood with a false and cheap forgiveness.[11] What is the difference? Cheap for-

---

10. See Raymond E. Brown, SS, *The Death of the Messiah: From Gethsemane to the Grave. A Commentary on the Passion Narratives in the Four Gospels*, vol. 2 (New York: Doubleday, 1994), 985–989.

11. See Dietrich Bonhoeffer, *The Cost of Discipleship,* trans. R.H. Fuller, trans. rev. Irmgard Booth (New York: Simon & Schuster, 1995).

giveness forgives wrongdoing by saying it was only a mistake or a moment of weakness. Cheap forgiveness is powerless in the face of the wounds of deep injustice, horrible suffering, and the separation caused by death. Costly forgiveness recognizes the true injustice and harm done by humans and the resultant intergenerational conflicts and does something about it. Costly forgiveness recognizes the total holiness of God and the reality that we could not stand in his presence. Costly forgiveness was introduced into the world through the loving sacrifice of Jesus Christ, who opened up a new relationship with God.

Paul, Hebrews, and the Blood of Christ

It is often the later parts of a story that illumine and draw together all of the earlier parts. In this vein, as noted above, the animal sacrifices do not determine the meaning of Jesus' sacrifice, but it is Jesus' sacrifice that reveal the full meaning of the animal sacrifices. Moreover, it is Jesus' Resurrection and Ascension that help us understand Jesus' sacrifice. Paul affirms that Jesus has fulfilled—and thereby revealed—the interior meaning and purpose of Israel's animal sacrifices. According to Paul, Jesus has fulfilled their meaning first through his supreme love, reversing our rebellious pride. Jesus has also fulfilled their expiatory meaning, freely paying the penalty of sin—death—and healing the wound that sin inflicts upon human beings' relationship with God.

In harmony with the Gospels, Paul depicts Jesus' death as perfecting the earlier animal sacrifices, even while being radically different from them. The symbolic meaning of the animal sacrifices comes from their pointing forward to the sacrificial death of Jesus. This order is crucial. Jesus' sacrifice is not merely one more of many sacrifices. He freely wills his sacrifice out of love rather than merely

accepting death passively or ignorantly. His sacrifice is the everlasting sacrifice of the New Covenant.

Paul remarks joyfully that "our paschal lamb, Christ, has been
sacrificed" (1 Cor. 5:7). He knows we have been saved by Christ's
Blood, just as the Israelites were spared by marking their doors with
the blood of the Passover lamb. Whereas the original exodus was an
escape from slavery and idolatry in Egypt to communion with God
in the Promised Land, Paul teaches that Christ has accomplished the
true exodus. It is Christ who brings us to the true Promised Land
and the opening up of our everlasting dwelling in peace with God
by becoming the true Passover from death to life. Because Christ
was the innocent Son of God whose self-offering was done with the
utmost love, "one man's act of righteousness leads to justification and
life for all" (Rom. 5:18).

Using the categories of Israel's faith, Paul explains first the depth
of sin and second the power of the Blood of Christ: "All have sinned
and fall short of the glory of God; they are now justified by his grace
as a gift, through the redemption that is in Christ Jesus, whom God
put forward as a sacrifice of atonement by his blood, effective through
faith" (Rom. 3:23–25).[12] By Christ's expiatory Blood, his holy self-
offering as the incarnate Lord for all sin, we sinners have redemption,
freedom, and a share in God's glory.

The Letter to the Hebrews reflects at length on Christ's fulfillment of Israel's animal sacrifices.[13] Hebrews depicts Jesus as the
"great high priest" (Heb. 4:14) who opens up a fount of mercy and
grace for us. In particular, Hebrews contrasts Jesus' high priesthood
with the high priests of Israel. Jesus' priesthood operates spiritually

---

12. See Charles B. Cousar, *A Theology of the Cross: The Death of Jesus in the Pauline Letters*
(Minneapolis, MN: Fortress Press, 1990), 56–66.

13. For numerous helpful insights, though also a failure to appreciate the need for
expiation, see John Dunnill, *Covenant and Sacrifice in the Letter to the Hebrews* (Cambridge:
Cambridge University Press, 1992).

along the lines of Melchizedek, without need for a Levitical priestly lineage. The Levitical high priest has to offer sacrifices for his own sins as well as the people's sins and Levitical priests offer new sacrifices each day. By contrast, Jesus' one sacrifice on the cross suffices for sin "once for all" (Heb. 7:27). Hebrews emphasizes that Jesus is not a mere imitation of the Mosaic Law's sacrifices or temple; rather, the earlier sacrifices and temple prefigure the eternal reality of Jesus' sacrificial offering.

According to Hebrews, the crucified and risen Jesus "entered once for all into the Holy Place, not with the blood of goats and calves, but with his own blood, thus obtaining eternal redemption" (Heb. 9:12). Jesus' own Blood is infinitely more powerful than the blood of mere animals could ever be, for Jesus offered himself freely and with full understanding. In this way, the path of death became the path of everlasting life. Christ's justice trumped our injustice, for he lovingly bore the penalty of death on behalf of all of us who owed it, replacing our injustice with his justice and love. His sacrifice was consummated in perfect knowledge and perfect love when, "through the eternal Spirit," he "offered himself without blemish to God" (Heb. 9:14).[14] Jesus thereby established the long-awaited "new covenant" by his Blood (Heb. 9:15) and by his obedience in doing God's will (Heb. 10:9–10). Jesus' sacrifice is unique since he offered it out of loving obedience and so repaired the history of our discord.

The Levitical priests daily offered animal sacrifices that could not really take away sins. Christ offers one sacrifice—once for all and once for always—that purifies the interior heart, mind, and soul of the human being. Hebrews summarizes this new reality: "When Christ had offered for all time a single sacrifice for sins, 'he sat down at the right hand of God.' . . . For by a single offering he has perfected

---

14. See Mary Healy, *Hebrews* (Grand Rapids, MI: Baker Academic, 2016), 161–178.

for all time those who are sanctified" (Heb. 10:12–14). Christ opens up a new path of communion with God through his perfect offering of his life, sorrowing for all sin in his immense love.

Sharing in Christ's Sacrifice: Faith, Baptism, and the Eucharist

How then do we enter into the new communion with God established in Christ? This incorporation—literally, entering into the *corpus*, into Christ's Mystical Body—occurs in two ways: through faith and the sacraments.

Communion and incorporation through faith. In Paul's Letter to the Philippians, the Apostle uses the image of "the sacrificial offering of your faith" (Phil. 2:17 RSV-CE; cf. Rom. 12:1–2). Faith itself is an interior "sacrificial offering" by which we offer our lives to the God who loves us. In making this offering of ourselves, we confess with our lives "that Jesus Christ is Lord, to the glory of God the Father" (Phil. 2:11). Everything that we do in faith and love stands as "a sacrifice acceptable and pleasing to God" (Phil. 4:18). When we take up our cross and follow Christ, we can even be said to be "completing what is lacking in Christ's afflictions for the sake of his body, that is, the church" (Col. 1:24).[15] We do so by serving our brethren as Christ has served us and by our willingness to suffer or to endure hardship as a means to deeper communion with God.

In a real sense, once we are incorporated into Christ by faith, we are no longer alienated from one another and from God. As Paul says, our lives have been "hidden with Christ in God" (Col. 3:3). To be hidden in God means that Christ has opened up a new reality of communion with God so that our lives are no longer estranged from God. Paul describes this union with God in Christ elsewhere in even more striking terms: "It is no longer I who live, but it is Christ

---

15. See Christopher R. Seitz, *Colossians* (Grand Rapids, MI: Brazos Press, 2014), 107–108.

who lives in me" (Gal. 2:20). This is the real meaning of the New Covenant life of grace. Christ's loving self-sacrificial obedience continues in the hearts of his followers.

But Christ does not live in us merely in our existence as individuals. In making us members of his Body, he unites us both to God and to one another. For this reason, Paul can rightly describe the Church as "the body of Christ" (1 Cor. 12:27). In faith and love, he writes, we become "one body in Christ, and individually we are members one of another" (Rom. 12:5), so that we can extend Christ's mission of love, justice, and mercy to each other and to the whole world. Christ "nourishes and tenderly cares" for us "because we are members of his body" (Eph. 5:29–30). Now that we are incorporated into Christ who is at the right hand of the Father, we are already sharing in his reign of love and extending this reign as "the church, which is his body, the fulness of him who fills all in all" (Eph. 1:22–23).

Communion and incorporation through the sacraments. The New Testament presents Baptism as integral to our salvation. The First Letter of Peter affirms, "Baptism . . . now saves you" (1 Pet. 3:21). In the book of Acts, when the crowd at Pentecost asks what to do, Peter responds, "Repent, and be baptized every one of you in the name of Jesus Christ so that your sins may be forgiven; and you will receive the gift of the Holy Spirit" (Acts 2:38). The Apostle thus follows the example of the risen Jesus himself, who, when commissioning his Apostles at the end of Mark, links Baptism and salvation together: "Go into all the world and proclaim the Good News to the whole creation. The one who believes and is baptized will be saved" (Mark 16:15).[16]

Belief and Baptism are thus the means of our incorporation into the saving sacrifice of Christ. Paul unpacks the power of Baptism by

---

16. See Morna D. Hooker, *The Gospel According to Saint Mark* (Peabody, MA: Hendrickson, 1993), 390.

making explicit this incorporation into Christ: "Do you not know that all of us who have been baptized into Christ Jesus were baptized into his death?" (Rom. 6:3). This is the Good News. In Baptism we have died with Christ so that we might also rise with him into a renewed relationship with God in this life and in the next.

Just as Baptism is the entrance into Christ's saving death and Resurrection, the Eucharist extends Christ's loving sacrificial offering of himself for the redemption of the world.[17] When we are incorporated into Christ's saving action, we are elevated into the divine "sanctuary"—communion in the triune divine life—due to our sharing in the redemptive power of "the blood of Jesus" (Heb. 10:19). Baptism into Christ makes it possible for us to share in his Eucharistic presence.

To share in a sacrificial meal is to enter into the reality of the sacrificial worship. Paul points out that, in the Levitical sacrifices of Israel's cult, all who "eat the sacrifices" are "partners in the altar" (1 Cor. 10:18). Likewise, when we consume the Eucharist, Paul affirms that we are partners or sharers in the altar of the cross, participating in Christ's supreme self-offering in love.

Since we are sinners, we are incapable of making such a pure offering of ourselves to God on our own power. Christ therefore incorporates us into his own saving action, so that we can dwell with God who is infinite self-offering love. Paul rejoices that the Eucharist gives us a real communion with Christ in his self-offering. He explains, "The cup of blessing that we bless, is it not a sharing"—the word he uses for sharing also means *communion*—"in the blood of Christ?" Likewise, he adds, "The bread which we break, is it not a sharing in the body of Christ?" (1 Cor. 10:16). To participate in the Eucharist is to share in the one sacrifice of Christ.

---

17. For further discussion, see Robert Barron, *Eucharist* (Maryknoll, NY: Orbis Books, 2008).

The Catholic Church's celebration of the Eucharist gives us a participation in Christ's sacrificial action for the salvation of the world, the very action by which we are healed and elevated to share in the divine life. As such, the celebration of the Eucharist builds up the Church in God's own love. It strengthens our love and makes us more truly members of his Body, whose purpose is to manifest his love in the world and to abide fully in his love in everlasting life. The Eucharist thus deepens our unity in Christ. Paul comments, "Because there is one bread, we who are many are one body, for we all partake of the one bread" (1 Cor. 10:17). The Church's sharing in Christ's sacrificial action bonds it together in his love.

In John 6, we again find these two inseparable modes of incorporation into Jesus' saving sacrifice: faith and the sacraments. Speaking to a crowd of his fellow Jews, Jesus repeatedly emphasizes the need for faith. For example, he states that "the work of God" is "that you believe in him whom he has sent" (John 6:29). When his audience asks him what sign he will do so that they might believe in him, Jesus indicates that he will be the new manna, the new Passover bread. To feed upon this "true bread from heaven" (John 6:32), one must believe that Jesus is God's Word, the Savior of the world.

James echoes this understanding of God's wisdom coming down from heaven when he writes, "The wisdom *from above* is first pure, then peaceable, . . . full of mercy and good fruits" (James 3:17; emphasis added). Jesus himself is the new manna, the true bread, the living wisdom that comes from above, as he teaches in John 6: "I am the bread of life. Whoever comes to me will never be hungry, and whoever believes in me will never be thirsty" (John 6:35). Jesus is the wisdom—the Word—of God himself, who must be believed in order to have eternal life.

Jesus' teaching here unveils both the need for faith and Christ's true presence in the Eucharist. A sacrament can be misunderstood either by a false literalism or by a false skepticism. A false literalism would imagine that the communion in Christ's Body and Blood spoken about by Paul is cannibalism. A false skepticism would reject the real presence of Christ in the Eucharist. Faith is required to perceive a sacramental mode in which, under the signs of bread and wine, the reality of Christ in his once-and-for-all sacrificial action is continually re-presented.[18] Jesus says that "the bread that I shall give for the life of the world is my flesh." Thus to believe in him and to receive his Body become one and the same action. In this way, Jesus is both the bread of wisdom in which we must believe (John 6:35) and the bread of life that we must eat (John 6:51). The Flesh and Blood of Jesus are the means of our salvation.

Jesus emphasizes the reception of his Flesh and Blood, to the shock of his own disciples. He says, "unless you eat the flesh of the Son of Man and drink his blood, you have no life in you"; and he adds, "Those who eat my flesh and drinks my blood abide in me, and I in them" (John 6:53, 56). His hearers are offended by Jesus' words (John 6:61). But Jesus begins to show them that he will make his Body and Blood available to us in ways that do not involve cannibalism but instead open up a sacramental communion. His use of the language of flesh here recalls the beginning of John, which teaches that "the Word became flesh and dwelt among us" (John 1:14). The Incarnation extends into the Eucharist so that the Word may continue to dwell among us and offer us a sacramental sharing in his own eternal life and love. In this sense, Jesus clarifies to his disciples: "It is the spirit that gives life; the flesh is useless" (John 6:63). In the Eucharist,

---

18. For discussion, see Brett Salkeld, *Transubstantiation: Theology, History, and Christian Unity* (Grand Rapids, MI: Baker Academic, 2019).

the disciples will eat his flesh not in a cannibalistic manner but in the power of the Holy Spirit.

Why is it that Jesus chooses this way to be united to us? In the Gospel of Luke, Jesus, after breaking bread at the Last Supper, tells his disciples: "This is my body which is given for you. Do this in remembrance of me" (Luke 22:19). What does he mean in commanding his disciples to do this ritual in "remembrance" of him (and of his sacrificial body)? The Greek word translated as "remembrance" is *anamnesis*, which is linked with the Hebrew word *zikron*. Both words express the divine and human "remembering" that pertains to a cultic sacrifice. Let us examine this point a bit further.

When the institution of the Passover is recounted in Exodus, Moses says, "*Remember* this day on which you came out from Egypt, out of the house of slavery, because the LORD brought you out from there by strength of hand" (Exod. 13:3; emphasis added). Deuteronomy also places the act of remembrance at the heart of the annual commemoration of the Passover. God commands the Israelites that the people must celebrate the Passover each year and that they must offer the Passover sacrifice of a lamb. They must also reenact the hurried flight from Egypt by eating unleavened bread for seven days. The annual ritual made present the past saving action in the memories of the participants: "all the days of your life you may *remember* the day of your departure from the land of Egypt" (Deut. 16:3; emphasis added). This "remembrance" makes the day of the Passover present again for the people participating in the ritual, so that they are able to share in the event of Passover. When we "remember" in this liturgical sense, God's saving actions are truly made present to us.

Through liturgical remembrance, later generations become present to God's earlier saving acts. Deuteronomy emphasizes that God made a covenant "with us, who are all of us here alive today"

(Deut. 5:3). This covenantal communion will be made real for those who enact its liturgical remembrance. Moses states, "I am making this covenant, sworn by an oath, not only with you who stand here with us today before the LORD our God, but also with those who are not here with us" (Deut. 29:14–15). The "remembrance" of the Passover and of Sinai includes all Israelites of every generation. In God's eyes, all generations are present as God makes the covenant with Israel through Moses.

The power of such liturgical remembrance is present in both the Old and New Covenants. For example, Leviticus 24:7 (RSV-CE) describes twelve loaves of bread with frankincense that serve in Israel's cult as "a *memorial* portion to be offered by fire to the LORD" every day. The people pray for God to remember them while they also "*remember* the day" (Deut. 16:3; emphases added) that they came out of Egypt by God's saving power. For Christians, this day points forward to the day of Christ's Passover, the day of his saving cross and Resurrection.

Every Sunday, Catholics gather to obey the Lord's command to "Do this in remembrance of me" (Luke 22:19). His use of the word "remembrance" fulfills this theme of liturgical remembrance so vital to the Old Covenant. Yet Christ is not merely memorialized on the altar, let alone is he sacrificed again. God forbid! Instead, the one eternal sacrifice of Jesus Christ is made present again in every place in which the Mass is celebrated. We are no longer sharing in the Passover lamb slain by the Israelites when they were delivered from slavery to Egypt; we are now sharing in the "the Lamb of God who takes away the sin of the world" (John 1:29), the "the Lamb that was slaughtered from the foundation of the world" (Rev. 13:8; alternate rendering). When the Israelites remembered the historical Passover, they became present to God's historical saving actions. How much more will those who liturgically remember the new Passover of Jesus Christ become present, by the power of the sacrament, to his unique sacrifice, at once historical and eternal.

Paul, when teaching the young church in Corinth about the Eucharist, refers to the "remembrance" commanded by Jesus. He writes, "I received from the Lord what I also handed on to you, that the Lord Jesus on the night when he was betrayed took bread, and when he had given thanks, he broke it, and said, 'This is my body that is for you. Do this in remembrance of me'" (1 Cor. 11:23–24). As Paul says, Jesus did the same with the cup, saying, "This cup is the new covenant in my blood. Do this, as often as you drink it, in remembrance of me" (1 Cor. 11:25). The Apostle understands this to be a liturgical or ritual command. Christians must undertake this ritual "remembrance" as part of their incorporation into Christ's saving Passover. Paul observes that "as often as you eat this bread and drink the cup, you proclaim the Lord's death until he comes" (1 Cor. 11:26). This liturgical proclamation of "the Lord's death" in the Eucharistic celebration gives believers a real communion in Christ's sacrificial Body and Blood.

Yet in writing to the Corinthians, Paul warns that the Eucharist, like the sacrifices of Israel, cannot be celebrated properly without charity and justice. In the Eucharist, we partake in the Body and Blood of Christ (1 Cor. 10:16). Yet this communion has no saving efficacy if we are in grave sin. The objective remembrance is real, but our subjective remembrance of Christ's Body and Blood is out of alignment. We are receiving true love itself, and yet we are not doing so in love. When we are in grave sin, the Eucharist stands in judgment upon our disobedience and lack of love. It reveals precisely what is missing in us. Paul makes the point clear: "Whoever . . . eats the bread or drinks the cup of the Lord in an unworthy manner will be answerable for the body and blood of the Lord" (1 Cor. 11:27). Before communing, therefore, we must attend to the state of our soul, repent, and be reconciled to Christ and each other.

The call to receive the Eucharist is thus a call to deeper conversion. Paul bemoans the selfishness and greed of the Corinthians. When the Corinthians partake in the Eucharist, says Paul, "each of you goes ahead with your own supper, and one goes hungry and another becomes drunk. What! Do you not have homes to eat and drink in? Or do you show contempt for the church of God and humiliate those who have nothing?" (1 Cor. 11:22). It appears that they were bringing their own bread and wine for the ritual and were not sharing with the poorer members of the community. Paul exhorts, "Examine yourself, and only then eat of the bread and drink of the cup. For all who eat and drink without discerning the body, eat and drink judgment against themselves" (1 Cor. 11:28–29). The subjective condition of the recipient does not affect whether the bread and cup are "the body and blood of the Lord." The gravely sinful person who receives Jesus' Body and Blood thus profanes the Lord and reveals, unto judgment, his or her lack of love. Jesus comes to us in the Eucharist in his Body and Blood, calling us to share in his divine mercy and love. In this way, Paul's reminder of judgment invites us to seek forgiveness first and then enter into communion with Jesus and with his Body, the Church, in the Eucharist.

Conclusion

This chapter asked whether Christian celebration of the "blood of Christ" makes sense. We have learned that God is not bloodthirsty, that God does not want the death of his innocent Son, and that receiving the Body and Blood of Christ is not cannibalism. What then is the sense of Christ's sacrificial death and our sharing in his sacrifice in the Mass?

Through biblical Israel's long history, God taught his people about the gravity of sin. During this time, the sacrificial cult was always present. When Abraham went forth to offer up his son Isaac, God himself provided the sacrificial animal—thereby making clear both that the sacrifice of a child was unacceptable and that God would provide the perfect sacrifice. The sacrifice of the Passover lamb saved the people from death in Egypt. Likewise, God, through prescribing the cultic ritual of the scapegoat that symbolically bore the sins of the whole people, revealed to the people their need for atonement and reconciliation. The temple cult sought to address the ongoing sinfulness of the people.

In all these ways, God prepared the people to understand the cross of Jesus Christ. The Psalms and prophets argued that God does not need animal sacrifice but rather wants the offering of a pure heart, filled with love and thanksgiving. The animal sacrifices represented the sacrificial offering of the self to God in love; they expressed the need to heal the wound of alienation and death caused by our turning away from the divine life-giver. Isaiah prophesies that the suffering servant will bear the people's sins and reconcile them to God. The depth of sin requires a Redeemer who goes to the very heart of death and reverses our deepest alienation from within.

At the center of Christ's death is love—Christ's love of the Father, Christ's love of each one of us. Christ's love perfects his sacrifice. His "blood" is his free payment of our penalty of death; by shedding it in his supreme self-offering for us, Jesus reverses our sinful cleaving to self and opens up a path to divine love. In light of Christ's perfect love in his redemptive action on the cross, we may be incorporated into the Body of Christ. Such incorporation enables us to share in his loving self-surrender to God. We are united to the death by which he has healed our condition of injustice by bearing its penalty for us. His Blood has established the path of eternal life.[19]

Why does our faith proclaim that "we have redemption through his blood" (Eph. 1:7)? Why does Christ teach that "those who eat my flesh and drink my blood have eternal life, and I will raise him up on the last day" (John 6:54). Once we understand the connections between sin (rebelling against the Giver of life), alienation and death, and the Messiah's work of redemption that bears our sorrow and reestablishes the just relationship of the human race to the Creator, then we discover the true meaning of Christ's Blood. Through its restorative justice and love, his sacrifice cleanses us, heals us, and elevates us to a communion with God as Father in the Holy Spirit. We enter into this communion through the Eucharist. Thus, salvation is indeed "a sharing in the blood of Christ" (1 Cor. 10:16).

---

19. For further background, see Martin Hengel, *The Atonement: The Origins of the Doctrine in the New Testament*, trans. John Bowden (Philadelphia: Fortress Press, 1981); Simon Gathercole, *Defending Substitution: An Essay on Atonement in Paul* (Grand Rapids, MI: Baker Academic, 2015); Khaled Anatolios, *Deification Through the Cross: An Eastern Christian Theology of Salvation* (Grand Rapids, MI: Eerdmans, 2020).

CHAPTER 5

Why Would God Hold Our Faults Against Us?

"Be reconciled to God"
(2 Corinthians 5:20)

It can be difficult to believe that God actually cares about what human beings do or how they live. Even if we admit that we do sin, does it really matter to God?

As the atheist author Richard Dawkins says, "Why should a divine being, with creation and eternity on his mind, care a fig for petty human malefactions? We humans give ourselves such airs, even aggrandizing our poky little 'sins' to the level of cosmic significance."[1] One lapsed Catholic man expressed a similar objection: "The thought that the creator of countless galaxies, stars, planets would be worried if I slept with a woman—or a man—outside marriage or missed Mass on Sunday is just not sustainable."[2] Dawkins and this man are likely unaware of it, but the Bible itself includes Job's complaint made to God many years ago: "If I sin, what do I do to you, you watcher of humanity? Why have you made me your target?" (Job 7:20).

God knows that humans are easily subject to temptation. We are prone to overindulge in seeking pleasure, in holding on to resentments, and in wanting everything to be our way. Each of us does

---

1. Richard Dawkins, *The God Delusion* (Boston: Houghton Mifflin, 2006), 238.

2. Stephen Bullivant, Catherine Knowles, Hannah Vaughan-Spruce, and Bernadette Durcan, *Why Catholics Leave, What They Miss, and How They Might Return* (New York: Paulist Press, 2019), 40.

good things and bad things every day. Given that this is the way of the world, why wouldn't a reasonable God sympathize with us and not count our sins against us? Furthermore, since most human beings are a mixture of good and bad, surely God will not condemn everyone or even the majority of us. What would be the point, it seems, if God only allowed saints such as Mother Teresa into heaven? Besides, we tend to think of ourselves as being mostly good at heart, even if we make mistakes from time to time.

In *Soul Searching: The Religious and Spiritual Lives of American Teenagers*, Christian Smith coined the phrase "moralistic therapeutic deism" to describe a widespread religious perspective among Protestants and Catholics in the United States. On this view, God expects us to be nice to each other, occasionally helps us in difficulties, and generally wants us to find our own happiness in this life. Traditional notions of commandments and sin do not fit into the beliefs associated with moralistic therapeutic deism. Smith quotes a young Catholic named John who describes his view of God: "I don't think he's demanding at all. . . . I think most people are good and forgiving."[3] On this view, there is no need to be reconciled to God since we are already okay with God and God is okay with us.

Smith, in summarizing his findings, says Catholic teenagers exhibit a "greater religious laxity . . . compared to the other Christian teens we observed in this study."[4] He does not, however, blame the teenagers for this. As he points out, they are simply mirroring their parents. It seems that the days of so-called "Catholic guilt" are gone. We all know people—no doubt at times including ourselves—who have a much stronger sense of how God has failed them than how they might have failed God.

---

3. Christian Smith with Melinda Lundquist Denton, *Soul Searching: The Religious and Spiritual Lives of American Teenagers* (Oxford: Oxford University Press, 2005), 201.

4. Smith and Denton, *Soul Searching*, 215.

How does the Bible address the issues of human sinfulness and wrongdoing as well as the Creator God's care, forgiveness, and mercy? In this chapter, in light of the previous two chapters, we will continue our investigation of the truth about sin and its remedy in the reconciliation offered by Jesus Christ and in his Spirit—now focusing specifically upon the biblical portraits of sin and mercy, exile and restoration, and reconciliation and repentance.

On Sin and Mercy

Although King David is "a man after [God's own] heart" (Acts 13:22; cf. 1 Sam. 13:14), the great Israelite leader has to journey through the horrible recognition of his own sinfulness. When the prophet Samuel comes to anoint David as king, he passes over all of Jesse's older sons and chooses David since the "the LORD does not see as mortals see; they look on the outward appearance, but the LORD looks on the heart" (1 Sam. 16:7). Later, after David enters the service of King Saul, the young shepherd kills the Philistine hero Goliath in one-on-one battle. He will go on to win many more battles on behalf of Saul. Paradoxically, such victories lead to great persecution for David as Saul grows envious and attempts to kill him on multiple occasions. Eventually Samuel's prophecy is fulfilled as David replaces Saul as king of Israel's twelve tribes and wages a number of military campaigns against the Philistines.[5]

One spring, having refrained from going out to battle with his army, David sees the married woman Bathsheba bathing on a rooftop. Abusing his power as king, he calls Bathsheba to himself and has sexual intercourse with her. When she becomes pregnant, he arranges to have her soldier husband, Uriah, return from the

---

5. For historical-critical efforts to reconstruct the "historical David," see Jacob L. Wright, *David, King of Israel, and Caleb in Biblical Memory* (Cambridge: Cambridge University Press, 2014); Baruch Halpern, *David's Secret Demons: Messiah, Murderer, Traitor, King* (Grand Rapids, MI: Eerdmans, 2001).

battlefield so that it will appear that Uriah is the father of the child. But when Uriah refuses to sleep in his home, arguing that it would be a breach of his soldierly discipline, David arranges to have the soldier killed in battle so that he can freely have Bathsheba.

The prophet Nathan then comes to David and tells him a story to help him see the wickedness of his deeds. In the story, David hears about a wealthy man with many flocks of many sheep and a poor man with only one young lamb, which he raised as part of his family. When a traveler visited, the wealthy man stole the lamb from the poor man and slaughtered it. Seeing the injustice of the action, David exclaims, "The man who has done this deserves to die" (2 Sam. 12:5). Nathan responds with the last words David expects to hear, "You are the man!" (2 Sam. 12:7). Although David immediately saw the sin of the fictional rich man, he was at first blind to his own sins of murder and adultery.

Convicted by Nathan's story and words, David says, "I have sinned against the Lord" (2 Sam. 12:13).[6] As king, David possessed great power and wealth, so he was capable of sinning on a large scale. How often do we sin on a small scale only because we lack David's power to commit greater ones? Like David, we are much better at seeing others' sins than our own.

The Bible does not stop with David's recognition of his own sin but continues onward to David's recognition of God's mercy. David's repentance is exemplary, for the people of Israel and for the Church, as we see in many of the Psalms linked with the king.[7] Just as David cries out "I have sinned" when confronted by Nathan, so he pleads in Psalm 51, "Have mercy on me, O God, according to your steadfast

---

6. See Robert Barron, *2 Samuel* (Grand Rapids, MI: Brazos Press, 2015), 107–115.

7. For the view that David did not author the Psalms, see Susan E. Gillingham, "The Levites and the Editorial Composition of the Psalms," in *The Oxford Handbook of the Psalms*, ed. William P. Brown (Oxford: Oxford University Press, 2014), 201–213.

love; according to your abundant mercy blot out my transgressions" (Ps. 51:1). "Steadfast love" here translates *hesed* from the Hebrew and recalls a loving-kindness not rooted in an emotion but bound by God's own sworn covenant. By saying "according to your covenantal love," David does not plead for God's mercy because he deserves it. The king instead responds to Nathan the prophet, "The man who has done this deserves to die." David makes his plea for mercy because of God's very own mercy, because of God's goodness, because of God's covenants with Abraham, with Moses, and with David himself (2 Sam. 7). We seek God's loving mercy not because we are good but because he is. Psalm 32 says, "Happy are those whose transgression is forgiven" (Ps. 32:1). To have sins forgiven is to return to blessedness—the state of genuine happiness with God and others.

The Bible offers hope of real forgiveness, of real blessedness through repentance. Here we discover a key biblical principle: the more that human beings recognize their sin, the more God bestows mercy. David continues in Psalm 51, "Against you, you only, have I sinned, and done what is evil in your sight, so that you are justified in your sentence" (51:4). When the sinner says, "Against you . . . have I sinned," God bestows mercy because he is all goodness. David prays, "Create in me a clean heart, O God, and put a new and right spirit within me. Do not cast me away from your presence, and take not your holy spirit from me" (Ps. 51:10–11). God's mercy renews our spirit according to the Spirit by whom we were created.

The Proliferation of Sin and Mercy in the Old Testament

Let us consider some other paradigmatic instances of sin and mercy in the Old Testament. One common misunderstanding that we have encountered when teaching the Bible is the belief that Adam and Eve's sin unfairly ruined it for the rest of us. The Bible instead goes out of its way to show that original sin is not, in fact, terribly original. Sin repeats itself in each new generation.

The Bible teaches us about the proliferation of sin by showing how human beings fall from grace again and again. Put simply, humans routinely make a mess out of God's gifts. Whether as individuals or as societies, we seem to rise only in order to fall. When the Bible tells of a great blessing, it almost always and shortly afterward describes a great transgression. The transgression of the blessing then leads to tragic curses and divisions. In this way, the Bible reveals the deep brokenness of the human race, for we cannot even receive good gifts from God without immediately returning to our old ways.

The story of Noah follows such a pattern of blessing and brokenness. Noah displays heroic courage and great faithfulness in trusting God and so surviving the great flood. After the flood, the Bible narrates how God then blesses Noah and his family and renews his covenant with them. The language echoes the original creation story, "God blessed Noah and his sons, and said to them, 'Be fruitful and multiply, and fill the earth'" (Gen. 9:1). God promises Noah and his sons, "As for me, I am establishing my covenant with you and your descendants after you" (Gen. 9:9).

Maybe this time human beings will get it right? Not so fast. After this blessing, Noah plants a vineyard, makes wine, and becomes drunk and passes out. His son Ham sees his father as "he lay uncovered in his tent" (Gen. 9:21), which in this context may mean that Ham attempts to exploit his father's weakness and claim for himself Noah's authority. By contrast, Noah's sons Shem and Japheth "covered the nakedness of their father" (Gen. 9:23). It is no surprise, then, that Noah gives his blessing to Shem and Japheth and announces a curse upon Ham and his descendants. From Ham's lineage comes the Canaanites, the Philistines, the Babylonians and so many other of Israel's enemies. The divine blessing meant for all of Noah's sons now excludes Ham. After explicitly telling the reader that God made his covenant with "Noah and his sons," in the very same chapter the Bible shows how Noah's sins were followed by the sins of his son Ham. The family that was blessed for its faithfulness immediately breaks apart in tragic enmity. Despite receiving God's gifts, they reenact the primordial stories of Adam and Eve, of Cain and Abel. The gift of grace gives way to another fall. Blessing gives way to transgression and subsequent division.

This pattern repeats itself all too often. As we saw earlier, God makes a covenant with Moses and the people of Israel in Exodus, promising to make Israel "a priestly kingdom and a holy nation"; the people respond, "All that the LORD has spoken we will do" (Exod. 19:6, 8). After the animals are sacrificed and the covenant is sworn, Moses goes up to the mountain with God to receive the Ten Commandments and instructions for building the tabernacle for forty days and forty nights. As the people become impatient, they convince Aaron to make them a golden calf so they might worship and follow a new god (Exod. 32). This is staggering disloyalty. Something is deeply wrong with humanity. As a result of Israel's infidelity and idolatrous worship, henceforth only the tribe of Levi would serve as priests (Exod. 32:25–29).[8] Rather than being a kingdom of priests taken from each household among all twelve tribes, now Israel has only one tribe of priests. God's blessing, again, precedes transgression and subsequent division.

The pattern repeats in the story of King Solomon. When the young king is asked by God to name what his heart most desires, Solomon does not ask for wealth and power but heroically asks for wisdom so that he may govern his people with justice. In 1 Kings 8,

---

8. For background, see Brevard S. Childs, *The Book of Exodus: A Critical, Theological Commentary* (Louisville, KY: Westminster, 1974), 553–72, especially 571.

he builds the temple of the Lord and offers great sacrifices for its con-
secration. He enters into a solemn renewal of the covenant that God
made with David. The Bible tells how the priests could not enter the
temple since the cloud of the Lord's glory filled the temple. Solomon
closes his dedicatory prayer, "that all the peoples of the earth may
know that the Lord is God; there is no other." (1 Kings 8:60). What a
glorious moment of Solomon's faithfulness and God's blessing!

The Bible, however, immediately goes on to describe Solomon's
use of forced labor, extreme taxes (666 talents of gold annually), and
many foreign wives and concubines. Solomon would eventually
attempt to bring the gods of these non-Israelite women into Israel's
worship, by building shrines to these gods. The king renowned for
his great wisdom and for building the great temple for God tragically
draws the people of Israel into idolatry. After his death, Solomon's
kingdom splits into the northern kingdom of Israel and the southern kingdom of Judah. Never again are the twelve tribes united in
the Old Testament. The fall comes quickly after the grace. As with
Noah and Moses, divine blessing gives way to transgression and subsequent division.

Understanding this pattern of blessing and division helps us to
turn the Bible's pages back to the start of Genesis and read the story
of Adam and Eve with greater understanding. Adam and Eve receive
an unmerited blessing from God in their very lives and in the garden
with its fruits, which they are "to till it and keep it" (Genesis 2:15).[9]
The narrative shows that marriage itself is a blessing, a divine gift:
"Therefore a man leaves his father and cleaves to his wife, and they
become one flesh" (Gen. 2:24). Human beings were in harmony with

---

9. "To till and to keep" may also be translated as "to work and to guard." The latter words
echo the priestly role in Numbers 8 and 16 when the Levites are assigned "to work" the
liturgical service and "to guard" the sanctuary. For discussion, see Steven C. Smith, *The
House of the Lord: A Catholic Biblical Theology of God's Temple Presence in the Old and New
Testaments* (Steubenville, OH: Franciscan University Press, 2017).

the earth and its plants and animals, with each other, and with God. As the author eloquently puts the matter, "the man and his wife were both naked, and were not ashamed" (Gen. 2:25). Harmony means to be without shame, in communion with God and one another.

The blessing of Eden acknowledged the possibility of transgression since Adam and Eve were commanded not to eat of the tree of the knowledge of good and evil. This tragic possibility edges toward reality as the serpent enters the garden and tempts Eve by denying that she would die if she disobeyed God's command. Eve sees the desirability of the fruit and eats it and then gives some to her husband who eats it. "Then the eyes of both were opened, and they knew they were naked" (Gen. 3:7). The story shows that this knowledge is more than merely awareness of physical nakedness. It is an awareness of an interior shame, since they remain afraid of God even after they had sewed together fig leaves to cover themselves.

Since the first humans lost their harmonious relationships with the world, with each other, and with God, they now feel shame. As will happen throughout history, such shame begets further sins. And as is likewise all too frequent, such shame leads not to repentance but only to regret. Both Adam and Eve fail to take personal responsibility for their actions. Adam blames the woman who gave him the fruit, and Eve the serpent—"The serpent tricked me, and I ate" (Gen. 3:13). The Bible points out this same failure to take responsibility when it narrates Israel's idolatry of the golden calf. When Moses confronts Aaron, the high priest simply says that the Israelites gave their gold to him, he tossed it into the fire, "and out came this calf" (Exod. 32:24). Aaron thus fails to take responsibility for leading the people of Israel in idolatrous worship.

The failure to take responsibility is only the beginning of the divisions and consequences of sin. These consequences describe human history as we know it, a history filled with suffering and death, blood and deceit, pain and infidelity. The great message of Genesis, however, is that the history of sin does not ultimately define the history of the world. God has plans for his creation.

When read in light of God's eventual action in Jesus Christ, Genesis does not merely teach us about the reality of original sin but also the original goodness of creation. Moreover, all of these instances of sins following upon blessings reveal that the history of sin is somehow humanity's shared fault—and, believe it or not, this is good news.

How can it be good news that this history of suffering is our fault in some way? If human suffering and betrayal were simply part of the universe all the way down to its creation, then there could be no hope for their being overcome. But if they instead are somehow the fault of misdirected free will, a fall from grace that marred the human condition, then they may be overcome by the greater work of the Creator. The patriarch Joseph expresses this truth to his brothers when speaking of how, after they sold him into slavery, he rose to become second in command to Pharaoh: "Even though you intended to do harm to me, God intended it for good, in order to preserve a numerous people, as he is doing today" (Genesis 50:20).

The good news, then, is that the evil and sin in the world result from the shared fault of free will (angelic and human) used against God. God did not create us for alienation and death. This hidden truth is unveiled in Wisdom of Solomon: "God did not make death, and he does not delight in the death of the living. . . . God created us for incorruption, and made us in the image of his own eternity, but through the devil's envy death entered the world, and those who belong to his company experience it" (Wis. 1:14, 2:23–24).[10] How many

---

10. For historical-critical background, see David Winston, *The Wisdom of Solomon: A New Translation with Introduction and Commentary* (Garden City, NY: Doubleday, 1979), 107–108, 121–123.

people struggle to believe in the existence of a good, all-powerful God in the face of human suffering? The beginning of any answer to the problem of evil has to distinguish between the world as God created it to be and the world that presently exists due to the abuse of free will, a world in which human death is marked by the threat of radical alienation and loss of communion.[11]

Even the revelation of the curses of Genesis is good news. People with severe symptoms sometimes experience a dramatic improvement in their physical health once they learn the actual disease from which they suffer and thus are able to limit its effects. The consequences of sin, as described in Genesis, impair three areas of existence—marriage and family, work and production, and life and death. Each case unveils a deep rupture. Childbirth includes great pain and danger to the health of the mother. The relationship of husband and wife includes dominance and betrayal. Human labor includes toil and sweat. Finally, human life includes death. "You are dust, and to dust you shall return" (Gen. 3:19).

When we learn to see each of these hardships as curses, we come to understand that the world is not now as it was created to be. Jesus teaches from this same perspective when he says, "You were so hard-hearted that Moses allowed you to divorce your wives, but from the beginning it was not so" (Matt. 19:8). A good God and the goodness of creation are older than sin. "God saw everything that he had made, and indeed, it was very good" (Gen. 1:31). Sin and suffering are not the whole of our story.

---

11. For further discussion, see the essays in *Evil and Creation: Historical and Constructive Essays in Christian Dogmatics*, ed. David J. Luy, Matthew Levering, and George Kalantzis (Bellingham, WA: Lexham, 2020), especially Gavin Ortlund's "Augustine on Animal Death" (84–110). Augustine believes animal death to be a natural part of God's good creation. See also B. Kyle Keltz, *Thomism and the Problem of Animal Suffering* (Eugene, OR: Wipf and Stock, 2020).

The Bible reveals human life as a life in exile. Man and woman no longer live in the home that was created for them. A notable feature of human existence is that many people today and across history find themselves desiring something much different from our present world—a place of righted wrongs, fulfilled hopes, restored lives. If there were nothing more than this current world, it would be strange indeed that human beings would find it so dissatisfying. Not only do we choose against the harmony of the Creator-creature relationship, we also exist within the rupture of that same harmony. We are exiles: exiles from God, from our neighbors, from ourselves.

The Genesis story portrays this exile from Eden by showing its bitter fruits in the story of Cain and Abel, the first two sons of Adam and Eve. Cain is the first-born and a tiller of the ground. Abel is the younger and a shepherd. Both offer sacrifices to God, yet Abel's is accepted and Cain's is not. In response, Cain becomes angry and resentful. The Lord then tells him, "If you do well, will you not be accepted? And if you do not do well, sin is lurking at the door; its desire is for you, but you must master it" (Gen. 4:7).

With a painful simplicity, the narrative immediately continues, "Cain said to Abel his brother, 'Let us go out to the field.' And when they were in the field, Cain rose up against his brother Abel, and killed him" (Gen. 4:8). Cain has a strong inclination to sin, but still might master it. Instead, as Cain masters Abel, sin masters Cain. The words of the serpent have been fulfilled in a twisted manner: Adam and Eve have indeed ended up with an intimate knowledge of evil. As parents, they now grieve the loss of one son who is murdered and of another son who murders his brother.

Our ability to recognize Cain's actions as evil does not mean that we are necessarily in the position of Abel and not of Cain. Jesus offers us some wisdom on this point: "You have heard that it was said to those of ancient times, 'You shall not murder'; and 'whoever murders shall be liable to judgment.' But I say to you that if you are angry with a brother or sister, you will be liable to judgment" (Matt. 5:21–22). What is Jesus teaching about the nature of unjust anger? He is teaching that anger is aimed at harming another. Cain was similarly first angry with his brother before killing him. In our anger, we can fall into Cain's situation. Like Cain, we must not offer gifts to God when our relationships are not in order. Jesus teaches, "So when you are offering your gift at the altar, if you remember that your brother or sister has something against you, leave your gift there before the altar and go; first be reconciled to your brother or sister, and then come and offer your gift" (Matt. 5:23–24). Recall that Cain's jealousy of Abel came when both were offering their gifts to God.

Jesus' words here gently put his listeners in the position of the envious and eventually murderous Cain. We might think of ourselves as Abel suffering at the hands of Cain, and, without doubt, we do suffer at the hands of others. But we are all also Cain. This might explain why so many took offense at Jesus! Jesus invites his hearers to say with David in the first person, "*I have sinned against the* LORD." The words of the Mass repeat this personal recognition: *my* fault, *my* fault, *my* most grievous fault. Jesus acts as the divine physician, a doctor of souls, who unveils the drama of sin in our own hearts. Jesus shows a path away from the resentment that marks our life in exile, a path from Cain to Abel, a path from destructive anger toward our brother to sacrificial thanksgiving to God. Jesus opens up this path of reconciliation and healing when he sheds his Blood, innocent Blood even greater than that of Abel (Heb. 12:24).

Exile and the Promise of Return

The stories of Adam and Eve and of Cain and Abel serve as a miniature version of the entire Old Testament. As we have seen, the pattern of blessing, transgression, curse, and separation is repeated continually. Separation leads to exile. Adam and Eve and their descendants are exiled from the garden. The descendants of Abraham end up exiled in Egypt, away from the promised land. Exile is both personal and communal. Yet at the same time that the Bible deepens the story of our exile, it also unfolds an even greater story of return and restoration.

The Babylonian exile forms one of the most pivotal points in the history of Israel. Recall that after the reign of Solomon ended around 931 BC, the kingdom split into the northern kingdom of Israel and the southern kingdom of Judah. Then in 722 BC, the northern kingdom's capital of Samaria was captured by Assyria. Most of the survivors of the northern kingdom of Israel were forcibly resettled by the Assyrians and intermixed among the Gentile peoples, whereas Gentiles were moved into what had been the northern kingdom. The result was that the ten northern tribes' distinct identity was lost. In the time of Jesus, the descendants of the few Israelites who had remained in the northern kingdom (rather than being forcibly resettled), who themselves had mixed with Gentile settlers, would be known as the Samaritans.

In 587 BC, the Babylonian armies attacked the southern kingdom of Judah and surrounded the walled city of Jerusalem. After a terrible and long-lasting siege, Babylon destroyed both Jerusalem and the famous temple of Solomon; then they deported the surviving captives from Judah and had them live together in Babylon. This became known as the Babylonian captivity. During this time, the people of Judah, eventually known as the Jews, preserved and edited many of the great writings of the prophets as well as the histories of the kings. These people came to see clearly that their exile from Jerusalem resulted from the sins of the kings and of the people themselves.

Among the sins of Judah that are described in the Old Testament, two stand out: idolatry against God and injustice against neighbor, especially the poor. The sins of idolatry and injustice are a comprehensive rejection of the two tablets of the Ten Commandments: idolatry fails in loving God above all things; injustice fails in loving our neighbor for God's sake. Living in exile, the people come to see that their situation is the result of their collective sins. The prophet Daniel reinforces this truth: "Righteousness is on your side, O Lord, but open shame, as it is this day, falls on us, the people of Judah, the inhabitants of Jerusalem, and all Israel, those who are near and those who are far away, in all the lands to which you have driven them, *because of the treachery* which we have committed against you" (Dan. 9:7; emphasis added).[12] Judah's people have recapitulated the story of Adam and Eve.

The people in exile kept their hope alive that God would remove them from exile and return them to the promised land. This happened partially under King Cyrus who sent them back to Jerusalem in 539 BC. Under Ezra and Nehemiah, the people of Judah rebuilt what would be known as the second temple, which fell far short of the first temple. The older Israelites who returned from the Exile and remembered the first temple wept when they saw the rebuilt temple because the second was not nearly as glorious (Ezra 3:12–13). There was no longer a son of David on the throne, and indeed there was no kingship at all. By contrast, the prophets had promised a great return from exile. They spoke of a coming restoration that would exceed anything known in the days prior to the exile. Some prophets spoke of the coming of a Davidic king (a Messiah or anointed

---

12. See N.T. Wright, *The New Testament and the People of God* (Minneapolis, MN: Fortress Press, 1992), 271. For a critique of Wright's approach to the theme of return from exile, while agreeing with him on some significant points, see James D.G. Dunn, *Jesus Remembered* (Grand Rapids, MI: Eerdmans, 2003), 472–477.

one) who would put everything to rights. Almost unanimously, the prophets foretold an extraordinary personal and communal return to right relationship with God and with neighbors. They described this restoration with language about a peace and abundance never seen in this world.

As we have seen, Jeremiah promises a New Covenant. The idea of a *New* Covenant was in certain ways shocking. It would have made sense to speak of a return to—a renewal of—the original covenant. God, however, wished to reveal bigger plans through his prophet. Jeremiah was a prophet around the time of the Babylonian destruction of Jerusalem. His prophecy teaches that the Lord will make "a new covenant with *the house of Israel and the house of Judah*" (Jer. 31:31; emphasis added). In other words, he prophesies, among other things, a healing of the division between the two southern tribes of Judah and the ten northern tribes of Israel. Since the ten northern tribes were lost, such a reunion was impossible on the level of earthly history and politics. The prophecy is of a New Covenant that is greater than a new constitution of an earthly political kingdom. The New Covenant requires a new kingdom of God—as will be later preached by Jesus.

The New Covenant would end the breach caused by sin. Jeremiah describes this exile of our own hearts in pointed language, "The heart is devious above all else; it is perverse—who can understand it?" (Jer. 17:9). Jeremiah promises a "new covenant" that will include the forgiveness of sins and a renewal of the people: "I will put my law within them, and I will write it upon their hearts. . . . For I will forgive their iniquity, and remember their sin no more" (Jer. 31:31, 33–34). This New Covenant recalls God's original covenant with creation. Jeremiah teaches that just as God will not break his covenant with the day and the night, he will not break his covenant with

Jacob and David. God the Creator will also be the Redeemer. The Lord says simply, "I will restore their fortunes, and will have mercy upon them" (Jer. 33:26). The exile due to sin is real, but God's mercy is greater. God's mercy does not merely forgive but heals, renews, and restores.

In a manner similar to Jeremiah, the prophet Ezekiel also speaks of the forgiveness of sins and an interior renewal. Ezekiel employs a striking image of an exchange of hearts: "I will sprinkle clean water upon you, and you shall be clean from all your uncleanness. . . . I will remove from your body the heart of stone and give you a heart of flesh" (Ezek. 36:25–26).[13] The exile from God is not merely a physical displacement from our homeland but an internal exile in which God has been exiled from our hearts. According to Ezekiel, God will work to restore the goodness of his original created order, washed and healed of the wounds of sin and division.

The prophet Isaiah promises a coming "everlasting covenant" and a "covenant of peace [shalom]" (Isa. 55:3; 54:10). As with Jeremiah and Ezekiel, Isaiah emphasizes that this covenant will be established by God's mercy and forgiveness. There is a way to return to God since he is a God of mercy: "Seek the LORD while he may be found, call upon him while he is near; let the wicked forsake their way, and the unrighteous their thoughts; let them return to the LORD, that he may have mercy on them, and to our God, for he will abundantly pardon" (Isa. 55:6–7). Isaiah reveals that the promise of mercy and restoration exceeds the logic of human existence: "For my thoughts are not your thoughts, nor are your ways my ways, says the LORD. For as the heavens are higher than the earth, so are my ways higher than your ways and my thoughts than your thoughts" (Isa. 55:8–9). This evocative passage reveals that God's plan of forgiveness

13. See Joseph Blenkinsopp, *Ezekiel* (Louisville, KY: John Knox, 1990), 166–169. Blenkinsopp suggests that Ezekiel is influenced by Jeremiah 31 here.

is so extraordinary that it cannot be grasped fully by our thoughts. Humans simply cannot solve the horrible sins and wounds of our history. God, however, is so much greater than we can imagine. His mercy and power can forgive sins, heal our wounds, and restore the dead to life.

Isaiah promises that the New Covenant will both include and exceed the Old Covenant with David. He speaks of the covenant with David (Isa. 55:3), yet shows that the end of the exile will exceed earthly political realities. In the name of the Lord, he prophesies, "I am about to create new heavens and a new earth; the former things shall not be remembered or come into mind" (Isa. 65:17). Thus the New Covenant will be a radical renewal and transformation of God's creation. Isaiah emphasizes the reversal of the curses of Genesis: "They shall not labor in vain, or bear children for calamity; for they shall be the offspring of the blessed of the LORD—and their descendants as well" (Isa. 65:23). God will bring the consequences of sin to an end; humans will no longer be doomed to exile from the fruits of their labor, from each other, and from God. The New Covenant will be a covenant of God's mercy, a covenant of peace, in ourselves, with our neighbors, and most importantly with God. Mercy will end the exile of sin.

Paul Preaches Reconciliation to Sinners

Paul preached the Good News that this promise of a New Covenant has now been fulfilled in the death and Resurrection of Jesus Christ. Writing from prison, Paul asks the Colossians to "remember my chains" (Col. 4:18).[14] Nonetheless, Paul had come to believe that he was free in Jesus Christ. In powerful language, Paul taught the

---

14. For differing positions on Pauline authorship, see Margaret Y. MacDonald, *Colossians and Ephesians* (Collegeville, MN: Liturgical Press, 2000), 6–18; and N. T. Wright, *Colossians and Philemon* (Grand Rapids, MI: Eerdmans, 1986), 21–39.

Colossians, "[The Father] has rescued us from the power of darkness and transferred us to the kingdom of his beloved Son, in whom we have redemption, the forgiveness of sins" (Col. 1:13–14).

There is a profound paradox in Paul's saying that he has redemption while still in chains. As he wrote to Timothy, for the Gospel "I suffer hardship, even to the point of being chained like a criminal. But the word of God is not chained" (2 Tim. 2:9).[15]

The simplest meaning of "redemption" is to have purchased freedom from captivity. Paul's words reveal that beyond the conflict of earthly kingdoms, there is a deeper conflict between the kingdom of darkness and the kingdom of Jesus Christ. The "power of darkness" describes the human exile of alienation from right relationship with God and neighbor. In this context, Paul defines redemption as "the forgiveness of sins," which liberates us from our slavery to sin. The Greek word for sin is *hamartia*, which means missing the target or failing to achieve that which is properly sought after. Sins describe the individual and collective loss of right action and harmony. Yet the dominion of sin and darkness does not have the final word. Paul's message is that we may leave the old dominion and enter a new dominion in Jesus Christ.

Paul concludes this passage in Colossians about the kingdom of darkness and the kingdom of his beloved Son with a beautiful hymn. In this hymn, Paul emphasizes the power of Christ and his work of reconciliation:

He is the image [or icon] of the invisible God, the firstborn of all creation; for in him all things in heaven and on earth were created, things visible and invisible, whether thrones or dominions or rulers or powers—all things have been created

---

15. See Luke Timothy Johnson, *The First and Second Letters to Timothy: A New Translation with Introduction and Commentary* (New York: Doubleday, 2001), 374–375, 381.

through him and for him. He himself is before all things, and in him all things hold together. He is the head of the body, the church; he is the beginning, the firstborn from the dead, so that he might come to have first place in everything. For in him all the fullness of God was pleased to dwell, and through him God was pleased *to reconcile to himself all things*, whether on earth or in heaven, by making peace through the blood of his cross. (Col. 1:15–20; emphasis added)

Much could be said about the compact profundity of these verses. Here we will simply draw out the theme of reconciliation. First, the one in whom we have redemption is revealed to be the one through whom we were created. All things are created in him; all things are now reconciled in him. Second, the one who made the world is also the one who made the Church. The Church denotes that new community that has been reconciled to God; the Church is the kingdom of God's peace. Third, redemption comes at a great price. Christ accomplishes our reconciliation by his Blood.

God blesses us by reconciling us to himself. When you have someone's blessing, you are in right relationship with that person. As we have seen, however, in the history of the Israel, moments of blessing repeatedly led to transgression and exile. God's blessings were never fully received since their reception was limited by the sinfulness and weakness of human beings. In the New Covenant, for the first time, God's blessing has been perfectly received and returned by humanity in the incarnate Word, Jesus Christ. Thus, the New Covenant uniquely accomplishes God's promises of a covenant of peace, communion with him and with neighbor.

This New Covenant will be one of spiritual adoption, by which God the Father renews creation within the communion he shares with his Son and his Holy Spirit. Paul describes how God "has blessed us in Christ with every spiritual blessing" (Eph. 1:3), and has "destined us in love to be his sons through Jesus Christ" (Eph. 1:5). The New Covenant blessing is the blessing of divine sonship—natural in Christ and adoptive in us. Paul goes on to say that "we have redemption through his blood, the forgiveness of our trespasses, according to riches of his grace that he lavished on us" (Eph. 1:7–8). The New Covenant blessing is realized in the perfect obedience of Christ who accomplished the forgiveness of sins through his Blood. Paul concludes that this is "a plan for the fullness of time, to gather up all things in [Christ], things in heaven and things on earth" (Eph. 1:10).[16]

Thus the New Covenant established in the loving sacrifice of Jesus Christ decisively overcomes the ugly history of division and exile. Christ has risen from the dead and ascended into heaven where he sits in glory at the right hand of the Father. In him, the exile of human beings from God has ended. With the gift of the Holy Spirit at Pentecost, Christians begin to share in the communion of the Son and the Father.

Yet the perfect realization of the New Covenant will come about only in the new heavens and the new earth. Since the kingdom has been inaugurated but not yet consummated, there remain sins and divisions among Christian communities and in the world as a whole—just as Christ warned his disciples to expect and as Paul frequently encountered. We still encounter great cruelty and endure tremendous suffering, both physical and emotional, due to the fact that we must wait for "the redemption of our bodies" (Rom. 8:23). Peter thus speaks of Christians as "aliens and exiles" on the earth, but no longer exiles from God. Rather, we are waiting for the day of God's consummation of his kingdom, which is the true home

---

16. For background to Ephesians 1:1–14, (over)emphasizing the relation of this text to the worldview of the Qumran sectarians, see MacDonald, *Colossians and Ephesians*, 191–214.

in which we already share (1 Pet. 2:11–12).[17] "Our citizenship is in heaven, and it is from there that we are expecting a Savior, the Lord Jesus Christ" (Phil. 3:20).

As Catholics, we believe that we have received the free gift of salvation in Christ and have risen with him from spiritual death to spiritual life. Paul describes the reality of our salvation in a concise summary of the Christian faith: "But God, who is rich in mercy, out of the great love with which he loved us even when we were dead through our trespasses, made us alive together with Christ—by grace you have been saved—and raised us up with him" (Eph. 2:4–6). The beauty of God's mercy contrasts with the ugly reality that we were truly dead in our sins. Despite all of our attempts to rationalize away our own shortcomings and misdeeds, apart from God's grace, we would be spiritually dead.

Paul does not mince words about our situation. He simply says that we were dead before receiving redemption in Jesus Christ: "You were dead through the trespasses and sins in which you once lived, following the course of this world" (Eph. 2:1–2). Notice that Paul uses the second-person form of address, "you." Our response to such an address should be in the first-person, "I." This is an opportunity to say, "Yes, I was dead in my sins"—and now, "Yes, Jesus Christ has made me alive." Paul proclaims that God has "made us alive together with Christ" (Eph 2:5).

Paul's Letter to the Romans likewise contrasts the darkness of human sin and the light of God's grace. The Apostle intensifies his description of our disorder by showing that not only were we dead in our sins but we were even enemies of God. How could it be the case that we were God's enemies? Paul explains that since we are

---

17. For background, drawing a connection to Genesis 23:4 and Psalm 39:13 (LXX) as well as to Hebrews 11:13, see Daniel A. Keating, *First and Second Peter, Jude* (Grand Rapids, MI: Baker Academic, 2011), 58–59.

able to know of God's existence from the visible creation, we have no excuse for worshiping creatures (Rom. 1:20–23). Moreover, since all peoples have the natural law, again, there is no excuse for disobedience (Rom. 2:14–16). Even the Jewish people were without excuse since they knew God's Law but could not keep it. Paul concludes, "All, both Jews and Greek, are under the power of sin" (Rom. 3:9). Just as Colossians said that we were in the "power of darkness" and as Ephesians said that we were "dead in our sins," Romans describes our fallen state as being "under the power of sin."

Opposed to the power of sin stands Jesus Christ who is the righteousness of God, the justice of God. Christ renews human beings in relationship to God, no longer being enemies, no longer worshiping created goods, no longer disobeying the Law. Paul explains that "since all have sinned and fall short of the glory of God; they are justified by his grace as a gift, through the redemption that is in Christ Jesus, whom God put forward as a sacrifice of atonement by his blood, effective through faith" (Rom. 3:23–25).

To understand Paul's meaning, it may help to consider the word "justify" in its ancient Jewish legal context. If someone stole a lamb from another person, the person from whom the lamb was stolen could seek justice from a judge. The judge would then *justify* the injured person by restoring the lamb and punishing the thief, thereby showing who is in the right and reestablishing justice.[18] When seen in this context, justification means a real restoration of relationship.

What does it mean then to say that God justifies us in Jesus Christ? Consider what we have lost through original sin and through our own personal sins: our birthright as children of God; the harmony that ought to shape our relationships among our families and societies; and everlasting life with God. We ourselves are both the

---

18. See James B. Prothro, *Both Judge and Justifier: Biblical Legal Language and the Act of Justifying in Paul* (Tübingen: Mohr Siebeck, 2018), especially chapter 2.

victim who has suffered these losses and the thief who stole them. God, too, is the victim, so to speak, of our thievery, since our sins destroyed our relationship with him. Thus, despite our countless efforts at justifying our own actions and intentions, we cannot ultimately justify ourselves. We cannot restore our broken relationship with God nor heal our own wounds. Only God can justify us in Christ, and he does so as "an expiation by his blood." Expiation here means the cleansing of, or taking away of, our sins through the sacrifice of Jesus Christ. Thus, Paul writes, our reception of God's redemption in Christ comes through faith: "[God] justifies the one who has faith in Jesus" (Rom. 3:26).

Paul will have much more to say regarding justification by faith. He writes, "For we hold that a person is justified by faith apart from works prescribed by the law" (Rom. 3:28). When God justifies the sinner, he restores the righteousness that was forfeited by the sinner himself. Justification thus truly justifies: its recipients are moved from a state of rebellion to one of reconciliation. Enemies of God become friends; disinherited children become welcome children and heirs of God (Rom. 8:16–17).

What does it mean to say that we are justified or restored to right relationship with God "by faith apart from works prescribed by the law"? Here "works prescribed by the law" does not refer to human works in general but to the works of the Mosaic Law in its ritual prescriptions, in particular circumcision. Although circumcision demarcated ritually one's entrance into the Old Covenant, it would not be the entrance into the New Covenant. Paul continues, "[God] will justify the circumcised on the ground of faith and the uncircumcised through that same faith" (Rom. 3:30). The Apostle thus does not oppose faith to love but rather opposes faith to circumcision as the ground of justification. Later in the same letter, he will encourage the Christians in Rome to follow the moral legal precepts in the highest manner possible: "The one who loves another has fulfilled the law" (Rom. 13:8).

Paul makes a similar argument about justification when he shows that God justified Abraham for his faith before the patriarch was circumcised (Rom. 4:1–12). Trust in God's promises allows us to say "yes" to God and to receive his gift of redemption. Paul's emphasis on justification by faith does not exclude living that faith in obedience and charity. That is why James is not disagreeing with Paul when he teaches, "You see that a person is justified by works and not by faith alone" (James 2:24).[19] God justifies us "by his grace as a gift" (Rom. 3:24), not as our due. It is by the obedience of faith that we receive the free gift of God given in Christ. Our justification is a free gift of grace that we accept by faith and let transform us through works of love.

Paul describes the fruit of justification as "peace with God" (Rom. 5:1). This helps us understand why this was only accomplished through Christ. If justification brings about peace, then the state of sin is shown to be war—and not just any war, but war with God. Paul describes the reality of our history and the essential role played by the death of Christ: "While we were still weak, at the right time Christ died for the ungodly. . . . God proves his love for us in that while we were still sinners Christ died for us. . . . For if while we were enemies, we were reconciled to God through the death of his Son, much more surely, having been reconciled, will we be saved by his life" (Rom. 5:6, 8, 10). We have indeed fallen short of the glory of God, and yet Christ died for us and offered us reconciliation with God.

Christ is the new Adam. Reconciliation is a re-creation. As through Adam's disobedience death and sin entered the world, so

---

19. For background, see William F. Brosend II, *James and Jude* (Cambridge: Cambridge University Press, 2004), 71–82.

through Christ's obedience forgiveness and grace have entered the world (Rom. 5:12–21). Paul describes Adam as a figure or type (*typos*) of Christ who was to come (Rom. 5:14). All human beings received their life from Adam; so all who are reborn will receive their new life from Christ. Justification accomplishes divine adoption. When Adam sinned and brought death into the world through his disobedience, he lost divine sonship for the human race. When Christ acts through obedience, he restores us as children of God. Christ does so by suffering the result of Adam's sin and disobedience in his death, marked by supreme love (Rom. 5:10). Christ is a greater Adam since he offers "the free gift of righteousness" unto "eternal life" (Rom. 5:17, 21).

How do we leave behind our lineage in Adam and receive our new identity as children of God in Jesus Christ? Baptism. Paul has already told us that we are justified by faith and not by works of the Law or circumcision. He does not mean, however, that it is by faith alone. Paul shows that Baptism necessarily complements faith. Rather than opposing faith to Baptism, Paul presents both as efficacious means of receiving God's gift of divine sonship. He writes to the Galatians, "In Christ Jesus you are all children of God, through *faith*. As many of you as were *baptized* into Christ have clothed yourselves with Christ" (Gal. 3:26–27; emphasis added).

Baptism is the sacrament of the New Covenant by which we enter into Christ's death and Resurrection. The connection between Baptism and Christ's dying and rising is greater than we often realize, for Baptism depicts a going-under and rising-from the waters. It is as much a drowning and rebirth as it is a cleansing. The baptismal waters recall the water from the flood that drowned those not in the ark with Noah and the water from the Red Sea that drowned the

Egyptians who were threatening the destruction of Israel. So also the sins of the baptized Christian have been drowned and put to death.

By Baptism, the Christian shares in Christ's bloody death in a bloodless manner. Paul reminds the early Christians, "Do you not know that all of us who have been baptized into Christ Jesus were baptized into his death?" (Rom. 6:3). Death is not the end, however, since we also rise with Christ in Baptism. "As Christ was raised from the dead by the glory of the Father, we too might walk in newness of life" (Rom. 6:4). Having been servants of sin, we are now servants and sons of God. Paul says that the Spirit helps us call God "Abba! Father!" since "we are children of God, and if children, then heirs, heirs of God, and joint heirs with Christ—if, in fact, we suffer with him in order that we may also be glorified with him" (Rom. 8:15, 17).[20] By faith, by Baptism, by works of love we are able to receive the free gift of salvation opened up through Christ's suffering.

Sin and Reconciliation in Jesus' Ministry

Jesus inaugurates the New Covenant of the children of God. The angel Gabriel announces to Mary, "You will conceive in your womb and bear a son, and you will name him Jesus. He will be great, and will be called the Son of the Most High, and the Lord God will give him the throne of his father David . . . and of his kingdom there will be no end" (Luke 1:31–33 RSV-CE). He is the Son of God who will sit on the renewed Davidic throne. This throne is not a physical throne but the kingdom of everlasting peace between God and the human race. As the new king, Jesus ends the exile of the human race: the exile of Judah and Israel, the exile of the nations from knowledge of the true God, and the exile of all of the descendants of Adam and Eve from God as Father.

---

20. See Ben C. Blackwell, *Christosis: Engaging Paul's Soteriology with His Patristic Interpreters* (Grand Rapids, MI: Eerdmans, 2016).

Jesus' words and actions reconcile sinners to God. When Jesus heals a paralyzed man, he also forgives the man his sins. When the Pharisees object that God alone can forgive sins, he states that he has done this "that you may know that the Son of Man has authority on earth to forgive sins" (Luke 5:24). Soon afterwards, the Pharisees complain that Jesus is eating with sinners and tax collectors. They seem unwilling to acknowledge that Levi, the former tax collector and host of the dinner, had in fact just left everything to follow Jesus. Such turnings from one way of life to another are repeated throughout Jesus' ministry. Jesus answers the Pharisees, "Those who are well have no need of a physician, but those who are sick; I have come to call not the righteous, but sinners to repentance" (Luke 5:31–32). "Repentance" here translates *metanoia*, which means a change of mind and heart, turning around from one way of life to another and seeing the world anew.

Conversion forms the heart of the Christian message of reconciliation. John preached, "Repent, for the kingdom of heaven has come near" (Matt. 3:2). Jesus began his preaching by calling sinners to repentance: "The kingdom of God has come near; repent, and believe in the good news" (Mark 1:15). Peter continues this preaching of repentance once he has been given the gift of the Holy Spirit at Pentecost: "Repent, and be baptized every one of you in the name of Jesus Christ so that your sins may be forgiven; and you shall receive the gift of the Holy Spirit" (Acts 2:38).

Jesus clarifies that the call to conversion is a call to become children of God. He proclaims, "Truly I tell you, unless you change and become like children, you will never enter the kingdom of heaven" (Matt. 18:3). In speaking of "the kingdom," he is referring to the renewed covenantal communion with God. Our entrance into that kingdom necessarily comes through the path of repentance, a path opened up by Jesus.

It may be hard to acknowledge our own sinfulness; we can easily lose hope of being able to overcome sin. This way of looking at it, however, focuses on our ability and on our sins, not on God's power and mercy. We may be powerless, but we are not helpless. We may call upon the Lord. Christian repentance does not lean on our own willpower but on God's initiative, on Jesus' loving sacrifice to reconcile us with God.

In Luke 15, Jesus tells profound stories of reconciliation—stories of finding lost sheep, lost coins, and even lost sons. A man with one hundred sheep loses one and then leaves the ninety-nine to find the one that was lost. When he finds the lost sheep, he rejoices. He calls his friends and neighbors and invites them to rejoice with him (Luke 15:3–7). A woman with ten silver coins loses one and then searches her entire house until she finds the lost coin. When she finds it, she invites her friends and neighbors to rejoice with her (Luke 15:8–10). Jesus concludes both stories by saying there will be "joy in heaven over one sinner who repents" (Luke 15:7, 10). The man and the woman each lose something dear to them; then they search for what was lost, find it, and then call others together to rejoice. Have we ever thought about repentance as an occasion for joy in heaven? Do we remember that God delights in each person who repents?

In a real sense, our story is more a story about God than about us. If we consider what Jesus is trying to tell us in speaking of the man with his lost sheep and the woman with her lost coin, we can recognize that God himself loses something dear to him, sets out to find it, finds it, and then rejoices in his recovery of what was lost. The children of Adam and Eve and even the children of Abraham become separated from God. They are lost. In the Incarnation, Jesus enters the world on a search-and-rescue mission. Find the lost sheep, find the lost coin. Restore it to the flock, to the home, and rejoice. Find the lost members of the human race, not only in our separation from God, but in our separation from each other and even from ourselves. As the prophets Jeremiah and Ezekiel described, we need new hearts of flesh, hearts with the Law written on them, hearts reconciled to God. And as Jesus makes clear, it is not only the tax collectors and sinners that need finding but also the Pharisees and the scribes. All of us need to discover that we are lost and to let ourselves be found by God.

It is thus to be expected that Jesus moves from speaking of lost sheep and coins to speaking of lost sons. In the parable of the prodigal son, Jesus reveals us to be lost sons of God the Father. He does this through telling a parable about a father who has lost his son and a son who has lost his father. The younger son in the story asks for his inheritance. Inheritances are typically conferred upon death, so to ask for an inheritance early is akin to saying, "I wish you were dead now so I could have what belongs to me." Yet just as God permits us to use our free will wrongly, the father acquiesces to the younger son's request and divides his estate between his two sons.

The younger son's sins do not merit much mention in the parable. Jesus merely says he went to a "distant country" and there spent his inheritance on "dissolute living" (Luke 15:13). Eventually, the younger son finds himself in a famine, without money, feeding pigs (which Jews were forbidden to eat), and so hungry that he hungers for the very husks he feeds to the pigs. The downward journey and humiliation push the son to the brink of despair. At that point, however, the son remembers his father and how his father would feed his servants generously with "bread enough and to spare" (Luke 15:17).

Perhaps it was his father's generosity that the younger son earlier chose to exploit, but here it is that same generosity that sparks his conversion, his literal turning around and heading home. The son comes to himself and says, "I will get up and go to my father" (Luke 15:18). The Greek word for "get up" is *anistemi* or "to stand again," used also when Jesus says he will be rejected, killed, and "after three days *rise again*" (Mark 8:31; emphasis added). This word choice foreshadows what the father will confirm at the end of the parable, namely, that the son was dead and now is alive. The son then takes full responsibility for his life and repeats to himself, "Father, I have sinned against heaven and before you; I am no longer worthy to be called your son; treat me like one of your hired hands" (Luke 15:18–19).

As the son is returning, the father sees him and has "compassion" on him and kisses him (Luke 15:20). Refusing to let him return as a servant, the father recognizes him as his son. He puts a robe on him and puts a ring on his hand and shoes on his feet. The father then invites others to rejoice with him, "for this son of mine was dead and is alive again; he was lost, and is found" (Luke 15:24). He slaughters the fattened calf, and together the household celebrates the return of his son. The father rejoices.

The return of the lost sheep, the lost coin, and the lost son all tell us about what God is doing in and through the ministry of Jesus Christ. We are the lost sinners, estranged from God our Father, exiled in a "distant country." Unlike the sheep and the coin, however, we are to blame for our exile. Like the son, we rebelled against our Father and his guidance. We demanded our inheritance to use as we pleased apart from him. The sheep and the coin may be found against their will, so to speak; the son, however, may not be found until he remembers his father's generosity, recognizes his sins, and returns home. So also Christ merited the forgiveness of our sins on the cross, but that forgiveness can become ours only when we remember God's generosity, recognize our sins, and return home.

Coming back home, however, is hard for the human creature, swollen with pride. For this reason, toward the end of the story of the prodigal son, Jesus includes a story about the son's older brother. When the older brother hears of the celebration in honor of the younger son's return, he is angry and refuses to join. In another amazing display of humility on the part of the father, the father goes out and pleads with the older son to come home as well. The older brother, however, refuses. He cannot see the father's generosity, but only what he perceives as the father's stinginess. In the older son's mind, he himself always served his father, never disobeyed, and yet never had even a small feast with his friends. He refuses to acknowledge his brother, but refers to him as "this son of yours . . . who has devoured your property with prostitutes" (Luke 15:30). The older son's memory thus sees the story only in part. He remembers his own good deeds, the father's stinginess, and his younger brother's sins. He fails to see the father's generosity, his brother's return, and the celebration that results when conversion meets mercy.

That same mercy of the father restores relationships while recognizing the freedom of both sons. The father refuses to coerce obedience from his adult sons. The father reminds his older son that everything he has is the older son's. The consequences of the younger son's actions remain; his half of the inheritance is gone. Yet these realities pale in comparison to the reality of the father's reconciliation with the younger son. Perhaps we might say that the mind of the older brother (who often represents our own self-justifying perspective) is still too small to perceive the greatness of God's mercy and forgiveness. As we observed earlier in Isaiah, as high as the heavens are above the earth, so are God's ways of forgiveness above our sense of our own righteousness. Through Christ's work of reconciliation, God is creating a new heaven and a new earth. The exile from God is over; we are called to dwell with God as his beloved sons and daughters.

Conclusion

In his letter to the young Church in Corinth, Paul offers a powerful summary of how God offers us a genuine new beginning in Christ:

> So if anyone is in Christ, there is a new creation; everything old has passed away; see, everything has become new! All this is from God, who reconciled us to himself through Christ, and has given us the ministry of reconciliation. . . . We entreat you on behalf of Christ, be reconciled to God. (2 Cor. 5:17–18, 20)

It is fascinating that Paul chooses to depict our reconciliation to God as a new creation. This shows that our human condition had become so deeply wounded that God needed to give it a restart. If we have trouble understanding why God would care about our sins, we may begin by recalling the story of what God has done for us in Jesus Christ. When we remember that Christ died and rose to bring about our peace with God, then we discover how we are more broken than we might want to admit and how much God cares about each and every part of our story.

The Bible teaches us that we are currently in exile in this world. We no longer enjoy a trusting relationship with God, with each other, and with ourselves. Yet as the Bible explains, we have reason for joy, for Christ has overcome our exile. He has walked our path of suffering and death and returned to his Father. No longer exiled, we may return home. No longer enemies of God, we may become his friends. No longer orphans, we may become sons and daughters of God.

This chapter has investigated the good news of sin and reconciliation. Sin has happened and continues to happen. Sin wounds and even devastates persons and communities. Our defects and failures are real. Their consequences do not go away by denial or wishful thinking. Our failings, however, are not the last word. God's reconciliation turns out to be a far greater story than that of human failure. In Jesus Christ, God redeems and re-creates his creation. Christ's death and Resurrection make possible the forgiveness of our sins and our adoption as children of God. Let us seize upon God's mercy and live according to the Spirit of Christ, in justice, mercy, and love. As Paul encourages us, "on behalf of Christ, be reconciled to God" (2 Cor. 5:20).

CHAPTER 6

Why Not Live and Think Like Everyone Else?

"Do not be conformed to this world"
(Romans 12:2)

Despite what can be said about our need for reconciliation in Christ, moral conversion no longer seems relevant to many Catholics. This is so for various reasons. For one, why turn away from the ways of the world when they offer quick gratifications, intense pleasures, and seemingly endless diversions and entertainments? Even more, why question the prevalent morals of our culture when it seems as though society keeps progressing while the Church remains stuck in the past?

No one doubts that the Catholic Church, in its human dimension, is always in need of reform and improvement. In making such changes, the Church may draw positive inspiration from the particular wisdom and longings for justice characteristic of each age. But the history of the Church is not simply a record of competition with the broader world to see which entity can make the most progress. As we have shown above, the Catholic Church has its foundation in the definitive revelation and reconciliation offered in Jesus Christ. Jesus Christ is the true standard by which we must judge any claims to progress.

In our chapters on the transforming power of the Spirit and our need for Christ's reconciliation, we proposed that we know the real condition of the world when we look into our own hearts. The Catholic writer Heather King puts it beautifully when she says of her life prior to conversion, "The fact that I had so egregiously gone against my own deepest soul lay squarely, forever, with me."[1] King experienced the reality that the modern world is, like all human cultures, built in part upon lies—not least upon the lie that following our (fallen) sexual desires wherever they lead will make us happy. All of us in various ways, small and large, have acted against the true longing of our own deepest soul. Christ offers us the chance to reclaim our true selves through his mercy along paths that truly will make us happy—happy with the beatitude of self-giving love in communion with God.

In light of our own inordinate desires and deep-seated resentments, we cannot find true happiness or contentment if we remain "worldly." As noted above, therefore, we need conversion through the grace of the Holy Spirit. Conversion means coming to love rightly, so as to be able to be a friend of God and neighbor in a new and powerful way. Along these lines, King remarks, "We all know what happens when you love someone. You turn into a fool! You make crazy sacrifices!"[2] Conversion opens up a new path of love.

The "world" in us and in others resists the claim that our desires need conversion. As a result, in each epoch of history, including our own, the Church faces pressure from within and without to normalize the sins that particularly afflict its members in that time period. Again Heather King is of help here, since she recognizes that many people accuse the Church's moral teaching of being oppressive and restrictive, and of leading to unnecessary suffering. King puts it succinctly: "Nothing will get you killed faster than suggesting that the meaning of life is to be found in our relationship to suffering. Nothing

---

1. Heather King, *Ravished: Notes on Womanhood* (n.p.: Holy Hell Books, 2019), 39.
2. King, *Ravished*, 40.

challenges the existing order more."[3] Jesus says that the path of holiness and the path of happiness involves suffering out of love. It is not that we want to suffer or that we want others to suffer, but we have to learn self-giving love and give up self-centered sentimentality and sensuality. In order truly to be happy, truly to live in a way that opens up to the superabundant and magnificent love of God, the followers of Jesus are called to "deny themselves and take up their cross daily" (Luke 9:23).

This can sound intimidating, even with the Spirit's help! It can be especially off-putting when, as is understandable, we want to avoid suffering and fit in with the cultural norms around us. In fact, Christians can and do enjoy the good things of life in accord with their created purpose. But the issue is how to embrace the things of this world in a truly life-giving manner. We cannot allow lust, greed, ambition, vanity, and so on to deflect us from the path of actual love. Christ invites us to turn from seeing everything and everyone as centered on our own ego, and to learn to see ourselves and our neighbors as created by God and for God.[4]

What does the Bible teach about what the "world" means and how we should relate to it as a people called to be holy? This chapter will emphasize the way in which the Christian life involves a continual call to conversion and holiness: to turn away from the well-worn patterns of fallen human nature, and to turn to Christ who is "the way, the truth, and the life" (John 14:6). No doubt, the "world" will always, as Robert Cardinal Sarah observes, oppose "the radical nature of the Gospel message and seek to anaesthetize it."[5] This chapter will continue our biblical exploration of what it means

---

3. King, *Ravished*, 41.

4. See Robert Barron, *The Strangest Way: Walking the Christian Path* (Maryknoll, NY: Orbis, 2002).

5. Robert Cardinal Sarah, *God or Nothing: A Conversation on Faith with Nicolas Diat*, trans. Michael J. Miller (San Francisco: Ignatius Press, 2015), 280.

when Christ teaches, "Take courage, I have overcome the world" (John 16:33).

The Call of Israel to be Holy

At the center of the first five books of the Old Testament stands Leviticus, a book about law and worship. This book teaches the people of Israel how they ought to live, which is what we call morality, and how they ought to relate to God, which is what we call liturgy or spirituality. Whereas in our society many people think of morality as unrelated to spirituality, the Bible knows no such separation. Sacred Scripture helps us to discover that morality and spirituality are two sides of the same coin. How we live and how we worship define our relationships with God and with our neighbor, for better and for worse.

At the center of Leviticus stands a startling invitation: "You shall be holy; for I the LORD your God am holy" (Lev. 19:2). What does it mean to "be holy"? The call to holiness forms a central aspect of the biblical revelation. Let us break down holiness into three components to help us understand it better. First, holiness is not a human project but a response to God's initiative, an imitation of who God is. Second, holiness is a separation from the unholy. Third, holiness is the perfection of love.[6] Let us consider each in turn.

Holiness as imitation of God. When God appeared to Moses in the burning bush, he told Moses, "Come no closer! Remove the sandals from your feet, for the place on which you are standing is holy ground. . . . I am the God of your father, the God of Abraham, the God of Isaac, and the God of Jacob" (Exod. 3:5–6).

The call to holiness is a call to imitate God's holiness. Yet it is common to encounter Catholics today who speak comfortably about

---

6. For further discussion, see Jacob Milgrom, *Leviticus 17–22* (New York: Doubleday, 2000), 1602–1608.

a God who is love and yet stumble over talking about a God who is holy. How might we rediscover the good news of God's holiness?[7]

We might begin by looking at the Exodus verse that we have just read and considering its implications. When God is present, we need to take off the shoes from our feet, for we are standing on holy ground. God is holy; he is other. To say God is holy is to say that he is not like the rest of the world. Although he continually holds creation in being, he is not the cause of our sinful and wounded human experience. Rather, he invites us to see beyond the ambiguities and corruptions that are so much a part of our collective and individual self-understandings. To say that God is holy is also to say that he is *wholly*—wholly uncompromised, wholly unambiguous, wholly incorrupt and incorruptible. God's holiness is sheer goodness and light without any hint of evil or darkness.

The prophet Isaiah shares his vision of God's holiness and how it transformed his life. Isaiah describes how he saw the LORD in his temple with the angels worshiping him and saying, "Holy, holy, holy is the LORD of hosts; the whole earth is full of his glory" (Isa. 6:3). By repeating the word "holy" three times, the angelic exclamation emphasizes that God's holiness surpasses all others. God is not simply holy, not simply holier, but the holiest of the holiest. Holiness means that the Lord is morally pure in a way different from human beings and our disordered loves. Thus, to confront God's purity is also to confront our sin. It is not surprising, then, to see that Isaiah turns from the declaration of God as "holy, holy, holy" to a confession of his sin: "Woe is me! I am lost, for I am a man of unclean lips, and I live among a people of unclean lips; yet my eyes have seen the King, the LORD of hosts!" (Isa. 6:5). In his vision, one of the angels then took a burning coal from the altar and touched Isaiah's lips and

---

7. For further discussion, see John Webster, *Holiness* (Grand Rapids, MI: Eerdmans, 2003).

said, "Now that this has touched your lips, your guilt has departed and your sin is blotted out" (Isa. 6:7).

God's encounter with Isaiah demonstrates how his immense holiness shines into our world and exposes our defects and sins. In his relationship with Israel, God reveals his holiness not merely to condemn but to transform. His very presence, his very gaze has the power to transform the person who encounters him. When the Lord looks upon Isaiah, he sees what Isaiah can be if he allows God to forgive his sins. In that same encounter, Isaiah becomes conscious of his own sinfulness as he witnesses the Lord's holiness.

As a result, this encounter transforms Isaiah into a suitable instrument for God's plan to announce his judgment and his salvation. The Lord asks Isaiah, "Whom shall I send, and who will go for us?" Isaiah responds, "Here am I; send me!" (Isa. 6:8). Isaiah's prophetic vocation, his "yes" to God, follows upon God's merciful transformation of Isaiah. The encounter thus presents to us a pattern that should give us hope: seeing God's holiness, confessing our sins, receiving God's forgiveness, and being sent on a mission.

Holiness as separation from the unholy. Since God is holy, all that is not holy is separated from him. The part of human activity that is most dramatically separated from God is the domain of idolatry. Idolatry, however, is not limited to false worship of God; it includes corrupt practices among human beings. Worship of idols in the ancient world often included sexual immorality and abuse in the way of cultic prostitution, child sacrifice, and ritual intoxication (Exod. 32; Num. 25). As we saw earlier, how we relate to God is intertwined with how we relate to our neighbor. In the biblical understanding, the call to live in holiness thus includes more than merely worshiping God. It also includes abiding by the moral laws that prohibit sins such as sexual incest, murder, and theft, and that promote good works such as the care of one's parents as well as of widows and orphans.

Just as acting rightly toward God is linked with acting rightly toward neighbor, so too, acting wrongly toward God is linked with acting wrongly toward neighbor. In Leviticus, God calls the Israelites to separate themselves from the types of disordered and unholy human relations that constitute so much of the fallen human experience. He gives his laws to make his people a people set apart: "You shall keep all my statutes and all my ordinances, and observe them. . . . You shall be holy to me; for I the LORD am holy, and I have *separated* you from the other peoples to be mine" (Lev. 20:22, 26; emphasis added).

Holiness thus necessitates a separation from that which is unholy. Think of the efforts that communities make to separate pollutants from their drinking water—even a little sewage in the supply is most unwelcome! In a similar manner, to be rightly related to God and neighbor requires removing oneself from disordered relationships.

The separation that holiness entails, however, is never for its own sake. God separates Israel from the other nations for a purpose; it is, as we have just seen him say to his people, "to be mine." Holiness requires separation because God has called his people into a covenantal relationship with him. Moses describes this calling, this election: "For you are a people holy to the LORD your God; the LORD your God has chosen you out of all the peoples on earth to be his people, his treasured possession" (Deut. 7:6). Hence, to be "a people holy to the LORD" requires Israel to be "a people for his own possession," or "his treasured possession." Israel is to stand out from among the nations by enjoying an intimate and treasured relationship with the Creator.

Israel's separation *from* the other nations is *for* the other nations.[8] It is called to be holy for the sake of the whole world that is under darkness due to confusion and blindness. Isaiah describes a servant of Israel who will help it become "a light to the nations." To this servant, God says, "I am the LORD, I have called you in righteousness, I have taken you by the hand and kept you; I have given you as a covenant to the people, a light to the nations, to open the eyes that are blind, to bring out the prisoners from the dungeon, from the prison those who sit in darkness" (Isa. 42:6–7). Because the Lord has called the servant to righteousness, the servant can help bring the other nations out of the prisons of division and sin and into an ordered knowledge and love of the true God.

Holiness as perfection in love. Loving God requires worshiping him alone as opposed to created things. Loving our fellow human beings requires recognizing their proper worth above other goods of the world. It is in the Ten Commandments that we find the connection between these two loves. Stealing from one's neighbor, committing adultery with one's neighbor's spouse, murdering one's neighbor—all are failures to love one's neighbor. Worshiping other gods and forgetting the Sabbath are failures to love God. In keeping with this thrust, Leviticus includes the second greatest commandment, which will be at the core of Jesus' teaching: "You shall love your neighbor as yourself" (Lev. 19:18). As Jesus and his hearers knew well, God's word in Leviticus continues, "You shall love your neighbor as yourself: I am the LORD." This teaching thus is not a

---

8. The book of Tobit describes the scattering of Israel among the nations so the nations may come to know the Lord: "Acknowledge him before the nations, O children of Israel; for he has scattered you among them. He has shown you his greatness even there" (Tobit 13:3–4). Tobit indicates that Israel's witness will bear fruit in the conversion of the Gentile nations: "Many nations will come to you from far away, the inhabitants of the remotest parts of the earth to your holy name, bearing gifts in their hands for the King of heaven" (Tobit 13:11).

generic humanitarian affirmation. True love of neighbor flows out of recognition of the true God.

We have stated some right ways to understand the connection between love of God and love of neighbor. There are also wrong ways. The connection may be falsely taken to imply that those who do not believe in God are entirely immoral and behave worse than believers. Or, it may be falsely understood as implying that believers cannot figure out for themselves that they ought to love their neighbors and behave decently. Each of these misunderstandings draws a false dichotomy between God's commands and our inner conscience.

The truth is that revelation does not mute our moral conscience: it *enlightens* it. To love our neighbor as ourselves implies that we recognize the good proper to us and that which is proper to our neighbor. To do so in light of God's wisdom does not detract in any way from the dignity of our moral choices. Rather, God's wisdom brings us to see that both we ourselves and our neighbor were created by God and for God.

To be honest, it is not always easy to love our neighbor—especially when our neighbor has wronged us, or when we desperately want something that belongs to our neighbor. Loving our neighbor out of love for God assists us in overcoming such temptations.

Reading beyond Leviticus, we will find that the Psalms offer profound meditations on holiness.[9] The first Psalm contrasts the way of blessedness to the way of wickedness. It begins, "Blessed is the man who walks not in the counsel of the wicked, nor stands in the way of sinners, nor sits in the seat of scoffers" (Ps. 1.1 RSV-CE). From the path of holiness, there is a threefold decline: walking in sin, standing in sin, and then sitting and taking our place squarely as a sinner among sinners. The threefold repetition forms a contrast with

---

9. See Christopher R. J. Holmes, *The Lord Is Good: Seeking the God of the Psalter* (Downers Grove, IL: IVP Academic, 2018).

Isaiah's vision: just as God is "holy, holy, holy," human beings are often "wicked," "sinners," and "scoffers."

The way of holiness, however, is not simply good behavior or good intentions. What is necessary is to receive the gift of God's Law, which is the condition for staying in God's covenant. God's holiness initiates a response of holiness. God initiates his covenant and gives his people the Law as a way to live and love rightly. The blessed person "delights in the law of the LORD, and on his law he meditates day and night" (Ps. 1:2 RSV-CE). Psalm 40 echoes this theme of delight: "I delight to do your will, O my God; your law is within my heart" (Ps. 40:8).

When we consider holiness as the blessedness obtained through meditation on God's Law, we see God's Law in a new light, no longer as a constraint but as a path to true joy. God's Law comes into our world as a lifeline in the midst of suffering and confusion. Blessedness does not mean a fleeting, subjective feeling of happiness that occurs when things happen to go our way. Rather, it is the stable and objective disposition of richly fulfilling the purpose for which we are made. It is not simply the satisfaction of our desire for pleasures but the satisfaction of the deepest longings in the heart—to love and to be loved, to know the truth and to be known by it. The path of holiness is the path to authentic happiness.

When we read the Psalms in light of their fulfillment in the New Covenant, Jesus Christ becomes both their subject and their speaker. "Blessed is the man." Jesus is that blessed man. "On his law he meditates day and night." Jesus is that Law. As Christians, we may pray Psalm 1 in order to meditate upon and enter into the holiness of Jesus' right relationship with the Father as that blessed man.

Psalm 16 reveals the path of God as the path to joy amid the hardships of this life. The Psalmist begins by asking for God's help as he makes the decision to choose God: "Preserve me, O God, for in you I take refuge. I say to the LORD, 'You are my LORD; I have no good apart from you'" (Ps. 16:1–2). With those words, the Psalmist recognizes the deepest truth that nothing other than God is truly good, for God is goodness itself. Jesus echoes this same truth when he says, "No one is good but God alone" (Mark 10:18).

Only a relationship with the living God will satisfy us in all that we seek, for he is the unlimited source of all of the limited perfections of creatures. Even the closest of human lovers, friends, and family can never satisfy all our deepest desires, because they, too, are subject to suffering and death, as well as their own wounds and sinful inclinations. Although human love may satisfy many longings and heal us of many immaturities, human love cannot heal our deepest wounds of sin and death. Only God is a sure refuge. In the language of the Psalm, to God alone may we unconditionally cry out, "Preserve me," "Save me," "Help me."

Psalm 16 concludes by emphasizing the connection between holiness and happiness. "You show me the path of life, in your presence there is fullness of joy; in your right hand are pleasures forevermore" (Ps. 16:11). Holiness is not a path of deprivation but a path of life. The "path of life" is filled with God's presence, a path to "fullness of joy" and "pleasures forevermore."

In a similar way, Psalm 4 indicates that seeking holiness helps one find true happiness. "Put your trust in the LORD," says the Psalmist, and he testifies to the joy that God has put into his heart (4:5, 7).

The Bible invites us to discover the call to holiness as a call to abundant life. Holiness in the Old Testament means saying "yes" to God's invitation to this abundance. It is an invitation that God will ultimately convey in person through Jesus, who says, "I came that they may have life, and have it abundantly" (John 10:10). To accept this invitation is to imitate God's holiness, his purity, and his love. By this acceptance, one is transformed by God's love so as to love God with one's whole heart, mind, and strength and to love one's neighbor as oneself. It is true and lasting happiness, a blessedness that God alone gives because it is a blessedness that God alone is.

Holiness and Conversion in the New Testament

Primary in the New Covenant's call to holiness is the call to conversion. Tax collectors and prostitutes enter the kingdom of heaven ahead of the Pharisees, not because of their past sins of extortion and fornication but rather because of their present acceptance of the Good News. Jesus preaches conversion: "Repent, the kingdom of heaven has come near" (Matt. 4:17). We might prefer that he would simply give us a gentle acknowledgment of our good efforts or a pat on the back for trying to be decent folk. Instead, we hear the profound truth that Jesus calls us to a decisive moment—and an ongoing journey—of conversion.

The New Testament presents Jesus as the one in whom the earlier prophecies of Isaiah are fulfilled. Blind people receive their sight (Luke 4:18–19) and the nations begin to worship "in spirit and truth" (John 4:24). Moreover, Isaiah prophesies that the true servant will not only restore the twelve tribes of Israel, but also that the Lord will give the servant as a light to the nations, "that my salvation may reach to the end of the earth" (Isa. 49:6).[10] Jesus fulfills this prophecy as well. When the prophet Simeon sees the child Jesus in the temple, he announces, "My eyes have seen your salvation, which you have prepared in the presence of all peoples, a light for revelation to the Gentiles, and for glory to your people Israel" (Luke 2:30–32).

---

10. See Christopher J.H. Wright, *The Mission of God: Unlocking the Bible's Grand Narrative* (Downers Grove, IL: IVP Academic, 2006), 519–520.

Christ continues this mission to be a light to the nations after his Ascension by way of his Apostles. Paul and Barnabas, inspired by the Holy Spirit, apply to themselves the prophecy of Isaiah: "I have set you to be a light to the Gentiles, so that you may bring salvation to the ends of the earth" (Acts 13:47).[11] Jesus' mission—and its extension through his Apostles—is unintelligible apart from Jesus' fulfilling in his person Israel's vocation to be holy, as in set apart *from* the nations and holy *for* the nations.

The New Testament presents holiness as love and love as holiness. Let us look at the famous expression from John's letter, "God is love." What is the actual context of this often-repeated teaching? The full verse offers union alongside separation. John writes, "Beloved, let us love one another, because love is of God; everyone who loves is born of God and knows God. Whoever does not love does not know God, for God is love" (1 John 4:7–8). Like holiness, love separates. In this case, the truth that "God is love" divides those who love their neighbor from those who do not. The truth that "God is love" does not offer generic comfort but calls us to be on God's side. And yet the truth that "God is love" is indeed our ultimate comfort. John writes to the early Christians, "In this is love, not that we loved God but that he loved us and sent his Son to be the atoning sacrifice for our sins" (1 John 4:10). God loved us and sent his Son to take away our sins. John invites us to say yes to God's love.

Christian life is a struggle to respond to the Gospel's call to holiness in order to draw closer to God. The author of Hebrews summarizes this reality: "Pursue peace with everyone, and the holiness without which no one will see the Lord" (Heb. 12:14). This verse teaches another aspect of holiness: holiness makes it possible to see the Lord. As we seek holiness, we also seek peace, a harmony within

---

11. See David W. Pao, *Acts and the Isaianic New Exodus* (Grand Rapids, MI: Baker Academic, 2002), especially 96–101.

ourselves and among our relationships with others, including those who may appear above us or below us in society. Peace does not come easily. Without such peace, however, we project our disordered passions, darkened vision, and clouded judgment upon others and God. This is why Hebrews says we must strive for the "holiness without which no one will see God." It is not that we break an arbitrary rule when we worship something or someone other than God; rather, we fail to see the true God and instead only see that which serves and pleases us. When we have idolatrous hearts, we only see idols. The gift of holiness in Jesus Christ renews our hearts so that they may see God. Hebrews here echoes Jesus' words, "Blessed are the pure of heart, for they will *see* God" (Matt. 5:8; emphasis added). Biblical revelation teaches that it is much harder for us to see God than we might think. Authentic vision requires holiness.

We are called to approach the holiness of God with reverence and trust. The author of Hebrews says something that might surprise us at first: "It is a fearful thing to fall into the hands of the living God" (Heb. 10:31). God's holiness, however, should fill us with awe and holy fear, not discouragement or servile fear. Remember that Hebrews exhorts us to pursue holiness so that we might see God. Such striving and struggle need to be understood properly since they are a response to God's initiative. The gift of holiness is received when God transforms us by his grace from ungodly into godly people. And yet to fall into God's hands remains "a fearful thing." God's holiness is "fearful" in the sense that it is profoundly wondrous and awe-inspiring. Hebrews, at the same time, encourages us to have great trust in the mercy of God: "We have confidence to enter the sanctuary by the blood of Jesus. . . . Let us approach with a true heart in full assurance of faith" (Heb. 10:19, 22). With true awe and respect and a deep confidence and assurance—this is how we may approach God's holiness in Jesus Christ.

This combination of awe and confidence is also present in Paul's teaching on how we are to approach God in Jesus Christ. One sentence in his Letter to the Philippians illustrates confidence in—as well as awe in the presence of—God in our journey of salvation. Paul echoes the same theme of fear and striving that we saw in Hebrews, "Work out your own salvation with fear and trembling" (Phil. 2:12). In this way, he puts the emphasis on our work to remain in the covenant. But he doesn't end his thought there; rather, he continues, "for it is God who is at work in you, enabling you both to will and to work for his good pleasure" (Phil. 2:13). This is not a vicious circle, however, since God acts first. The result is a holy trust.

Christ's death and Resurrection are the pattern for—and make possible—our own conversion. Jesus has already died in a perfect gift of self and has been raised victoriously. Paul shares a mystery—namely, that Christ rises from the dead to become the Lord of all creation: "That at the name of Jesus every knee should bend, in heaven and on earth and under the earth, and every tongue should confess that Jesus Christ is Lord, to the glory of God the Father" (Phil. 2:10–11). With those words, Paul invites us to make Jesus Lord of our entire person, of our mind and of our body.

And so, "If God is for us, who is against us?" (Rom. 8:31). God is indeed for us, so let us be for God. He never wishes to be separated from us; it is we who are liable to separate ourselves from him by spurning the call to holiness, the call to conversion. For our own personal thriving, to live up to the fullness of the life for which God created us, we need to answer his call with a "yes" that encompasses our entire person.

It is helpful to remember that conversion is not merely an event; even when it is sparked by an event, that event is only the beginning of a process. An initial decision to follow Christ begets countless more.

We are invited to convert again each day when we pray the prayer that Jesus taught us: "Forgive us our debts, as we also have forgiven our debtors" (Matt. 6:12). In this way, through our seeking forgiveness for sins, we may come to see our total dependence upon God's assistance as we pray, "And lead us not into temptation, but deliver us from evil" (Matt. 6:13 RSV-CE). Our conversion is not the result of our own initiative but our response to the gift of God's mercy.

Holiness and Imitation

The call to holiness invites us to turn from imitating the world and to begin to imitate Christ. Such imitation does not reject the world in itself, the world as it was created to be. Rather, when we imitate Christ, we help to renew the world, to claim it back by seeing the beauty of the human person and the glory of God.

Nonetheless, there is part of the world, part of our societies, and part of us that is disordered, rebelling against the good order of creation and the provident care of the Creator. To find true happiness and discover God's plan for us, we need to turn away from that disordered "world," that part of creation rebelling and turning away from God. Paul powerfully summarizes this truth, "Do not be conformed to this world" (Rom. 12:2). The Apostle does not stop there, however, but invites us to change: "Be transformed by the renewal of your mind, that you may discern what is the will of God—what is good and acceptable and perfect" (Rom. 12:2).

Jesus Christ introduces into human history the perfect image of God. In Colossians, Paul teaches that "[Christ] is the image of the invisible God, the firstborn of all creation" (Col. 1:15).[12] Unlike the rest of humanity, Jesus Christ is not created in the image of God (cf. Genesis 1:27) but simply is the image of God. The word used for

---

12. For historical-critical background, see Margaret Y. MacDonald, *Colossians and Ephesians* (Collegeville, MN: Liturgical Press, 2000), 58–59.

"image" translates the Greek *eikon*, the source of our word "icon." When we worship Jesus Christ, we are not worshiping an idol but an icon. His human nature is fully united to his divine nature. As the true image and true icon of God, he is God's true and eternal Son.

Hebrews emphasizes the Son's completely faithful reflection of the Father: "in these last days [God] has spoken to us by a Son, whom he appointed heir of all things, through whom he also created the worlds. He is the reflection of God's glory and the exact imprint of God's very being, and he sustains all things by his powerful word" (Heb. 1:2–3).[13] Notice how Hebrews says that the Son is "the reflection of" God's glory and "the exact imprint" of the God's being. God's perfect reflection or image has now entered our history.

Christian conversion thus renews the image of God in us according to the true Image of God, Jesus Christ. As rational creatures we reflect and imitate God's glory by coming to know and love him with all our heart, mind, soul, and strength. Listen to how Paul describes the image of God as something that we put on (like a garment), as we put off our sinful habits. Paul writes, "Do not lie to one another, seeing that you have put off the old nature with its practices and have put on the new nature, which is being renewed in knowledge after to the image [*eikon*] of its creator" (Col. 3:9–10 RSV-CE). More than a mere picture, religious icons of Jesus Christ and the saints serve to make present the person represented. In this manner, Paul calls us to be true icons of God, making the Creator present in our lives rather than obstructing God's presence through our perverted wills. Paul invites us to put off our old nature.

What does it mean for our natures to be renewed in the image of God? The word "nature" describes the sorts of activities and operations that are typical of a living thing. So a bird has a bird-nature

---

13. See Harold W. Attridge, *Hebrews* (Minneapolis, MN: Fortress Press, 1989), 41–45.

and acts in bird-like ways, such as flying, building nests, laying eggs, and so on. The more the biologist comes to understand the infinitely complex operations and activities of the bird and how they interact with the surrounding environment, the more the biologist comes to know the nature of the bird.

Natures go hand-in-hand with activities. Jesus makes reference to this when he says that good trees bear good fruits and bad trees bear bad fruits. So when Paul speaks of our "old nature" and "its practices," he is showing that our sinful tendencies run deep. We stand in need of the renewal of our image in Jesus Christ. We need a new identity in Christ.

Paul contrasts the evil practices of our old identity with the loving actions that should characterize members of the New Covenant. This is not a mere moral exhortation but more a reminder of believers' new identity. Paul is teaching Christians that they are now free to cease behaving (or, rather, misbehaving) in their old ways since they now have new natures, new selves, renewed according to the image of God. The observance of the Law follows from the new identity of the person in now properly imitating the one God.

In the Second Letter of Peter, we likewise are invited to consider the new nature that God is calling us to put on. Peter asks, "What sort of persons ought you to be in leading lives of holiness and godliness?" (2 Pet. 3:11). When we look at our actions and the fruits we bear in our lives, we can begin to recognize the difference between what sort of person we are and what sort of person we might become.

Paul urges us to go ever deeper to find our new identity in our Christian vocation. "Put off your old nature which belongs to your former manner of life and is corrupt through deceitful lusts," he writes, "and be renewed in the spirit of your minds, and put on the new nature, created after the likeness of God in true righteousness and holiness" (Eph. 4:22–24 RSV-CE). Let us pay attention here to two themes: putting off "deceitful lusts" and being "renewed in the spirit of your minds."

Putting off "deceitful lusts." The Greek translated here as "lusts" is *epithumia*, from the root word *thumos*, or spiritedness, and might be translated as "intense desires." Thus, the difficulty is not that our desires are too intense but that we have two types of such desires—truthful desires and deceitful desires—and too often we desire wrongly. The wounds to our human nature produce a chilling of the heart and a darkening of the mind. Rather than immediately moving to what is highest—namely, God and neighbor—our desires are captivated by lesser things such as physical pleasures and comforts. We are often unduly attached to our own sense of being right rather than letting our intellects be receptive to the truth about reality. We are quick to excuse our own behavior and slow to evaluate our actions in light of God's standards.

The peculiar difficulty, however, is that since it is our own thoughts and desires that are darkened, we cannot enlighten them ourselves. When we try to clean a mirror with oily and dirty hands, it only gets dirtier. So with the mirrors of our minds and psyches. We need God to wash us and enlighten us, to restore the mirror in us. Yet God does not wash us as we might wash an inanimate mirror. He washes us *with* us, not *without* us.[14] He asks for our cooperation, for our willingness "to put off" our old ways of thinking and acting.

Paul shows how our clouded vision impacts our ability to see the goodness of God's plan for us. "The minds of the unbelievers," he writes, are darkened and cannot see "the light of the gospel of the glory of Christ, who is the image of God" (2 Cor. 4:4). We need to ask

---

14. See *Catechism of the Catholic Church*, no. 1847, which quotes Augustine: "God created us without us: but he did not will to save us without us" (*Sermo* 169, 11, 13: *PL* 38, 923). *Catechism of the Catholic Church*, 2nd ed. (Washington, DC: USCCB Publishing, 1997), 452.

God to enlighten our minds to see the true icon of God, Jesus Christ in his glory. To love God means to work to leave behind our deceitful desires and to be renewed in the image of God "in true righteousness and holiness." The more we share in Christ's holiness, the less we obscure God's goodness. Paul writes, "And we all, with unveiled face, beholding the glory of the Lord, are being changed into his image from one degree of glory to another; for this comes from the Lord who is the Spirit" (2 Cor. 3:18 RSV-CE).[15] As our deceitful desires give way to truthful desires, we may both behold and reflect to a greater degree the Lord's glory.

Becoming renewed. According to Paul, our conversion requires not only turning away from "deceitful desires" but also "the renewal of our minds." In our contemporary culture, we tend to value sincerity over truth. Yet if we do not know the truth, at least at some level, what value is our sincerity? How can we love what we do not know? To know God as he reveals himself in Jesus Christ is to be renewed "in the spirit of your minds." This renewal of our minds allows us to receive a new identity, to become a new person. Our new nature is according to the likeness of God "in true righteousness and holiness." The call of Leviticus, "Be holy as the LORD your God is holy," is thus fulfilled in Jesus Christ, for he is the holiness of God.

Paul thus develops this call to imitate God with a directness that may surprise us at first. He writes, "Therefore be imitators of God, as beloved children" (Eph. 5:1). We may imitate God because we are his beloved children (cf. Rom. 8:28–29). Paul's next words show us that we are to carry out this imitation through following Christ's example: "And live in love, *as* Christ loved us and gave himself up for us,

---

15. See Michael J. Gorman, "Paul's Corporate, Cruciform, Missional Theosis in Second Corinthians," in *"In Christ" in Paul: Explorations in Paul's Theology of Union and Participation,* ed. Michael J. Thate, Kevin J. Vanhoozer, and Constantine R. Campbell (Tübingen: Mohr Siebeck, 2014), 181–208, especially 188–193.

a fragrant offering and sacrifice to God" (Eph. 5:2; emphasis added). This is not a mere moral burden, for it flows from God's love. Christ loved us and gave himself up for us—for you and for me.

In this way, the New Testament presents us with a revolution in our understanding of true holiness and in how we live that holiness. Popular belief has it that those who are holy are perfect people who walk around with a halo. Paul is opening up a new way of thinking about holiness. We do not achieve holiness on our own but receive it as a gift. We are called to accept the gift of Christ's holiness and let it transform us.

Here again, we see that an attitude of holiness says "yes" to Christ's love for us. Paul encourages us to continue to put off old sinful habits and live in accord with Jesus Christ. Holiness allows for a new separation, a separation within each person, away from evil and toward good. The call to holiness is thus a continual call to separate from the old nature and its actions and to embrace the new nature and its actions (Rom. 7:13–8:17).

Holiness and Imitating Jesus

If holiness calls for the renewal of the image of God in human beings according to Jesus Christ, then we need to have an authentic image of Jesus before us. Happily, we are not left to our own devices to develop this image, since Jesus leaves it for us at the beginning of his Sermon on the Mount. In his Beatitudes, Jesus paints a picture of the true nature of holiness and of the true flourishing of the human creature.

Blessed are the poor in spirit, for theirs is the kingdom of heaven.

Blessed are those who mourn, for they will be comforted.

Blessed are the meek, for they will inherit the earth.

Blessed are those who hunger and thirst for righteousness, for they will be filled.

Blessed are the merciful, for they will receive mercy.

Blessed are the pure in heart, for they will see God.

Blessed are the peacemakers, for they will be called children of God.

Blessed are those who are persecuted for righteousness' sake, for theirs is the kingdom of heaven. (Matt. 5:3–9)

The Beatitudes are a self-portrait of Jesus. They depict the way that Jesus truly images God. As such, they also are Jesus' portrait of Christians called to live in the divine image.[16] The Beatitudes powerfully call us to deeper and ongoing conversion of heart.

Let us view these eight Beatitudes as they apply to Jesus. Through each of them, Jesus invites his followers to enter into the perfect relationship with God and neighbor that he alone made possible. He shows himself to have lived each beatitude:

- Jesus is the blessed one who is poor in spirit: "In his anguish, he prayed more earnestly" (Luke 22:44).

- Jesus is the one who mourns: he wept over Jerusalem for its failure to receive his coming (Luke 19:41–44).

- Jesus is the one who is meek: for he is "gentle and lowly in heart" (Matt. 11:29).

- Jesus is the one who hungers for God: "My food is to do the will of him who sent me" (John 4:34).

- Jesus is the one who shows mercy: he says to the woman caught in adultery, "Neither do I condemn you. Go your way, and from now on do not sin again" (John 8:11).

---

16. See Jonathan T. Pennington, *The Sermon on the Mount and Human Flourishing: A Theological Commentary* (Grand Rapids, MI: Baker Academic, 2019).

- Jesus is the one who is pure of heart and able to see God: "Father, I thank you that you have heard me. I know that you hear me always" (John 11:42 RSV-CE).

- Jesus is the one who is a peacemaker: "For he is our peace; in his flesh he has made both groups into one" (Eph. 2:14).

- Finally, Jesus is the one who is persecuted. He will "be rejected by the elders, the chief priests, and the scribes, and be killed" (Mark 8:31).

Jesus thus reveals how true happiness and blessedness is found in his identity as the true Son of God and how this identity is characterized by each of the Beatitudes. In proclaiming the Beatitudes to us, he invites us to share in his own rich relationship with God the Father by becoming children of God and so bringing our lives into correspondence with our Father's will for his beloved children.

These blessings, however, come at a cost. The believer has to turn away from a pattern of sinful attitudes and deceitful desires. As we saw with the Psalms, the Beatitudes disclose two ways. One way leads to true life and communion with God, whereas the other leads to death and alienation from God. For this reason, when Jesus presents the Beatitudes in Luke, Jesus speaks not only of blessings, but also of anti-blessings or woes (Luke 6:24–26). The Beatitudes call for a turning away from sin and a turning toward God, turning away from woes and turning toward blessedness. Blessed are the poor and the poor in spirit, but woe to the haughty in spirit and prideful who will lose the very self to which they cling. Blessed are those who mourn their own sins and the injustices of this world, but woe to those who rejoice in their sins and injustices. Jesus diagnoses our woes not to condemn us but to invite us to a deeper conversion.

The blessing of the meek opens up a new way of life that comes when we surrender our will to God's will. Meekness may be easily misunderstood as a call to let others trample upon us. This is not so. Meekness before the Lord corresponds to great strength. The Greek word translated here as "meek" is *praus* and describes an animal that is no longer wild but has been trained. A *meek* horse, for instance, is one that has been "gentled" or trained to come under human guidance. The meekest horse in a race thereby may well be the fastest horse and so win the prize. In the same way, a meek person is not a weak person, but one who willingly seeks to be trained by the Lord and come under divine guidance. Meekness overcomes our prideful tendency to trust in ourselves and in this world rather than in God. Jesus thus displayed meekness when he drove out the money changers from the temple and defended his Father's house (Matt. 21:12). Genuine meekness is powerful, filled with power received from above.

The remaining Beatitudes deepen the Christian call to conversion through mercy, purity, peace, and, in a different way, persecution. Jesus immediately sees through our own tendencies toward self-justification. In multiple parables, he illustrates how quick we are to ask for—and expect—forgiveness when we have done wrong and how slow we are to forgive others when we have been wronged. Only the merciful, however, are truly able to receive mercy.

As is the Gospel pattern for gifts from God (and, indeed, as is the pattern of the whole Bible), we do not initiate God's mercy. God is first merciful to us. His mercy is the standard, ours is the image, the reflection. Thus, his mercy has the capacity to make us merciful. It is because of this divine initiative that Jesus says, "Be merciful, just as your Father is merciful" (Luke 6:36).

Mercy leads to purity of heart. It allows us to see the world as God sees it and to let his mercy flow through us to those in misery, both the misery of sin and the misery of wounds and poverty. Instead of seeing the world and other people as objects for the gratification of our often disordered desires, purity of heart allows us to see the world and others as they truly are, created by God and loved by him. To see others as God's creatures means to see in them the image of God, a mirror of God's presence. The one with purity of heart no longer sees the world as an idol in competition with God but rather sees it in its authentic reality as an icon of God's glory.

The more our vision is purified, the more we may bring peace, the seventh beatitude. The angels declare to the shepherds at Jesus' birth, "Glory to God in the highest heaven, and on earth peace among those whom he favors!" (Luke 2:14). The peace that God establishes in Jesus Christ spreads through his disciples.

When we live the Beatitudes, we may help make true peace, even when it requires confrontation and difficult decisions rather than seeking the path of maximal comfort. The same Jesus who teaches that "blessed are the peacemakers" also says that "I have not come to bring peace, but a sword" (Matt. 10:34). As we have seen, holiness requires us to reflect God's identity as opposed to our sins and the sins of others.

Holiness enables us to turn away from the sinful habits of our hearts, of our families, and of our societies. As Christians, we cannot make peace with—or simply cover up—our own sins or the sins of others. The very act of mercy is both to forgive and to attempt to alleviate the wounded condition. Mercy encourages us and others to "not sin again" (John 8:11). Such confrontation of sin takes place within the domain of mercy, of God's loving kindness. God's mercy allows us to accept the reality of our weaknesses as well as to strive to rid ourselves of those same weaknesses. The Beatitudes describe this ongoing conversion in multiple steps and stages: the deeper the conversion, the more the Christian receives the gift of peace that comes from God through Christ to his community of disciples.

Jesus, wishing to ensure that his followers understand that peace does not mean comfortable compromise with sinful patterns, concludes the Beatitudes with the final blessing for those who suffer persecution. For the Christian, to be persecuted for the sake of righteousness is not the end of the story. Rather, it is the gateway to the perfect peace of the kingdom of heaven.

Finally, Christ sums up his teaching on holiness when he says, "Be perfect, therefore, as your heavenly Father is perfect" (Matt. 5:48). To receive this teaching, we need to avoid a perfectionistic understanding of the call to holiness in which our inevitable imperfections would render void Jesus' command. Instead, the Greek word here for "perfect" is *teleios* from the word *telos*, meaning goal, purpose, or wholeness. Thus the meaning of "be perfect" is better captured by "be perfected" or "reach the goal for which you were created." Again, the call is to let God increasingly perfect in us the image of his Son as children of God. In this life, the way is of repentance, of conversion, of turning to God's promises in faith and then of making progress and living in hope of final perfection in eternal life.

Paul likewise depicts divine filiation—that is, living out one's Christian identity as a son or daughter of God—as progress toward holiness. In Galatians, Paul calls his readers to recognize who they are and then grow into their true nature. He teaches, "Because you are children, God has sent the Spirit of his Son into our hearts, crying, 'Abba! Father!'" (Gal. 4:6). He continues, "My little children, for whom I am again in the pain of childbirth until Christ is formed in you" (Gal. 4:19). To be perfected as our Father is perfect is to allow our wounded, sinful, and alienated selves to be healed by Christ who invites us to receive a share in his own perfect relationship with the Father in the Spirit. It is to be born anew in Jesus Christ and to let Christ be formed in us.

Conversion and Freedom

What about freedom in the moral life? Are we free when we merely do what we want? What if we want the wrong things, led astray by "deceitful desires"? What if these disordered desires conflict among themselves, and so lead to further chaos and confusion—or, worse, boredom? How are we to find purpose? How are we to find freedom?

To all those questions, Paul gives us the beginning of our answer when he teaches in his Letter to the Galatians, "For freedom Christ has set us free" (Gal. 5:1). This true freedom is not freedom *from* obligation but freedom *for* excellence—that is, for life in Christ.[17]

Paul challenges Christians to make a decision for this true freedom: "For you were called to freedom, brethren; only do not use your freedom as an opportunity for the flesh, but through love be servants of one another" (Gal. 5:13). The word "flesh" here includes all that is in us that is in rebellion against our deepest created inclinations to the good. As such, the flesh includes distorted bodily and spiritual desires. Paul thus will speak not only of sexual immorality and drunkenness as works of the flesh but also of envy and selfishness. He introduces the antidote: to be servants of one another through love. He teaches, "for the whole law is fulfilled in one word, 'you shall love your neighbor as yourself'" (Gal. 5:14).

Paul goes on to invite us to overcome the works of the flesh with the fruits of the Spirit: Will we walk in the flesh or in the Spirit (see Gal. 5:16)? As noted in an earlier chapter, he then makes the call to conversion more concrete by listing various works of the flesh— activities associated with the disordered state of affairs within our own hearts and communities. "Now the works of the flesh are plain: sexual immorality, impurity, licentiousness, idolatry, sorcery,

---

17. See Servais Pinckaers, OP, *The Sources of Christian Ethics*, trans. Mary Thomas Noble, OP (Washington, DC: The Catholic University of America, 1995).

enmity, strife, jealousy, anger, selfishness, dissension, party spirit, envy, drunkenness, carousing, and the like" (Gal. 5:19–21). These works of the flesh include both bodily and spiritual sins.

When a person sins, his or her action reveals a person still trapped within the worldly rebellion against the true order of creation, for creation is intended to give glory to God. Paul does not mince words about the reality of such disordered actions: "I am warning you, as I warned you before: those who do such things will not inherit the kingdom of God" (Gal. 5:21). The Apostle's logic is not that of extrinsic punishment but of the intrinsic consequences of living in rebellion against God. God's kingdom will be perfected in the glorious renewed creation, in which humans will live fully in accord with their call to love God and love neighbor. Those who in the present life do not live in this manner, but who instead continue to use their freedom to separate themselves from God, will not be forced into the presence of God.

Whatever or whoever we may love, ultimately we love either our own distortions of the created order or God and his plan for creation—namely, the redemption of the world he "so loved" (John 3:16). We must therefore make a choice either to love our own loves or to love God's loves. This is why Paul tells the Galatians that he glories only in "the cross of our Lord Jesus Christ"—by which, in his words, "the world has been crucified to me, and I to the world" (Gal. 6:14). What matters, he says, is not whether they rack up good deeds but that they are, from the inside out, "a new creation" (Gal. 6:15), transformed interiorly so as to express divine love in their lives.[18] Our fallen creation needs to be made new.

---

18. See N.T. Wright, *Paul and the Faithfulness of God: Book II, Parts III and IV* (Minneapolis, MN: Fortress Press, 2013), 1143–1145 (Wright's main focus is the context provided by Gal. 6:16 regarding "the Israel of God").

What then does the renewed creation look like now in the lives of Christians? "The fruit of the Spirit," Paul writes, "is love, joy, peace, patience, kindness, goodness, faithfulness, gentleness, self-control. There is no law against such things" (Gal. 5:22–23). Here we see the pattern for human beings living in peace with God and with neighbor—a pattern perfectly lived out by Jesus Christ. The bodily sins of disordered sexual relations and drunkenness have been set aside. Likewise, interior sins such as resentment, envy, and jealousy no longer dominate relationships with neighbor. Idolatry and efforts to harness occult powers no longer cloud the hearts and minds of human beings before God their Father. In the fruits of the Spirit indwelling the new creation, the cry of the Psalmist has been ful-filled: "When you send forth your Spirit, they are created; and you renew the face of the earth" (Ps. 104:30 RSV-CE).

Paul depicts the renewed state of being children of God in the Spirit who may call God "Abba, Father!" He urges his readers to let God's works be accomplished in us: "Those who belong to Christ Jesus have crucified the flesh with its passions and desires" (Gal. 5:24). This crucifixion of our rebellious hearts and bodies is not for its own sake—and it is certainly not because our hearts and bodies are inherently bad. Just as Christ did not die for the sake of dying, but so that he might rise again to eternal life, so our hearts and bodies are to die with Christ so they might live anew with Christ (Gal. 2:20; Rom. 6:3–4). Conversion allows God's plan to be manifested in us, a plan for living in harmony with God and with our neighbors (Rom. 8:18–23). Paul summarizes what it means to use our freedom well by living in the Spirit and continually turning from the works of the flesh. He writes, "Bear one another's burdens, and so fulfill the law of Christ" (Gal. 6:2). The law of Christ is the perfection of the love of God and the love of neighbor as oneself.

Conclusion

The prophet Jeremiah spoke to the people of God who were exiled from Jerusalem and were living as captives in Babylon. He offered them comfort that their captivity would end and that God would bring them back to Jerusalem where they would be free—and now actually able—to worship God properly and to follow his Law fully. In a celebrated phrase, Jeremiah writes, "For surely I know the plans I have for you, says the Lord, plans for welfare and not for harm, to give you a future with hope" (Jer. 29:11). These same words speak to us today. Despite the exile of this current world, its burdens and the burdens of our own sins, we are called to have great trust in God and in his plans for us, plans for good and not for evil, to give us a future and a hope in Christ.

The call to conversion is nothing other than the call to trust fully in God and to let him be Lord of our lives. Paul writes, "For this is the will of God, your sanctification" (1 Thess. 4:3). God wants us to be holy. This is surely good news! Since this is his will, it is not up to our strength but up to the strength of the Holy Spirit living in us. Paul writes to Timothy and to all of us who have been baptized, "for God did not give us a spirit of cowardice, but rather a spirit of power and love and self-discipline" (2 Tim. 1:7). When we respond to it, we discover that the call to holiness is actually a daring adventure[19] that fosters a bold relationship with God in Christ—our ongoing missteps notwithstanding.

This chapter has considered the call to conversion within the entirety of biblical revelation. God's calling of Israel was always a call for Israel to be holy as God was holy. In the Old Testament, holiness is especially a call to imitate God's holiness, to be separated from

---

19. See Daniel A. Keating, *The Adventure of Discipleship* (Steubenville, OH: Emmaus Road, 2018).

that which is not holy, in order to be a light for those nations and people outside God's renewed covenant. In the New Testament, the main pattern of holiness remains, but it is now transformed in the person of Jesus Christ. He is the perfect image of God's holiness and he calls for a separation inside each of us from our unholy and disordered desires and so also for a separation from participation in the sins of others. Jesus presents a picture of the renewed image of God in all that he says and does, but especially in his portrait of himself in the Beatitudes.

Paul teaches how the old self must be put away so that the new self may come to light. To say "no" to the disordered parts of ourselves and of our societies is to say "yes" to God. Paul's words reveal that the call to conversion is an ongoing call to delight God more and more: "Finally, brothers and sisters, we ask and urge you in the Lord Jesus that, as you learned from us how you ought to live and to please God (as in fact, you are doing), you should do so more and more" (1 Thess. 4:1). In this way, we will be conformed to God's love rather than being "conformed to this world" (Rom. 12:2).

CHAPTER 7

Why Care for the Poor?

"There was not a needy person among them"
(Acts 4:34)

It is difficult for some people today to see why the Christian faith should be anything more than loving our neighbor and helping the poor. Such actions are important, given Jesus' love for the poor as well as in light of the many saintly Catholics who have followed his example, such as St. Teresa of Kolkata. Indeed, saints who have served the poor are generally the saints most widely applauded. As Brandon Vogt remarks, "When most people say they have a problem with the Catholic Church, it isn't with the saints. They hear about people such as St. Lawrence, St. Damien, or St. Teresa and respond with admiration and enthusiasm. There is nothing wrong with *those* people. They're doing it right. It's everyone else that's wrong!"[1]

In this vein, consider the perspective of a fifty-four-year-old Catholic who no longer believes or practices his faith. He still admires "the fact that the Catholic Church is the biggest provider of health and education after governments in the world."[2] For this person, the message of Jesus is measured by its economic or political impact. He admires the Catholic faith insofar as it involves helping the poor, but he does not believe the truth claims of Catholicism.

---

1. Brandon Vogt, *Why I Am Catholic (And You Should Be Too)* (Notre Dame, IN: Ave Maria Press, 2017), 99.

2. Stephen Bullivant, Catherine Knowles, Hannah Vaughan-Spruce, and Bernadette Durcan, *Why Catholics Leave, What They Miss, and How They Might Return* (New York: Paulist Press, 2019), 76.

Without doubt, addressing political and economic injustice forms a necessary part of responding to the Gospel. Indeed, Catholics are called to be energized by the sight of poor individuals and families. In the United States and around the globe, it is profoundly distressing to see so many who lack necessities of food, water, opportunities for work, and basic health care. Catholics have a personal responsibility to get involved in caring for the poor and trying to alleviate their distress.

Nonetheless, Catholic faith contains many other elements. In fact, in his earthly ministry, Christ did not provide an economic or political program. He could have come to show people better methods of farming, to invent penicillin or anti-malarial drugs, or to lead a movement for world disarmament, but he did not. Instead, he focused on bringing reconciliation by his cross and overcoming death by his Resurrection, and he anticipated his death and Resurrection through many of his parables and miracles.

Where there is a lack of care for the poor, however, there is a lack of love. All Christians must embrace Christ's command to care for "the least of these who are members of my family" (Matt. 25:40).[3] The Letter of James puts matters succinctly: "Religion that is pure and undefiled before God, the Father, is this: to care for orphans and widows in their distress, and to keep oneself unstained by the world" (James 1:27). James warns that followers of Christ may easily fall into the trap of honoring the rich while neglecting the poor. Those who dishonor "the poor man" have not understood the ways of God, for God has often chosen the poor to be "rich in faith and to be heirs of the kingdom" (James 2:5–6), whereas the rich can be fatally self-satisfied. With sharp irony, James depicts a Christian complacently saying to a hungry and ill-clothed

---

3. See Curtis Mitch and Edward Sri, *The Gospel of Matthew* (Grand Rapids, MI: Baker Academic, 2010), 326.

Christian, "Go in peace; keep warm and eat your fill" (James 2:16)—without giving the needy person any food or clothing. This is a clear sign of lack of love and of a faith that is profitless.[4]

Therefore, Catholics should proceed by holding two points in tension. On the one hand, being Catholic is not primarily about economics or politics. The heart of Catholic faith is the divine Savior who came to redeem all people from the deepest poverty—namely, that of sin and death. On the other hand, care for the poor is central to being Catholic, because we desire life and salvation for all. Vogt, describing an encounter he had with a homeless man named Jimmy, rightly observes, "Christ identifies precisely with people like Jimmy—those without jobs, without hope, and without anyone to talk to."[5] In fact, Catholics are to reach out to people in the midst of every type of personal trial, whether it be economic trouble, mental illness, disasters, addiction, victimization, or political persecution.

What can the voice of the Bible—the full Old and New Testaments—teach us about care for the poor and its place within the Good News of Jesus Christ? The purpose of this chapter is to explore how Catholics might learn from the biblical teachings about the relationship of material needs and spiritual needs. What we will find is that it is in fulfilling spiritual needs—our own and those of others—that we come to care for the material needs of others. Otherwise, as Everett Fritz puts it, we will find ourselves "chasing after the next hedonistic thrill" rather than truly caring about the good of our neighbor.[6]

---

4. See Kelly Anderson, "James," in Kelly Anderson and Daniel Keating, *James, First, Second, and Third John* (Grand Rapids, MI: Baker Academic, 2017), 1–121, at 45–49, 56–57.

5. Brandon Vogt, *Saints and Social Justice: A Guide to Changing the World* (Huntington, IN: Our Sunday Visitor, 2014), 19.

6. Everett Fritz, *Freedom: Battle Strategies for Conquering Temptation* (San Francisco: Ignatius Press, 2015), 187. Fritz is here discussing the quest for chastity and purity of heart.

A Realistic Portrait of the Situation of the Poor in This World

The Psalmist emphasizes that "the Lord hears the cry of the poor" (Ps. 34:6 RSV-CE). In the Psalms, there are frequent, strong petitions calling upon God to "give justice to the weak and the orphan; maintain the right of the afflicted and the destitute" (Ps. 82:3). The Psalmist affirms that God's nature is to care for the weak and the poor. God is on the side of the oppressed.

The Psalms also, however, confront the painful reality that God allows the wicked to thrive in this world. In the mystery of his providence, God does not compel evildoers to change their ways. As such, evildoers continue to cause great suffering amidst the weak and the poor. That the wicked undeniably flourish can make God seem impotent or unknowing. But the Psalmist points out that this material flourishing of health and wealth does not last long; disease and death come relatively soon for all people. Ultimately, it is better to have God than an earthly good. "Whom have I in heaven but you? And there is nothing on earth that I desire other than you. My flesh and my heart may fail, but God is the strength of my heart and my portion forever" (Ps. 73:25–26).

In the book of Ezekiel, God describes the attributes of a righteous person as inextricably linked to care for the poor: a righteous person "does not oppress anyone, but restores to the debtor his pledge" and "gives his bread to the hungry and covers the naked with a garment" (Ezek. 18:7). The sinner, by contrast, is one who "oppresses the poor and needy" (Ezek. 18:12). But Ezekiel goes on to make clear that in certain situations no one is truly on the side of the just. He warns that the whole city of Jerusalem has sinned and merits its punishment of destruction and exile. The people are consumed by various habitual vices against the Decalogue: some commit idolatry, others show contempt for parents, others reject the Sabbath, others commit rape or adultery or incest, others take bribes and do wrong to widows and orphans, others oppress the poor. God seeks one righteous person in the whole city but cannot find one (Ezek. 22:23–31).

The book of Proverbs adds to this picture by considering situations in which people bring poverty upon themselves due to their lack of steady diligence and prudence. We read that "poverty and disgrace are for the one who ignores instruction, but one who heeds reproof is honored" (Prov. 13:18). Likewise, Proverbs teaches that poverty may also arise from self-indulgence: "Whoever loves pleasure will be a poor man; he who loves wine and oil will not be rich" (Prov. 21:17 RSV-CE). One might recall Jesus' parable of the prodigal son who quickly spent through an inheritance only to suffer want.

Thus, we find a multifaceted depiction of the poor in the Old Testament. Many of the poor are poor through the unjust persecution of the wealthy and powerful. Others end up poor through their own foolishness or immoderate desires. Finally, both rich and poor alike fall short of God's righteousness; we are all poor in this sense. In fact, true wealth is found in the spiritual treasure of God.

Care for the Poor

Those who love the Lord are called to care for the poor. Even Proverbs, despite its awareness that some people have brought poverty upon themselves by sinning, insists upon this command to serve the poor. Proverbs argues that the test of royal rule is how the king treats the poor: "If a king judges the poor with equity, his throne will be established forever" (Prov. 29:14). Similarly, the book argues that blessing consistently follows upon care for the poor: "Whoever gives to the poor will lack nothing, but one who turns a blind eye will get many a curse" (Prov. 28:27).

Proverbs recognizes that the wicked are also human beings dependent upon God. We read, "The poor man and the oppressor have this in common: the LORD gives light to the eyes of both" (Prov. 29:13). At the same time, Proverbs emphasizes that the wicked lack justice and such a lack is grievous: "Better to be poor and walk in integrity than to be crooked in one's ways even though rich" (Prov. 28:6). We are not made solely for wealth but are above all created for friendship and communion.

God will reward those who care for the poor: such good actions build up a treasury of divine reward for those who do them. "Whoever is kind to the poor lends to the LORD," Proverbs observes, "and he will be repaid in full" (Prov. 19:17).[7] The poor cannot repay a loan, but God will repay it abundantly. "Do not rob the poor because they are poor, or crush the afflicted at the gate," Proverbs warns, "for the LORD pleads their cause and despoils of life those who despoil them" (Prov. 22:22–23).

In terms of judicial and economic life, the Mosaic Law emphasizes the call to care for the poor. Instructing judges and also those who bring lawsuits, the Mosaic Law issues a warning: "You shall not pervert the justice due to your poor in their lawsuits" (Exod. 23:6). One of the central responsibilities of judges is to restore to the poor that which has been taken from them.

The Bible's message of care for the poor sometimes shows up in unlikely places or in implicit ways. For instance, the Mosaic Law sets apart the Sabbath day as a day of rest and worship. The Sabbath rest is for everyone, poor and rich alike. On that day, even the poor are to rest like kings. Although Jesus challenged the Pharisees' view of what constitutes work on the Sabbath—for he held that healing the sick and feeding the hungry should be done on the Sabbath as well— he observed the law concerning the Sabbath (see Matthew 5:17–18), setting an example for his disciples (see Luke 23:56). Much to the

---

7. See the discussion of this verse in Gary A. Anderson, *Sin: A History* (New Haven, CT: Yale University Press, 2009).

world's shame, however, in most cultures the poor often have to work on the Sabbath while wealthier people relax and spend time with family and friends.

In the Law, God also commands that fields be seeded and harvested for six years but that on the seventh year the fields must lie fallow. The purpose of this law is so that "the poor of your people may eat" (Exod. 23:11). This seventh-year rule applies to orchards as well, whose fruit on the seventh year belongs to the poor. Thus the Law inscribes the duty to provide for the poor into the very agricultural practices that sustain Israel's life.

The precepts about care for the poor include a concern for the distressing consequences of falling into debt. God, after commanding the people of Israel to care for widows and orphans, further instructs the wealthy, "If you lend money to my people, to the poor among you, you shall not deal with them as a creditor; you shall not exact interest from them" (Exod. 22:25). Lenders must remember the difficult situation of their poor debtors. In this vein, God commands, "If ever you take your neighbor's cloak in pawn, you shall restore it before the sun goes down; for it may be your neighbor's only clothing to use as cover; in what else shall that person sleep?" (Exod. 22:26–27).

In Leviticus 25, God outlines the laws for the jubilee year. In the jubilee year, the people must offer amnesty and the forgiveness of loans. Jubilee laws seek to ensure that God's gift of land to each part of Israel would not be lost. They also remind the people that God's gift of life and the personhood of the poor outweigh the rights of the creditor. God grants to people the right to "redeem" or repurchase any land that they sold because they fell into poverty. Every fifty years, moreover, land returns to its original owner. God insists that the rich must care for the poor: "If any of your kin fall into difficulty and become dependent on you, you shall support them. . . . Do not take interest in advance or otherwise make a profit from them, but fear your God; let them live with you" (Lev. 25:35–36).[8]

Similarly, Moses teaches in Deuteronomy that every seven years, whatever one owes to a creditor is released and no longer needs to be repaid. This law attempts to ensure that creditors will not become rich through the oppression of poor people. In Deuteronomy 15, we find numerous laws aimed at care for the poor. For example, Moses commands, "If there is among you anyone in need, a member of your community in any of your towns within your land that the LORD your God is giving you, do not be hard-hearted or tight-fisted toward your needy neighbor. You should rather open your hand, willingly lending enough to meet the need, whatever it may be" (Deut. 15:7–8).

Moses is aware that wealthy people will face the temptation not to lend when the jubilee year is approaching. In such a case, if the wealthy person refuses to lend, the Lord will count it as a sin. Moses additionally tells the wealthy person, "Give liberally and be ungrudging when you do so, for on this account the Lord your God will bless you in all your work and in all that you undertake" (Deut. 15:10).

Israel's Scriptures do not envision the possibility of eradicating poverty entirely in this earthly life. The Bible teaches that "there will never cease to be some in need on the earth" (Deut. 15:11). Personal charity toward the poor will therefore always remain at the heart of living under God's just law. Deuteronomy especially has in view poor persons who work for the wealthy. Moses commands, "You shall not withhold the wages of poor and needy laborers. . . . You shall pay them their wages daily before sunset, because they are poor and their livelihood depends on them; otherwise they might cry to the Lord against you, and you would incur guilt" (Deut. 24:14–15).

---

8. On Leviticus 25 and the jubilee, see Walter Brueggemann, *Theology of the Old Testament: Testimony, Dispute, Advocacy* (Minneapolis, MN: Fortress Press, 1997), 189.

Deuteronomy also has in view the care of widows and orphans, who easily fall into poverty.

The story of Tobit gives a powerful witness to the role of care for the poor in our lives as God's faithful. As Tobit nears his death, he gives his final words and guidance to his son Tobias. Tobit exhorts his son to give generously to the poor and compares a person's attitude toward the poor to God's attitude toward him. This is key to the Bible's view of the poor. We are all poor before God. We are all indebted to him and can never repay him. When we are generous, our actions toward the poor will mirror God's actions toward us.

Tobit reveals, moreover, that he understands giving to the poor as a sacrifice to God.[9] He tells his son, "Indeed, almsgiving, for all who practice it, is an excellent *offering* in the presence of the Most High" (Tobit 4:11; emphasis added). Along with the offerings in the temple, the faithful may sacrifice to God through their almsgiving and acts of charity. What we offer to the poor, we offer to God.

Failure to Care for the Poor

Israel's Scriptures do not conceal the perennial failure of God's people to care for the poor. Indeed, the Davidic king who is supposed to render justice to the poor often stands as an egregious oppressor of them. Under King Solomon, the wealth of the people began to flow into the state treasury. God warns in Deuteronomy, when Israel seeks to have a king, that such a ruler "must not acquire many horses for himself," neither may he take many wives; also, "silver and gold he must not acquire in great quantity for himself" (Deut. 17:16–17). Unfortunately—but not surprisingly—these things are precisely what Solomon did in his opulent regime powered by forced labor and

---

9. On Tobit 4, see Gary A. Anderson, *Charity: The Place of the Poor in the Biblical Tradition* (New Haven, CT: Yale University Press, 2017), 60–61; see also his extended discussion of the book of Tobit in 71–103.

exorbitant taxation. As we have seen, in the next generation, when representatives of the northern tribes went to complain to Solomon's son King Rehoboam about the heavy taxes, Rehoboam replied to them, "My father made your yoke heavy, but I will add to your yoke; my father disciplined you with whips, but I will discipline you with scorpions" (1 Kings 12:14). The result was the permanent fracturing of the kingdom of Israel into the ten northern tribes called "Israel" and the two southern tribes called "Judah."[10]

The prophets frequently denounced the deplorable record of both kingdoms—Israel and Judah—with regard to caring for the poor. The prophet Amos charges the elite of the northern kingdom with a deplorable selfishness. Despite their relatively thriving economy, they have not cared for the poor. Amos proclaims, "Hear this word, you . . . who oppress the poor, who crush the needy, who say to their husbands, 'Bring something to drink!'" (Amos 4:1). Amos warns that their wickedness toward the poor will result in their destruction. They will not be able to enjoy their ill-gotten gains. He proclaims, "You trample on the poor and take from them levies of grain, you have built houses of hewn stone, but you shall not live in them; you have planted pleasant vineyards, but you shall not drink their wine" (Amos 5:11). According to Amos, the wealthy people of the northern kingdom "lie on beds of ivory" and "eat lambs from the flock" while singing songs and drinking wine without any concern for "the needy in the gate" (Amos 5:12; 6:4–5) or for the moral ruin of God's people. As a result, their divine punishment will be a devastating exile. God will reduce to nothing those who, forgetting that the poor are God's people, dared to buy "the poor for silver, and the needy for a pair of sandals" (Amos 8:6; cf. 2:6).

---

10. For background, see Keith Bodner, *Jeroboam's Royal Drama* (Oxford: Oxford University Press, 2012).

Similarly, the prophet Isaiah communicates God's judgment on the kingdom of Judah for its idolatry, bribery, murder, thievery, oppression of widows and orphans, and other crimes. He imagines a courtroom scene between God and his people: "The Lord enters into judgment with the elders and princes of his people: It is you who have devoured the vineyard; the spoil of the poor is in your houses. What do you mean by crushing my people, by grinding the face of the poor?'" (Isa. 3:14–15). As with the northern kingdom, a fundamental crime of the Davidic kingdom consists in the treatment of the poor by the members of the elite.

Isaiah bemoans the perversion of justice toward the poor, especially in relation to the corruption of the practice of fasting. He chastises the leaders, "Behold, in the day of your fast you seek your own pleasure, and oppress all your workers" (Isa. 58:3). Ritual observances are part of God's covenant with Israel and thus must imitate his character. Isaiah's teaching here is worth quoting at length:

> Is not this the fast that I choose: to loose the bonds of injustice, to undo the thongs of the yoke, to let the oppressed go free, and to break every yoke? Is it not to share your bread with the hungry, and bring the homeless poor into your house; when you see the naked, to cover him, and not to hide yourself from your kin? Then your light break forth like the dawn, and your healing shall spring up quickly; your vindicator shall go before you, the glory of the Lord shall be your rear guard. (Isa. 58:6–8)

With these words, Isaiah shows us what is required for living in right relationship with God. He calls us to feed the hungry, house the homeless, cover the naked, take care of family and community members. When we do so, then we may have the glory of the Lord as our rear guard. Otherwise, Isaiah sternly reminds us that God's glory will not dwell in us if we fall into exploitation and oppression of the poor. The prophet urgently calls Israel to imitate God's justice and goodness. In caring for the poor, we will encounter the glory of the Lord.

The prophet Jeremiah credits King Josiah with doing "justice and righteousness" and rightly judging "the cause of the poor and needy" (Jer. 22:15–16). But Josiah's son King Jehoiakim is quite a different matter. Through Jeremiah, God condemns Jehoiakim. God proclaims, "Woe to him who builds his house by unrighteousness, and his upper rooms by injustice; who makes his neighbors work for nothing, and does not give him his wages" (Jer. 22:13). It is therefore fitting that when the people go into exile in Babylon, the ones who avoid exile are largely "the poorest people of the land" (Jer. 52:16), the agricultural laborers.

Looking forward to the day of God's victory, the prophets foretell a kingdom in which righteousness and justice will thrive. True justice excludes oppression of the poor. Excluding oppression makes way for love of neighbor; excluding the idolization of money makes way for proper love of God. When God's Davidic Servant comes, his coming will be known because "with righteousness he shall judge the poor, and decide with equity for the meek of the earth" (Isa. 11:4). The new kingdom will be one in which the poor and needy will be defended by the Messiah. Jeremiah teaches, "The days are surely coming, says the Lord, when I will raise up for David a righteous Branch, and he shall reign as king and deal wisely, and shall execute justice and righteousness in the land" (Jer. 23:5). Isaiah links possession of the Spirit with care for the poor: "The Spirit of the Lord God is upon me, because the Lord has anointed me to bring good news to the poor" (Isa. 61:1 RSV-CE).

The Old Testament prophets leave us looking forward to the promised kingdom of God and the merciful healing and restoration of the poor. Indeed, Isaiah makes clear that when God comes to redeem his people through his "servant," God will come in solidarity with the poor, as "a man of suffering and acquainted with infirmity" and as one who is "despised" and held "of no account" (Isa. 53:3). God will redeem the poor in a most unexpected way—by taking our poverty upon himself.

Christ and the Care for the Poor in Paul

Paul's preaching of the Gospel includes a great emphasis on care for the poor. As with all of Paul's preaching, he presents Christ as the exemplar we are called to imitate. Paul thus treats riches and poverty through the lens of Jesus Christ. On one occasion when Paul asks a local church to assist the church in Jerusalem, he remarks, "You know the grace of our Lord Jesus Christ, that though he was rich, yet for your sakes he became poor, so that by his poverty might become rich" (2 Cor. 8:9). Christ did not claim his divine prerogatives, but instead came among us as a poor man. He did so in order that we might be united to God and thereby become rich.

The first Christians, imitating Christ's setting aside material riches, were known for their personal care for the poor. In the Acts of the Apostles, we read that the first community of Christians held "all things in common" and sold their possessions so as to distribute them to the poor (Acts 2:44–45).[11] Although Paul's communities retained personal property, the Apostle encourages them to outdo each other in generous giving to the poor (see Eph. 4:28). Thus, Paul tells the Corinthians that he has been amazed and overjoyed by the generosity of the churches in Macedonia. These churches "volun-

---

11. See Joseph A. Fitzmyer, SJ, *The Acts of the Apostles* (New York: Doubleday, 1998), 269, 271–272.

tarily gave according to their means, and even beyond their means, begging us earnestly for the privilege of sharing in this ministry to the saints" (2 Cor. 8:3–4). They did so out of love for Christ and in obedience to Christ. Paul urges the Corinthians to compete with the Macedonians for the title of who is the most generous.

Paul not only asks *that* we share our money but also offers helpful guidelines for *how* Christians might do so. He points out that Christian care for the poor requires giving freely, without grudging the gift. A gift should be proportionate to the extent of the person's wealth. Paul is not asking the Corinthian families to impoverish themselves by giving away all that they have. He does not intend "that there should be relief for others and pressure on you" (2 Cor. 8:13). It is no help if, in order to serve the poor, one makes one's own family destitute. Instead, as Paul tells the Corinthians, "it is a question of a fair balance between your present abundance and their need, so that their abundance may be for your need" (2 Cor. 8:14). Such care for the poor will show that the Corinthians' "love . . . is genuine" (2 Cor. 8:8 RSV-CE).

Stirring the competitive spirit of the Corinthians, Paul writes that he fears that perhaps his boasting in their generosity might prove to be unjustified. He asks the Corinthians to "show them the proof of your love and of our reason for boasting about you" (2 Cor. 8:24). And he claims to be worried that, if their generosity does not exhibit itself, he (and they) will be humiliated before the Macedonians. At bottom, what Paul is doing is encouraging all Christians to strive to outdo each other in love (Rom. 12:10). Love requires helping the poor; helping the poor requires love. It is to be a "voluntary gift" (2 Cor. 9:5) or else it will have no value in God's eyes. We are justified in striving to outdo each other in love for the glory of Christ.

Giving to the poor has a specific name in the community of Israel and of the Church: "almsgiving." Almsgiving, Paul argues, accords with the law of love: "The one who sows sparingly will also reap sparingly, and he who sows bountifully will also reap bountifully" (2 Cor. 9:6). To sow sparingly means to do so not only minimally, but also grudgingly. In fact, people who "love" grudgingly do not love at all. Loving requires a generous spirit. Paul draws upon Proverbs 22:8 to emphasize this point: "Each of you must give as you have made up your mind, not reluctantly or under compulsion, for God loves a cheerful giver" (2 Cor. 9:7). The Apostle can no more compel cheerful giving than he can compel faith and love. But if faith and love are present, then bountiful giving will also be present. Lest those who give away their resources fear that they will have made themselves destitute, Paul says that God will ensure they receive abundant spiritual blessing. Above all, Christ will respond, as Paul tells the Corinthians, by increasing "the harvest of your righteousness" (2 Cor. 9:10). Those who give to the poor will receive everlasting righteousness, and no greater reward is possible. Paul promises that the Corinthians, through their generosity to the poor, "will be enriched in every way" (2 Cor. 9:11).

In caring for those who are suffering poverty, believers "glorify God" (2 Cor. 9:13). Catholics today are called to follow this path of giving God glory. When we give to others out of love for Christ, Christ himself rewards us, and the recipients of the gifts pray for us. In this virtuous circle, we discover how Christ's grace spreads through acts of charity that abound in blessing for others and for ourselves. Indeed, the true source of every act of generous giving to the poor is Christ himself. We can never give more than we have received, for we have received the gift of Christ. For every act of generosity, we can only exclaim with Paul, "Thanks be to God for his indescribable gift!" (2 Cor. 9:15). It is Christ who gives. It is Christ who receives.

Care for the poor begins with those in need within our family. Paul writes to Timothy, "And whoever does not provide for relatives, and especially for family members, has denied the faith and is worse than an unbeliever" (1 Tim. 5:8). This teaching occurs in Paul's exhortation to care for widows—namely, to "honor widows who are really widows" (1 Tim. 5:3). Rather than burdening the church community with supporting widows who have children or grandchildren, Timothy must insist that the children or grandchildren support their aging relatives. The aged who have no family ought to be supported by the community. How pertinent is this teaching in today's society, when so many senior citizens find themselves suffering from loneliness.

According to Paul, our trust in material possessions often rivals our trust in God. In 1 Timothy 6:10, we discover the profound teaching that "the love of money is the root of all kinds of evils." Might we pause for a moment to let this truth sink in? Think of love of money as the desire to find absolute security in this life or to have as much as or more than those we envy or admire. Paul warns the early Christians about the danger that riches can become in their lives: "Those who want to be rich fall into temptation and are trapped by many senseless and harmful desires that plunge people into ruin and destruction" (1 Tim. 6:9). The Apostle's concern is not with being rich or poor but with the "desire" for riches. Our hearts have the uncanny ability to love money and the security it promises with all our heart, mind, and strength. Only God is worthy of such love. Paul thus reminds us that we never truly possess our possessions, "for we brought nothing into the world, so that we can take nothing out of it; but if we have food and clothing, we will be content with these"

(1 Tim. 6:6–7). And he urges us to seek "godliness," not material "gain" (1 Tim. 6:5–6). Generosity with our possessions is a concrete manner of saying "no" to the love of money and "yes" to the love of God.

Jesus' Preaching and Poverty

For Jesus, it is not a matter of *whether* his followers will give gifts to the poor, but of *how* they will do so. In his Sermon on the Mount, Jesus urges us that we should care for the poor out of love for God and neighbor rather than as yet another way of seeking human recognition. Moreover, he makes clear in his parables that we will be judged by whether we have cared for the poor.

In Matthew 25, Jesus depicts the final judgment, identifying himself with the poor and outcast. He proclaims that he will welcome to eternal life those who loved him in their earthly lives by loving the poor and the outcast. Jesus depicts himself saying, "Come, you that are blessed by my Father, inherit the kingdom prepared for you from the foundation of the world; for I was hungry and you gave me food, I was thirsty and you gave me something to drink, I was a stranger and you welcomed me, I was naked and you gave me clothing, I was sick and you took care of me, I was in prison and you visited me" (Matt. 25:34–36). The blessed will profess not to remember when they did this to Jesus, but Jesus will tell them, "As you did it to one of the least of these who are members of my family, *you did it to me*" (Matt. 25:40; emphasis added).

Jesus thus perfects in himself the Old Testament attitude toward the poor. Gifts and service to the poor are now sacrifices and offerings to the incarnate God himself present in them.

The presence of Christ among the poor does not mean that care for the poor should replace the worship of God or that all the Church's resources should be given to the poor. The great example of this lesson comes by way of Judas Iscariot's darkened view. Judas was the leader of the disciples who complained when, a couple days prior to Passover, a woman anointed Jesus with a jar of expensive ointment. Judas and the other disciples complain aloud, "Why this waste? For this ointment might have been sold for a large sum, and the money given to the poor" (Matt. 26:8–9; cf. John 12:6). But Jesus, hearing their words, responds by observing that the anointing the woman has given him is an act that glorifies God. We rightly may devote ourselves in love to Jesus in various ways so long as we truly have love for him and his people.

Jesus' parables in the Gospel of Luke are similarly instructive. The father in the parable of the prodigal son shows us how we must behave to the poor: he kills the fatted calf for a feast for his younger son despite the son's being utterly undeserving, having done nothing but waste his resources (Luke 15:23). In the parable of the dishonest steward, the steward who will soon be fired by the landowner extends mercy toward all the landowner's debtors—from which Jesus draws the lesson that we must hurry to "make friends . . . by means of dishonest wealth" (Luke 16:9).[12] The point is that all the earth's resources belong to God, and in order to ensure ourselves a future after our death, we must give these resources to those who come to us in need. We must not serve material wealth (Luke 16:13); rather, we must use material wealth to serve God by serving the poor.

With the powerful story about the rich man and Lazarus, Jesus teaches us about the use of possessions (Luke 16:19–31). In this parable, the rich man does nothing for the poor man Lazarus, who begs food at the rich man's gate and has his sores licked by the rich man's dogs. The rich man dies and goes to everlasting punishment while

---

12. See Anthony Giambrone, OP, *Sacramental Charity, Creditor Christology, and the Economy of Salvation in Luke's Gospel* (Tübingen: Mohr Siebeck, 2017), 242–265.

Lazarus dies and goes to everlasting peace in Abraham's family.[13] When the rich man asks whether someone will warn his brothers not to follow the same path, Abraham replies that one who does not listen to Moses and the prophets would not listen even to someone risen from the dead. Moses and the prophets repeatedly spoke about giving to the poor. Those who will not listen to Moses and the prophets about the care for the poor will not listen to Jesus risen from the dead. Conversely, those who listen to the risen Jesus as the fulfillment of the Law and the prophets may see in him an even greater impetus to care for the poor.

In Luke, Jesus tells a parable about a gift of ten pounds, or sums of money, given to each of a landowner's ten servants (Luke 19:12–27). The Gospel of Matthew has a version of the same parable but described in terms of different amounts of talents, the largest unit of currency (Matt. 25:14–30).[14] In both parables, each servant receives a certain amount of resources to invest. Likewise, in both parables, the landowner praises the servants who invest what they have received and make more, but condemns the servant who hides the resources. The moral of the parable is that God wants us to use the resources he gives us. When we see our resources as gifts from God and so share them with the poor, we spread the generosity of God.

Mary's words in Luke reflect a deep concern for the poor. After she has said yes to God and conceived Jesus in her womb, she goes to visit her older cousin Elizabeth who is pregnant with John the Baptist. Upon their meeting, Elizabeth calls Mary "the mother of my Lord," the mother of the future king and Messiah. Mary responds by offering a song of thanksgiving, known as the Magnificat, for the gift

---

13. For background, see Matthew Ryan Hauge, *The Biblical Tour of Hell* (London: Bloomsbury, 2013).

14. See Nathan Eubank, *Wages of Cross-Bearing and Debt of Sin: The Economy of Heaven in Matthew's Gospel* (Berlin: De Gruyter, 2013), 100–102.

of her son Jesus Christ. Right at the heart of Mary's song of praise is
God's justice for the poor. She proclaims that God has lifted up the
lowly" and "has filled the hungry with good things, and sent the rich
away empty" (Luke 1:52–53).

Such reversal of earthly fortunes finds a parallel in Jesus' story
that we considered above about the rich man and the poor man,
Lazarus. Although the rich enjoy good things in the present life,
life in Christ involves a quite different ordering—namely, one based
upon faith and love. In Luke, Jesus offers both blessings and woes
based upon our poverty and wealth: "Blessed are you who are poor,
for yours is the kingdom of God. Blessed are you who are hungry
now, for you will be filled" (Luke 6:20–21). And he also says, "But
woe to you who are rich, for you have received your consolation. Woe
to you that are full now, for you will be hungry" (Luke 6:24–25). We
cannot receive the kingdom of God unless we recognize our poverty
before God.

Matthew, Mark, and Luke all tell of Jesus' encounter with the
rich young man, in which Jesus again overturns popular notions
of wealth and poverty by depicting wealth as a possible obstacle to
union with God. The man approaches Jesus and asks how he might
inherit eternal life. This is a clear instance of Jesus explaining how
we ourselves might attain salvation. He praises the rich young man
for following the commandments of the Decalogue, especially those
related to the love of neighbor. But Jesus presses further: "There is
still one thing lacking. Sell all that you own and distribute the money
to the poor, and you will have treasure in heaven; then come, follow
me" (Luke 18:22).

The rich young man turns away in sadness, unwilling to obey
this summons. Likewise, the crowd assembled around Jesus is
shocked at the extent of Jesus' demands, not least because wealth was

associated with Torah study and the corresponding ability to keep the commandments of God. Jesus, however, draws a lesson from the rich young man's unwillingness: "How hard it is for those who have wealth to enter the kingdom of God! Indeed, it is easier for a camel to go through the eye of a needle than for someone who is rich to enter the kingdom of God" (Luke 18:25).

Even if we allow for hyperbole, the crowd around Jesus is right to cry out in reply, "Then who can be saved?" (Luke 18:26). But Jesus answers, "What is impossible for mortals is possible for God" (Luke 18:27).[15]

Jesus did not expect all his followers to give away their entire possessions. This is evident in multiple ways. In his Sermon on the Mount, he presumes that all of the faithful will make almsgiving an ongoing part of their lives: "*When* you give alms" (Matt. 6:3; emphasis added). But if one has given away everything, one can no longer give regular gifts to the poor. Furthermore, wealthy women funded the ministry of Jesus and his disciples (see Luke 8:3), and they could not have done this had they been destitute after giving away all their possessions. Paul, too, knows that a prudent concern for "worldly affairs" is necessary, especially for those who have responsibility for the raising of children (1 Cor. 7:33).

As noted above, although Paul makes clear that the Corinthians who are wealthy do not need to give away all their possessions, he does aim at a certain "balance," so that Christians who have an "abundance" may supply the needs of fellow Christians who are lacking in material goods (2 Cor. 8:14). As a practical matter, Paul's call for generosity must have worked, since in Romans he reports that he is traveling to Jerusalem bearing material aid. He explains, "Macedonia and Achaia have been pleased to share their resources

---

15. See Joseph A. Fitzmyer, SJ, *The Gospel According to Luke X–XXIV: A New Translation with Introduction and Commentary* (Garden City, NY: Doubleday, 1985), 1205.

with the poor among the saints at Jerusalem. They were pleased to do this" (Rom. 15:26–27).[16]

Thus, although all are called to care for the poor, all are not called to do so in the same way. Jesus calls his followers to follow him in different ways. The call of the rich young man is a powerful call to radical discipleship: sell what you have, give to the poor, and follow Jesus. Yet it is important to notice that Jesus begins with obedience to the commandments. Keeping the commandments is a first stage to which all are called as disciples; giving up all one's possessions is a higher path of discipleship, one that was given to that particular young man. Regardless, all paths have the same goal—to respond affirmatively to Jesus' invitation: "Come, follow me."

When Jesus sat watching people give money to the temple treasury, he noticed "many rich people" giving "large sums" (Mark 12:41). This is good, but even better, he tells his disciples, is what a poor widow did. She could give only a penny, and yet she gave more than anyone: "For all of them have contributed out of their abundance; but she out of her poverty has put in everything she had, all she had to live on" (Mark 12:44).

Luke, in the very next chapter after the story of the rich man who was asked to give up all of his possessions and went away sad, tells the story of a rich tax collector named Zacchaeus. As we discussed briefly above, Zacchaeus also had a strong desire to meet Jesus. The story includes the detail that he was rather short, so he chose to climb a sycamore tree so that he could see Jesus through the crowds when he passed by. Jesus calls out to Zacchaeus and says, "Hurry and come down; for I must stay at your house today" (Luke 19:5).

Zacchaeus knows that he is a sinner and unworthy to have Jesus in his house. When Jesus calls him, he immediately repents and

---

16. See David J. Downs, *The Offering of the Gentiles: Paul's Collection for Jerusalem in Its Chronological, Cultural, and Cultic Contexts* (Grand Rapids, MI: Eerdmans, 2016).

exclaims, "Look, half of my possessions, Lord, I will give to the poor; and if I have defrauded anyone of anything, I will pay back four times as much." Jesus responds to Zacchaeus, "Today salvation has come to this house" (Luke 19:8). Salvation has come to Zacchaeus's home because he has repented and showed proper generosity to the poor and justice to those he had wronged.

Whereas Jesus had asked the man in the earlier story to give up all of his possessions, Zacchaeus gave up only a significant portion of his abundant wealth. The reader might ask why Jesus did not give this same option to the rich young man! We receive no explanation from the Gospel story but may trust in Jesus' wisdom. In reading of his encounter with Zacchaeus, we discover the reality that God calls each of us personally. There are different vocations in terms of how one should give away material possessions and practice care for the poor.

Regardless of our particular vocation, the Bible cautions us about the dangers of attachment to money. Because of our fears, insecurities, and disordered desires, we are prone to trust more in money than in God. The Bible invites us to turn from the illusory security offered by money. Whether we are rich or poor, whether we embrace voluntary poverty or own many possessions, our time in this world is short. God alone provides true and lasting contentment. Jesus, in the Sermon on the Mount, teaches us not to be anxious about or focused on material things. Jesus thus calls us to "strive first for the kingdom of God and his righteousness" and to trust that we will receive all else we need (Matt. 6:33). In this life, we may well not receive all we need to sustain earthly life, but we will receive everything in the life to come. He draws our attention away from fears about the future and encourages us to focus on the present moment:

"Do not worry about tomorrow. . . . Today's trouble is enough for today" (Matt. 6:34).

Jesus continually draws our attention to the ultimate reality of our lives before God. So much of the Sermon on the Mount invites us to see this world from the perspective of the world to come. Jesus teaches, "Do not store up for yourselves treasures on earth, where moth and rust consume and where thieves break in and steal; but store up for yourselves treasures in heaven, where neither moth nor rust consumes and where thieves do not break in and steal. For where your treasure is, there your heart will be also" (Matt. 6:19–21). We find peace when we find our treasure in the Good News of Jesus Christ and set our hearts on him.

In our fallen condition, we often would do anything in order to gain control over our uncertain futures, especially to avoid being poor or dependent on others. Poverty, including the radical existential poverty of death, often appears as the worst thing that can happen to us. We admire those who are wealthy and healthy, and we fear losing our material blessings. God's poor do not have this security to fall back upon. As such, the poor may well be more open to God's call.

Can it really be that if we seek to do God's will, rather than seeking earthly security, we will be blessed? We have seen all too often the tragedies that befall poor persons. They endure sufferings that damage their lives and welfare. We might wish to do everything in our power to avoid ending up in such poverty, and it is necessary to assist the poor and to serve their good. Yet all people are existentially poor; each human being must die. The path to life in Christ runs through care for the poor, not least because in caring for the poor we discover our own existential poverty and our utter dependence upon God's continual giving us all that we have.

God commands tithing, or giving to God and to the poor ten percent of our income, to remind us that we receive everything from him and so ought to give everything back to him. For example, he instructs Moses, "All tithes from the land, whether the seed from the ground or the fruit from the tree, are the Lord's; they are holy to the LORD. . . . And tithes of herd and flock, every tenth one that passes under the shepherd's staff, shall be holy to the LORD" (Lev. 27:30, 32).

Granted, if we "tithe mint and rue and every herb of all kinds, and neglect justice and the love of God" (Luke 11:42)—as Jesus says that some Pharisees have done—then our tithing is for naught, since we have missed the point. When the giving of such gifts is not rooted in faith and love, it is ultimately merely another act of pride. As Paul puts it, "If I give away all my possessions, and if I hand over my body so that I may boast, but do not have love, I gain nothing" (1 Cor. 13:3). Giving ten percent of our income to support the poor and the worship of God in the Church, however, remains a concrete way of expressing justice and mercy.

When we come to know ourselves in Christ, we discover that we, too, are God's poor. God, in creating us in his image, gave us "dominion" (as stewardship or leadership) over the whole earth (Genesis 1:28). To share in God's royal rule, by exercising leadership, thus ultimately means to love the earth, and particularly our fellow human beings, as God loves. And to reign with Jesus in love, we must care for the poor, recognizing that we too are poor by acknowledging our dependence upon the divine Giver. As we discover this biblical truth, it fuels our love for the whole Body of Christ.

Giving to others and to the poor is more than a mere human exchange. The Bible shows us that our gifts to others are extensions of God's gifts to us. Let us look carefully at Jesus' words to his followers concerning gifts to the poor: "When you give alms, do not let your left hand know what your right hand is doing, so that your alms may be done in secret; and your Father who sees in secret will reward you" (Matt. 6:3).

The New Testament word for gifts to the poor is often translated as "alms" and the practice of giving gifts as "almsgiving." Although those terms may sound odd to many of us, they have powerful meanings. The word for "giving alms" stems from the Greek *eleos*, which in the Septuagint (the ancient Greek translation of the Old Testament) is used to translate the Hebrew word *hesed*. In English, both *eleos* and *hesed* may also be translated as "mercy" or "merciful love." As an example, Psalm 13 in the Septuagint reads, "I have trusted in your merciful love [*eleos*]" (Ps. 13:5).[17] Likewise, the Septuagint version of Psalm 51, which recounts David's repentance after his sins of adultery and murder, begins, "Have mercy [*eleos*] on me, O God, according to your merciful love [*eleos*]" (Ps. 51:1). God has mercy on the sinner because God is merciful. So to give alms is to enact not merely our own mercy but to let God's mercy be communicated through us.[18]

The faithful people of God are called to imitate God's mercy both in their being and in their doing. Mercy plays the central role in Jesus' story of the Good Samaritan who took care of a man beaten by robbers and left for dead. When Jesus asks at the end of the parable, "Which of these three, do you think, was a neighbor to the man who fell into the hands of the robbers," the man replied, "The one who showed him mercy [*eleos*]" (Luke 10:36–37). Mercy seeks to comfort the afflicted and to restore what has been lost to the suffering.

---

17. The Psalms were written in Hebrew and later translated in Greek. The Greek version of the Old Testament is referred to as the Septuagint, which was used by the authors of the New Testament.

18. See Daniel Moloney, *Mercy: What Every Catholic Should Know* (San Francisco: Ignatius Press, 2020).

Sometimes people object to this promise of reward since it suggests that Jesus is encouraging his faithful to perform works of mercy only for some reward in heaven. But Jesus' words here in Matthew affirm that when we enact mercy, our works of mercy flow from God's mercy. The Father is the source of all mercy since he is the one who is "rich in mercy [*eleos*]" (Eph. 2:4). If we reflect upon this, we will understand that the reward Jesus speaks of is not an extrinsic reward such as money but the reward of friendship with God, of a covenantal and personal relationship with God our Father. That is why Jesus teaches us not to give money to the poor for the sake of earthly attention and honors. When we give money "in secret"—that is, in the sight of our Father—God rewards us with himself.

Jesus' teaching about care for the poor is helpfully understood within this theological orientation. It is not mere social work. It is about living in the covenant family of God. Jesus teaches in Luke, "Love your enemies, do good, and lend, expecting nothing in return. Your reward will be great, and you will be children of the Most High" (Luke 6:35). Acts of mercy are the pathway to becoming children of God. Jesus summarizes this teaching, "Be merciful, just as your Father is merciful" (Luke 6:36).

Conclusion

Poverty plays a central role in the Gospel. Since Jesus Christ became poor for our sake and died in utter poverty, to glorify Jesus is to care for God's poor, and vice versa. Giving to the poor is a path to love Jesus Christ and to enact his mercy in our lives.

Should the pope therefore sell all the treasures in the Vatican to feed the poor? We answer no, since these treasures show in a powerful way how much Christians have loved Jesus and since they bear witness to love. Even so, the Gospel calls us all to examine ourselves and see how we might be more generous with those in need.

We must heed the words of the Letter to the Hebrews: "Keep your life free from the love of money" (Heb. 13:5). This does not mean supporting a particular political agenda regarding the best economic path for alleviating poverty, though we should seek sincerely to practice and support sound economic policies for the sake of the poor. Instead, it means that Catholics are called to give personally to the poor and to care personally for them in the many ways that this may be done in each person's unique situation.

Mercy must be practiced in all of its dimensions, both material and spiritual. The greatest gift to the rich and poor alike is the Gospel of Jesus Christ since we are all poor in the sight of God. James emphasizes that faith in God and works of love go hand in hand. The gift of the Gospel ought not be given by itself, "if a brother or sister is naked and lacks daily food" (James 2:15). In proclaiming the Gospel, we must also seek to clothe and feed this brother or sister.

The Church's first ministry is that of preaching salvation through the death and Resurrection of Jesus Christ. Catholics are called to help the poor person to find himself or herself exalted in Christ and to help the wealthy person discover "being brought low, because the rich will disappear like a flower in the field" (James 1:10). The latter discovery—that we are all existentially poor—helps to awaken us to the love of Jesus Christ. God wishes to make all of us, both the poor and the rich, into sharers in the riches of his own life. The path to such sharing is to care selflessly for God's poor, just as Jesus has cared selflessly for us. Let it be said of us: "There was not a needy person among them" (Acts 4:34).

CHAPTER 8

Why Is the Church So Strict about Sex?

"Glorify God in your body"
(1 Corinthians 6:20)

It is no secret that a number of Catholics today consider the Church's teachings on sexuality to be outdated. Sociological studies show that one reason why people leave the Church has to do with current cultural norms regarding sexuality. In *Young Catholic America*, Christian Smith and his co-authors find "little evidence of genuine anger at the Catholic Church as an institution," but they frequently encounter young people who consider the Church's positions on premarital sex and homosexuality "to be 'narrow-minded' and even 'just ridiculous.'"[1] Likewise, in *American Catholics Today*, William D'Antonio and his co-authors interview a young Catholic woman named "Kate" who supports abortion, homosexual acts, and premarital sex. Kate observes, "The sex-outside-of-marriage issue is one that challenges a lot of young people in this country, and it's one that is forming a wedge between young people and the Church."[2]

In *Blessed Are the Bored in Spirit: A Young Catholic's Search for Meaning*, Mark Hart observes, "The numbers don't lie. A majority of Catholics disagree with fundamental, doctrinal teachings of the Church. Many cite the Church's 'refusal to change' as primary

---

1. Christian Smith, Kyle Longest, Jonathan Hill, and Kari Christoffersen, *Young Catholic America: Emerging Adults In, Out of, and Gone from the Church* (Oxford: Oxford University Press, 2014), 112.

2. William V. D'Antonio, James D. Davidson, Dean R. Hoge, and Mary L. Gautier, *American Catholics Today: New Realities of Their Faith and Their Church* (Lanham, MD: Rowman & Littlefield, 2007), 102.

reason for their disagreement."[3] The "refusal to change" that these Catholics have in mind definitely includes the Church's vision of sexuality and marriage.

Why do some sexual relationships pose an obstacle to authentic communion with each other and with God, whereas other sexual relationships foster genuine communion? In response, St. John Paul II, in writing his "theology of the body," realized that it is necessary to explore the meaning and purpose of body-soul human communion. Contemporary culture generally assumes that any sexual activity is fine as long as it has the consent of the individuals involved. The idea that consensual sex may be wrong is often not even seriously considered. What is often forgotten is that not all forms of sexual expression are actually good for human persons, families, and communities.

In seeking "God's original plan for the beauty of human love,"[4] we will find that sexuality and marriage are integral parts of the New Covenant established by Jesus Christ. Both sex and marriage are good and are to be valued and praised by Catholics. As a sacrament that causes grace, marriage is deeply honored by the Catholic Church. Sexual intercourse, too, has great honor since it allows the married couple uniquely to become "one flesh" and to "be fruitful and multiply" (Gen. 2:24, 1:28), in a relationship of profoundly intimate and life-giving love. For that reason, on the Catholic understanding, sex is properly called "the marital act" since it is part of the larger story of two persons becoming one. Paul, in opposition to some early Christians who wrongly denigrated sex, insists that husbands and wives ought to have sexual relations with one another (1 Cor. 7:3). He goes so far as to describe the union of man and

---

3. Mark Hart, *Blessed Are the Bored in Spirit: A Young Catholic's Search for Meaning* (Cincinnati, OH: Servant Books, 2006), 2. Hart goes on to observe, "The pews are emptying because the reality of sin has taken on an almost fairy-tale-like existence in our world today. The pews are emptying because where there is no sin, there is no need of a savior" (2).

4. Jason Evert, *Theology of the Body in One Hour* (Scottsdale, AZ: Totus Tuus Press, 2017), xv.

woman as a sign of the union of Christ and the Church (Eph. 5:32). Sexual intercourse within marriage is, or should be, an expression of mutual love, sealed by mutual enjoyment and pleasurable delight in the wonder of the other person.

In fact, nothing could be more positive than the Bible's understanding of sexuality—once we learn how to distinguish between sexuality in God's original creation, its present disordered state, and its call to renewal in Christ. For as Heather King says, "[Sexual] purity is the conviction that we are all pearls of great price: not to be violated, tampered with, used loosely, or given away for less than we are worth or to someone who's incapable of understanding our value. Christianity is all invitation and all gift."[5]

"Be Fruitful and Multiply"

In order to appreciate the realities of marriage and sexuality, let us begin with the beginning. Stories about creation pull back the veil of our present disordered human history and consider our original purpose as created by God. Genesis unfolds the mystery of man and woman as central to the creation of human beings: "God created humankind in his image, in the image of God he created them; male and female he created them" (Gen. 1:27). Man and woman are both made in the image of God. They were created not only to love God and to govern the creation but also to love one another and to enjoy marital intimacy. In fact, this marital intimacy becomes a manner in which man and woman love God and govern creation. Genesis continues, "God blessed them, and God said to them, 'Be fruitful and multiply, and fill the earth and subdue it" (Gen. 1:28). Since God is the author of life, the author of creation, he blesses the man and the woman so that they may share in his creative love. His intention is

---

5. Heather King, *Stumble: Virtue, Vice, and the Space Between* (Cincinnati, OH: Franciscan Media, 2015), 29.

that their sexual expression of love would be the means of generating new life. As God's love is creative, human love is to be pro-creative.

The call to be fruitful and multiply is not a concession to disordered lust; rather, it is in accordance with a natural desire of man and woman for one another, a desire without which the human race would have long since ended. After repeating that "God saw that it was good" at the end of each phase of creation, Genesis affirms at the creation of man and woman that God saw that "it was *very* good" (Gen. 1:31; emphasis added). Subsequently, the second chapter of Genesis describes how the Lord said, "It is not good that the man should be alone; I will make him a helper as his partner" (Gen. 2:18). When the man sees the woman, he cries out, "This at last is bone of my bones and flesh of my flesh" (Gen. 2:23). Genesis concludes that the man and woman are created for each other in marriage: "Therefore a man leaves his father and his mother and clings to his wife, and they become one flesh" (Gen. 2:24).

Thus the first two chapters of Genesis robustly announce to a fallen world the goodness of marriage and human sexuality. In case the reader was not paying attention to this goodness, the last verse of Genesis 2 reads, "The man and his wife were both naked, and were not ashamed" (Gen. 2:25). This lack of shame reveals that marriage and sexuality are part of the original harmony of creation. Within God's original plan for creation—in which human nature, unstained by sin, is free from the temptation to reduce another human being to an object for self-gratification—human sexuality is beautiful.

Furthermore, the Bible shows that the goodness of marriage persists after the fall, even though human beings, corrupted by sin, often misuse the gifts of marriage and sexuality. The story of Tobias and Sarah helps us see how marriage remains good and holy even when restored in God's covenant. Although the piety with which Tobias

and Sarah approach marriage and sex may feel alien to our sensibil-
ities, the story tells of the greatness of God's gift. When Tobias and
Sarah marry, they place their relationship under God and restore
sexuality to his original plan.

On their wedding night, Tobias and Sarah pray together next
to the marriage bed. This beautiful wedding prayer has three parts:
blessing God; remembering creation as it came forth from God; and
ordering their desires to God. First, they bless God: "Blessed are you,
O God of our ancestors, and blessed is your name in all generations
forever. Let the heavens and the whole creation bless you forever"
(Tobit 8:5). When Tobias and Sarah pray this prayer of blessing, they
are beginning to establish themselves in the proper role of creatures
called to give glory to God.

Second, the prayer of Tobias and Sarah calls to mind God's original plan. Their prayer is thus a prayer of remembrance: "You made
Adam, and for him you made his wife Eve as a helper and support.
From the two of them the human race has sprung. You said, 'It is
not good that the man should be alone; let us make a helper for him
like himself'" (Tobit 8:6). Although they live far from Jerusalem in a
foreign land, Tobias and Sarah do not look around at their culture to
learn about marriage. Instead they call to mind God's plan for marriage, the one he revealed in the story of creation of Adam and Eve,
an original union God described as "very good."

Third, Tobias and Sarah enter into God's plan. They order their
sexual desires within the lifelong covenant of marriage: "And now, O
Lord, I am taking this kinswoman of mine, not because of lust, but
with sincerity. Grant that she and I may find mercy and that we may
grow old together" (Tobit 8:7). The Bible shows an honest realism
in acknowledging that sexual relations often simply flow from lust,
without sincerity, without a desire to grow old together. Our feelings

of sexual attraction are quite vulnerable to disorder and are not a trustworthy guide for human action. The commitment to lifelong union, however, takes up this sexual desire into a harmonious relation. In marriage, husband and wife give themselves to each other in a unique way through sexual intimacy. Sexual intimacy within marriage is shown to be a blessing from God.

Calling Out Harmful Sexual Practices

But why do we need revelation to tell us about the goodness of marital sexuality? Unfortunately, in many ways, we all know the answer. The history of human sexuality is not a pretty one. The disordered character of human lusts jumps off the page in much of the Old Testament. The Bible is not condoning such disordered actions but diagnosing the human condition, which is in need of healing and redemption. Following with tragic haste upon the beauty of the "one flesh" marital union described in Genesis 1, Genesis 3 highlights the disruption of human sexuality in light of the fall of the human race.

We hear the punishment that God pronounces upon the first woman—not so much ordaining a forthcoming punishment as observing the intrinsic consequences of her sin, by which love becomes distorted through power: "Your desire shall be for your husband, and he shall rule over you" (Gen. 3:16).[6] What a sordid history of abuse, perversion, and lust are summarized in that one sentence! Human desires no longer reflect the intrinsic beauty and worth of the other person. The God-given desire to protect the other quickly shifts into a perverted desire to rule over the other. Already in Genesis 4, one of the offspring of Cain (Lamech) is depicted as the first to take more than one wife and also to boast of his exaggerated vengefulness: "I have killed a man for wounding me, a young man

---

6. See Walter Brueggemann, *Genesis* (Louisville, KY: Westminster John Knox, 2010), 51.

for striking me" (Gen. 4:23). Genesis thus presents polygamy and violence as entering our history side by side.

The Bible does not shy away from presenting the ugly side of our disordered sexual desires and lust for power over others. In the laws of Leviticus, we witnessed Israel's call to be holy as the Lord is holy. As part of that call to holiness, Leviticus places restraints on our fallen desires, especially as they relate to disordered sexual activities and sexual exploitation. Incestuous sexual practices were present in ancient cultures as they are around the world today. The biblical laws against sexual incest among families particularly protect the more vulnerable members of families. They also display a frank realism in recognizing and naming the reality of sexual abuse within families and communities. The restraint of sexual license does not bind Israel but rather frees it. Through it, the Law calls Israel back to those ordered sexual relationships that characterize the goodness of the created order.

Leviticus repeatedly and frequently condemns sexual incest and sexual abuse. The idiom it uses to describe the sexual act is "uncovering the nakedness" of another person. Knowing that men may well abuse the women and girls within their own families, Leviticus teaches, "You shall not uncover the nakedness of your sister, your father's daughter or your mother's daughter, whether born at home or born abroad" (Lev. 18:9; cf. 18:16). Again, Leviticus calls out disordered and abusive sexual relationships: "You shall not uncover the nakedness of a woman and her daughter, and you shall not take her son's daughter or her daughter's daughter to uncover her nakedness" (Lev. 18:17). With those words, Leviticus condemns those who exploit their power to prey upon women, especially upon girls and young women. How much sexual abuse, prostitution, and pornography is condemned in this one chapter of Leviticus!

Leviticus continues to disclose further disordered sexual relationships. "You shall not have sexual relations with your kinsman's wife" (Lev. 18:20). "You shall not lie with a male as with a woman" (Lev. 18:22). In this way, the book affirms a truth that Paul will emphasize in Romans: adulterous and homosexual sexual activities are not in accord with human flourishing. These can be difficult teachings for some contemporary Christians to accept. They might ask, why should people be bound to a marriage if they are no longer in love? Why not develop a relationship with someone new? With respect to homosexual activities, should not people be free to follow their deep-seated inclinations?

The biblical understanding of sex and marriage was no less countercultural in ancient times than it is today. Adulterous and homosexual practices were common in the ancient world, both by way of cultic prostitution and in other forms of life. But Sacred Scripture teaches that such acts are not in accord with the truth of our nature as originally created by God.[7]

At its core, human sexuality has a created ordering toward family that is affirmed throughout the Bible. Sadly, however, in our culture, the pursuit of sexual freedom is often valued above the needs of children. When we misuse our sexuality, it often results in unstable relationships and emotional trauma. As a result of such trauma and instability, children end up being raised without the full support of their mothers and fathers.[8]

---

7. For an unpersuasive but representative denial of the coherence of biblical sexual teaching, see John J. Collins, *What Are Biblical Values? What the Bible Says on Key Ethical Issues* (New Haven, CT: Yale University Press, 2019), chapter 4. For a better approach, see Robert A. J. Gagnon, *The Bible and Homosexual Practice: Texts and Hermeneutics* (Nashville, TN: Abingdon, 2002); and Wesley Hill, *Washed and Waiting: Reflections on Christian Faithfulness and Homosexuality*, 2nd ed. (Grand Rapids, MI: Zondervan, 2016).

8. See Matthew Levering, *Engaging the Doctrine of Marriage: Human Marriage as the Image and Sacrament of the Marriage of God and Creation* (Eugene, OR: Cascade, 2020).

Sex, Marriage, and Holiness in the New Covenant

The New Testament writings place sexuality squarely within the reality of the New Covenant. Paul writes to the early Christians in Thessalonica and addresses the matter of sexuality with a directness and forcefulness that may well surprise us:

> For this is the will of God, your sanctification: that you abstain from sexual immorality [*porneia*]; that each one of you know how to control your own body in holiness and honor, not with lustful passion, like the Gentiles who do not know God; that no one wrong or exploit a brother or sister in this matter, because the Lord is an avenger in all these things, just as we have told you beforehand and solemnly warned you. For God has not called us to impurity but in holiness. Therefore whoever rejects this rejects not human authority but God, who also gives his Holy Spirit to you. (1 Thess. 4:3–8; translation slightly altered)

This passage requires some unpacking in order for us to receive its full teaching. Language about the Lord being a judge or an "avenger" might well sound as though Paul is just using scare tactics. Not so. The starting point is God's will for us—namely, our sanctification. Everything that comes afterward follows from this initial call to holiness. Do we really believe that God wills our holiness? an intimate relationship with him? a renewal of our daily lives and practices? The call to holiness forms the context of any particular teaching about human sexuality. Paul thus exhorts us to control our bodies "in holiness and honor." God cares about what we do with our bodies and how we use them to relate to others.

Secondly, the Greek word translated above as "sexual immorality" is *porneia*, which is the root of our word "pornography." Sexual immorality does not merely harm our relationship with ourselves and with our neighbor; it disregards God and the purposes of created human nature. It is in this sense that Paul says that "the Lord is an avenger in all these things." When we turn away from God's good, orderly direction, we find ourselves out of touch with reality. Disordered actions have disordered consequences, but such consequences are not the end of the story. When Christians turn from disordered lusts and live sexuality in "holiness and honor," they share in the sanctification that God wills for them.

Paul wants us to live this witness to the reality of God's new creation in our communal life as the Church. The sexual immorality that he spoke about in 1 Thessalonians was also a reality in the young Christian community of Corinth. Paul addresses the matter directly: "It is actually reported that there is sexual immorality [*porneia*] among you, and of a kind that is not found even among pagans; for a man is living with his father's wife" (1 Cor. 5:1).[9] The Apostle instructs the community to deal with this situation, going so far as to quote Deuteronomy's command to "drive out the wicked person from among you" (1 Cor. 5:13; Deut. 17:7). How might we properly understand Paul's teachings here?

When we look to the beginning of Paul's First Letter to the Corinthians, we see the same call to holiness that forms the center of the Gospel. Paul writes "to the church of God that is in Corinth, to those who are sanctified in Christ Jesus, called to be saints" (1 Cor. 1:2). Despite that, Paul knows full well the sinful activities among the Christians in Corinth, and he reminds them of their calling: they have been sanctified and called to be saints. Paul preaches "Christ crucified" to the Corinthians, "Christ the power of God and the wisdom of God" (1 Cor. 1:23–24).

---

9. See Frank J. Matera, *New Testament Ethics: The Legacies of Jesus and Paul* (Louisville, KY: Westminster John Knox, 1996), 144–147.

God's initiative in the gift of salvation is crucial to understanding the call to sexual purity. Paul explains that God "is the source of your life in Christ Jesus, who became for us wisdom from God, and righteousness and sanctification and redemption" (1 Cor. 1:30). Whatever holiness Christians possess is a gift from God, and not some generic gift, but the gift realized in and through Jesus Christ. Paul thus summarizes his preaching: "I decided to know nothing among you except Jesus Christ, and him crucified" (1 Cor. 2:2). The gift of Christ is something we receive by believing that he died for our sins and rose again unto eternal life, by entering into his death and Resurrection through Baptism. Our life is a looking forward to the full realization of the gift of God in eternal life in Christ.

With this in mind, we can understand Paul's directive to "drive out the wicked person from among you." Moreover, Paul says that the man living with his father's wife is to be delivered "for the destruction of the flesh, so that his spirit may be saved in the day of the Lord" (1 Cor. 5:5). This destruction of the flesh is a sharing in the Crucifixion, a saying-no to disordered desires of the flesh, so that the person may share in the Resurrection of the body, which is God's yes to the deepest human longing. Paul shows that the entirety of our lives ought to be ordered to "the day of the Lord." His words open up a new vista that looks forward to our resurrection, to the day of the Lord Jesus. Sexual fidelity is now a way to live within the renewal of creation made possible through Christ's death and Resurrection.[10]

Paul invites those who have fallen into sexual sin to begin again. Unlike the command in Deuteronomy 17 in which the wicked person is simply to be driven out of the community of Israel, Paul quotes this verse to call the person to repentance. The person enmeshed in

---

10. For further discussion of openness to life within marriage, see Michael Dauphinais, "Married Sexuality within the Drama of Creation and Redemption: *Humanae Vitae* through the Lens of *Gaudium et Spes*," *Nova et Vetera* 16, no. 1 (2018): 113–140.

habits of sexual sin is to struggle against his or her disordered sexual passions in order to be "saved in the day of the Lord." Here is a great message of conversion and renewal displayed in the lives of Christians. Even those living in disordered sexual sins "not found even among pagans" are not barred from the hope of redemption.

Walking the path to redemption is not easy. It means accepting the guidance and direction of the Lord exercised through the Christian community. Such a path to renewal is surely good news today in the midst of deep confusion about sexual morality, the disappearance of common expectations for sexual purity, and the high rates of pornography use, all of which undermines the possibility of happy, mature, and fulfilling relationships between men and women— relationships that are central, in all kinds of ways, to human happiness.[11]

Today's challenges of living sexual purity amidst a sexually permissive culture are not, however, new for Christians. The author of Hebrews includes among his final moral exhortations, "let the marriage bed be kept undefiled" (Heb. 13:4). Such an exhortation recognizes that marriage was in fact often defiled but nonetheless could be rendered holy. Paul and the early Christians faced tremendous challenges of disordered sexual practices both inside and outside the Christian communities. Past failures were not the end of the story then, and they are not the end of the story now. In Paul's letters, we find the good news that Christ the power of God offers us forgiveness and strength and that Christ the wisdom of God instructs us how to live rightly with God and with neighbor.

Paul describes both concrete prohibitions against sinful bodily acts and the ultimate purpose of the body. Let us consider the goal of the body first and then see whether certain negative teachings become more intelligible. In Romans 12, Paul speaks of our bodies as

---

11. See William M. Struthers, *Wired for Intimacy: How Pornography Hijacks the Male Brain* (Downers Grove, IL: InterVarsity Press, 2009).

instruments of true worship: "I appeal to you therefore, brothers and sisters, by the mercies of God, to present your bodies as a living sacrifice, holy and acceptable to God, which is your spiritual worship" (Rom. 12:1). What an amazing calling! The body is not an accident of creation but is part of God's plan and part of our relationship with God. Worship is not merely an intellectual phenomenon. Instead, when we love God with all our hearts, mind, and strength, we order our whole selves, body, soul, and spirit, to love God. Our bodies may become living sacrifices, "holy and acceptable to God."

In the state of fallen nature, however, we are not yet holy and acceptable to God. As a result of the fall, our bodily desires are often disordered. When we follow such disordered desires, we harm our relationships with others, with ourselves, and with God. Thus we need to have our desires ordered by the teachings of Christ and his Church. Paul continues with an exhortation to leave behind the worldliness that afflicts us: "Do not be conformed to this world, but be transformed by the renewing of your minds, so that you may discern what is the will of God—what is good and acceptable and perfect" (Rom. 12:2). To present our bodies as living sacrifices to the Lord, we need to turn away from the disordered practices of this world. This call to turn from worshiping things of this world to worshiping God alone forms the fundamental theme of the covenant with Israel and with the Church.

Paul speaks about how idolatry and sexual immorality go hand in hand. After he speaks about how the invisible God can be known through his creation (Rom. 1:20), Paul emphasizes that many people, despite being capable of knowing God, did not turn to him but instead turned to idols. As indicated above, idolatry consists in worshiping something other than God as god. Any time that we make power, sex, or money our highest end, we are engaging in idolatry, even if we do not call it by that name. Paul, for example, will else-where say that greediness is idolatry since it makes us love money with our heart, mind, and strength (Col. 3:5). Discussing those who knew God through creation, Paul observes that "though they knew God, they did not honor him as God or give thanks to him, but they became futile in their thinking, and their senseless minds were darkened" (Rom. 1:21). He then connects this idolatry to sexual immorality: "Therefore God gave them up in the lusts of their hearts to impurity, to the degrading of their bodies among themselves, because they exchanged the truth about God for a lie and worshiped and served the creature rather than the Creator" (Rom. 1:24–25). In the mystery of his love, God respects the free wills of his creatures so much that he allows us to reject the truth about God and his plan for marriage and sexuality. But God does more than this. He offers us the grace of forgiveness and conversion.

Here we see the real good news of what Paul teaches in Romans 12 when he says that we can turn from conformity to the world and present our bodies as "living sacrifices, holy and acceptable to God." Sexual immorality is not merely a private act but is a rejection of God's plans and commandments for his creatures. When we engage in sexual immorality, we set aside God's created order that alone allows the family of God to flourish.

What sorts of disordered sexual practices does Paul have in mind? As we saw earlier, he calls the Christians to avoid *porneia*, which is any form sexual immorality. Paul was not yet confronted with online pornography, but he would have recognized it as a disordered form of sexual practice. The Apostle specifically addresses two distinct modes of *porneia*, homosexual actions and prostitution, and calls the early Christians to abandon these practices. In writing of those who exchanged the truth about the Creator to worship creatures, he says, "For this reason God gave them up to degrading passions. Their women exchanged natural intercourse for unnatural, and in the same way also the men, giving up natural intercourse with women, were consumed with passion for one another" (Rom. 1:26–27).[12] Just as this criticism would have sounded strange to the Romans of Paul's day, it sounds strange to many people today. The role of divine revelation is often to remind us of deeper truths of human nature that have been lost amidst confused societal practices and customs. Homosexual relations take the sexual act out of its created order revealed in Genesis and inscribed in our complementary bodily constitution as male and female. Of course, to experience homosexual attraction is not thereby to commit sin—by no means! The difficulty of practicing chastity can seem impossible for people who do not feel called to singleness and who are attracted solely to persons of the same sex. Yet by grace, it is indeed possible to habituate our sexual desires in such a way that we can live and thrive within the bounds set by the good of persons and families.

So, too, prostitution and pornography remove the sexual act from its divinely instituted created order, in a different way. In the port city of Corinth, prostitution was socially accepted, "normal" behavior without any shame or stigma. In our day, a parallel would be sexual activity outside of marriage or even a committed relationship. Paul challenges the social norms of Corinth in his day as well as those of our day in light of God's created order. God did not create man and woman to commit sexual acts that were separated from

---

12. Brendan Byrne, SJ, among others, tries to argue that Paul's view of homosexual actions can today be ignored by Christians, either because Paul had in view only a particular kind of homosexual relationship, or because Paul's views were culturally conditioned: see Byrne, *Romans* (Collegeville, MN: Liturgical Press, 1996), 70. For a correction of this approach, see N.T. Wright, "The Letter to the Romans," in *The New Interpreter's Bible: Volume X*, ed. Leander E. Keck (Nashville, TN: Abingdon, 1994); Richard B. Hays, *The Moral Vision of the New Testament: Community, Cross, New Creation. A Contemporary Introduction to New Testament Ethics* (New York: HarperCollins, 1996), 379–406.

permanence and from offspring. Sexuality has an intrinsic order to unity and fertility—that is, to family. Paul writes, "Do you not know that your bodies are members of Christ? Should I therefore take the members of Christ and make them members of a prostitute? Never! Do you not know that whoever is united to a prostitute becomes one body with her?" (1 Cor. 6:15–16). What we do with our bodies matters. What we do with Christ's body matters. Since we have been baptized into Christ, we are really members of his body. This same approach calls Christians away from sexual activity outside of the permanence of the vows of marriage, in which the husband and wife complement each other in the raising of children or in other tasks of building family and community.

Paul discloses the inherent reality of sexual unions in the midst of cultures that downplays their importance. Sexual intimacy is inherently ordered to union, even when the sexual act is disordered. Sex is never merely casual since it impacts the person body and soul.

To understand why sex outside of marriage is a sin, it is helpful to view it as a kind of falsehood.[13] As we have explored, the act of sex is intrinsically ordered so that "the two may become one" and for the propagation of human life. Yet sex outside of marriage does not match that unity and, instead, leaves the two as two. Our bodies are promising unity while our souls fail to make the corresponding promise. So also with respect to openness to children within marriage. Whereas the act of sex is ordered to "be fruitful and multiply," sex without openness to children and without marriage says no both to fertility and to the commitment to child-rearing that it entails. Granted, the unmarried couple that has children may intend to stay together, and may actually do so. However, their union is weaker without the public commitment (and grace) of marriage, and their

---

13. See Pope John Paul II, *Male and Female He Created Them: A Theology of the Body*, trans. Michael Waldstein (Boston, MA: Pauline Books & Media, 2006).

children are thereby at greater risk of suffering the breakup of their parents' relationship. Sexual activity outside of marriage between man and woman thus misses the true target of marital union and openness to children that reflects the order of creation, in which marriage and children truly flourish.

Paul writes succinctly, "Shun immorality [*porneia*]" (1 Cor. 6:18 RSV-CE). The Greek word here actually means "to flee." Flee from sexual immorality! The brevity and choice of words reminds the reader of the Old Testament story of when the Pharaoh's wife attempted to seduce Joseph. The Bible simply records that Joseph "fled and got out of the house" (Genesis 39:12). Christians are not called to argue and debate with sexual temptation and sexual immorality, but simply to flee. Paul explains why: "Every other sin which a man commits is outside the body; but the sexually immoral [*porneia*] man sins against his own body" (1 Cor. 6:18 RSV-CE). Notice that Paul says sexual sins offend not only God but also our very selves. Many Christians today feel trapped within addictions to pornography and masturbation or unhealthy sexual relationships. They themselves suffer; their partners suffer.

Within the New Covenant, sexual intimacy is for the glory of God. Our bodies express an intrinsic ordering toward marriage and offspring and thus form part of the call to "be fruitful and multiply and fill the earth." When we sin sexually, we remove our body from its created purpose, its manner of giving glory to God. We harm the good of the family, and we harm our own good. That is what we do when we trade a real relationship for pornographic depictions on a screen; when we undermine the right of children to be raised by their mother and father; when we engage in a psychologically and physically detrimental promiscuity; and when we suffer spiritual wounds from using our bodies in ways for which they were not made. Yet at any time, we can repent and begin again in response to the Spirit's call. Cleaving to chaste friendships and to holy sexuality, we can at any time heed the word of the Lord: "If any want to become my followers, let them deny themselves and take up their cross and follow me. For those who want to save their life will lose it, and those who lose their life for my sake will find it" (Matt. 16:24–25). We may present our bodies anew as "living sacrifices, holy and acceptable to God."

Paul explains our true calling by teaching us that we are temples of the Holy Spirit, both individually and together. Writing to the oft-confused Corinthians, he says, "Do you not know that your body is a temple of the Holy Spirit within you, which you have from God, and that you are not your own? For you were bought with a price; therefore glorify God in your body" (1 Cor. 6:19–20). Our bodies are the temples of the Spirit! Thus, it is not sexuality in itself that does not give glory to God but disordered sexual practices. When sex is placed within the marriage covenant, when the two become one, Christ becomes one with them. The Holy Spirit dwells within the marriage and renders it fruitful in diverse ways. Christian marriage thus becomes a way for the body to glorify God.

Marriage as a Great Mystery in the New Covenant

Sexual fidelity is not only a path to holiness and honor, a way of preparing for the resurrection, and a path of beginning again. Paul describes marriage as "a great mystery," a marvelous unveiled secret, of God's love for human beings. In Ephesians, Paul harkens back to the original language of Genesis: "For this reason a man will leave his father and mother and be joined to his wife, and the two will become one flesh" (Eph. 5:31, quoting Gen. 2:24). He then immediately continues, "This is a great mystery, and I am applying it to Christ and the church; Each of you, however, should love his wife as himself, and a wife should respect her husband" (Eph. 5:32). The love between husband and wife is a real sign of the love between Christ and his Church. Moreover, the perfect love between Christ and his Church reverberates in the renewed love between man and woman.

Since Paul has told us this great truth that Christian married love flows from the love between Christ and his Church, we are invited to look anew at Christ's love for the Church, in particular as it is expressed in the book of Revelation. Revelation presents the new heavens and the new earth as a great wedding feast between Christ and his Church.[14] The multitudes of heaven cry out, "'Let us rejoice and exult and give him the glory, for the marriage of the Lamb has come, and his bride has made herself ready; to her it has been granted to be clothed with fine linen, bright and pure'—for the fine linen is the righteous deeds of the saints" (Rev. 19:7–8). As the great wedding is unveiled, we see that the bride is the Church, adorned with the faithful deeds and witness of her members. Now we begin to see why sexuality and marriage matter so much to the Church: heaven is a great wedding! The two become one. Christ becomes one with his Church for all eternity.

The entirety of the marriage between Christ and his Church is a relationship of gift. Christ gives himself entirely through his death so that he might offer forgiveness of sins and eternal life to his followers; the Church gives herself back to Christ in faith and love. The exchange of gifts, however, is never symmetrical, for God's gifts are efficacious. It is always the love of God manifested in Christ that makes possible the return gift of the Church. In this way, God makes the unholy holy so that the Church may participate in the nuptial union with Christ.

---

14. For background, see Phillip J. Long, *Jesus the Bridegroom: The Origin of the Eschatological Feast as a Wedding Banquet in the Synoptic Gospels* (Eugene, OR: Pickwick, 2013).

Marriage as presented in the Bible is thus more than a legal contract; it is a covenant. The two truly become one flesh. As Paul teaches at the beginning of Ephesians, God's plan is "to gather up all things in him, things in heaven and things on earth" (Eph. 1:10). This is indeed the great mystery: God unites us to himself in Christ's marriage to his Church. Furthermore, since Christ's marriage to his Church is eternal, so is its celebration.

The book of Revelation, recounting a vision given to the Apostle John, follows the wedding of Christ and his Church with the great banquet supper. In John's vision, the multitudes in heaven announce, "Blessed are those who are invited to the marriage supper of the Lamb" (Rev. 19:9). Christ is not only the Bridegroom; he is also the Feast. The marriage supper of the Lamb is nothing other than an eternal Eucharistic celebration. The Eucharist is the reality whereby the Church becomes one with Christ, in which all who receive become members of the one Body. Revelation helps us to avoid the mistake of limiting our view of the Church to what we see in this world. The Church already exists as united to Christ's Body in heaven. When this world ends and the Church on this earth ceases to be, the Church will be united to Christ in ecstatic love for all eternity.

Revelation continues to unfold the reality of Christ's marital relationship with his Church as an angel says to John, "'Come, I will show you the Bride, the wife of the Lamb.'" "And in the Spirit," John continues, "he carried me away to a great, high mountain, and showed me the holy city Jerusalem coming down out of heaven from God" (Rev. 21:9–10).[15] The bride of the Lamb is the new Jerusalem, the heavenly Jerusalem, the Church now unveiled (or revealed, hence

---

15. See Peter S. Williamson, *Revelation* (Grand Rapids, MI: Baker Academic, 2015), 347–349. Peter J. Leithart, mistakenly in our view, reads Revelation 21:9 as an indication of a millennium of earthly peace that will take place prior to the final events: see Leithart, *Revelation 12–22* (London: Bloomsbury, 2018), 357–360.

"revelation") in its true nature. We see through this image that the Church on earth is an earthly presence of a heavenly reality. What is more, this heavenly reality is not only the goal of our earthly life but also unveils the truth about our earthly realities.

Looking back to John's Gospel, at the wedding at Cana we witness the heavenly reality erupting into our earthly existence. This will be Jesus' first sign, when he first reveals his glory to his disciples. At the urging of his mother Mary, Jesus blesses earthly marriage with an overflowing abundance. Just as heaven is revealed to be the marriage of Christ and the Church, so Jesus reveals himself in the blessing of a marriage. John describes the miraculous wine as follows: "Jesus did this, the first of his signs, in Cana of Galilee, and revealed his glory; and his disciples believed in him" (John 2:11).[16] The celebration of marriage was the occasion of Jesus' first miracle. This was surely a sign of the goodness of marriage. It is hardly surprising that, if the final consummation of creation is the marriage supper of the Lamb, Jesus' first miracle was at a marriage supper.

Marriage and Virginity in the Kingdom of God

When Jesus preaches the kingdom of God, he both renews the institution of marriage and complements it with a call to virginity. In a debate with the Pharisees about divorce, he teaches about the authentic nature of marriage by recalling the revelation of Genesis: "Have you not read that he who made them from the beginning 'made them male and female,' and said, 'For this reason a man shall leave his father and mother and be joined to his wife, and the two shall become one flesh'" (Matt. 19:4–5).

When the Pharisees point out that Moses permitted divorce in Deuteronomy, Jesus responds again by recalling Genesis, "It was

---

16. See Francis Martin and William M. Wright IV, *The Gospel of John* (Grand Rapids, MI: Baker Academic, 2015), 59–60.

because you were so hard-hearted that Moses allowed you to divorce your wives, but from the beginning it was not so" (Matt. 19:8). In appealing to what God had made "from the beginning," Jesus reveals that his ministry inaugurates a renewal of creation. Within the context of the kingdom of God inaugurated by Jesus, the children of God are invited to leave behind accommodations to the sinful practices of humanity, even those that were permitted by Moses. Israel was always called to be a people set apart. They were to leave behind practices of incest and sexual abuse. They were to leave behind adultery, homosexual acts, and prostitution. Jesus here elevates this call once more in order to return marriage to what it was "from the beginning."

Within the context of the renewal of creation, Jesus reveals marriage to have a unity that precludes divorce. Jesus teaches, "So they are no longer two, but one flesh. Therefore what God has joined together, let no man one separate" (Matt. 19:6). After mentioning Moses' permission of divorce, he continues, "And I say to you, whoever divorces his wife, except for unchastity, and marries another commits adultery; and he who marries a divorced woman commits adultery" (Matt. 19:9).[17]

Rather than beginning with difficult cases, let us consider Jesus' teaching on marriage as another beatitude, another way in which God blesses his creatures. Jesus is revealing the authentic path to happiness. Real happiness means living rightly with God and with our neighbor. This means turning away from the practices in which we are inclined to use God for our own plans—the times when we act not for love of our neighbor but rather for improper ends. Right

---

17. See John P. Meier, *A Marginal Jew, vol. 4, Law and Love* (New Haven, CT: Yale University Press, 2009), 126–127; Ulrich Luz, *Matthew 1–7*, trans. James E. Crouch (Minneapolis, MN: Fortress Press, 2007), 250–259.

relationships within the kingdom of God turn worldly relationships upside down.

Jesus places divorce within these worldly patterns of broken relationships: "From the beginning, it was not so." His kingdom calls for the renewal of marriage, not by human effort alone, but as a corresponding gift that belongs to his inaugurated kingdom. Without the grace of the Holy Spirit, the prohibition of divorce and remarriage—as distinct from permanent separation (which can be necessary in particular situations)—would be too much for people to bear. But Jesus offers us his grace, which makes it possible to keep the vows that we have freely made to our spouse. This grace ensures that we will not be truly left alone, even if we have to bear the immeasurable hurt in the wake of spousal abandonment. Jesus will give us the strength to live out a relationship suited to his inaugurated kingdom, despite our failures and those of our spouse.[18]

The good news, therefore, is that sexuality and marriage are part of the inaugurated kingdom of God. By pouring out his Spirit, Jesus renews them so that they may be what God has meant them to be "from the beginning." Jesus' teaching on sexuality and marriage is not meant to condemn us but to save us. We are saved *from* our sinful desires and habits, which threaten to make it impossible for us to keep our commitments to each other, and saved *for* rightly ordered love that images the union of Christ and the Church.

The disciples, however, found Jesus' prohibition of divorce shocking. "If such is the case of a man with his wife," they responded, "it is better not to marry" (Matt. 19:10). If Jesus did not intend an actual prohibition of divorce, now was his chance to explain to his disciples that they had misinterpreted his meaning and that it was still okay to follow Moses's allowance of divorce. Instead, he does the oppo-

18. For further discussion, see Matthew Levering, *The Indissolubility of Marriage: Amoris Laetitia in Context* (San Francisco: Ignatius Press, 2019).

site. Not only does he refuse to back down on his unveiling of the indissolubility of marriage; he goes further and leads his disciples to a restored vision for marriage and virginity. Marriage in the inaugurated kingdom is revealed to be between one man and one woman, for life, and for the procreation and raising of children.

In addition to the renewed vision of marriage, Jesus also reveals the vocation of virginity in the newly inaugurated kingdom. One of the decisive shifts from the Old Covenant to the new is how common dedicated virginity becomes as a state of life within the Christian community. The Old Covenant occasionally honored dedicated virginity, but this was very exceptional. In the New Covenant, there appears a new phenomenon. Anyone among the baptized faithful may be called to forgo marriage—to be more available to follow Jesus in undivided contemplation and service, bearing witness to the primacy of our eschatological "marriage" with God.[19]

Jesus responds to his disciples' question of whether it is "better not to marry" by inviting them to consider life without marriage. This is surely surprising. After teaching that marriage is "from the beginning," he immediately explains to his disciples that some are called not to pursue marriage. Here lies a central truth about the inaugurated kingdom of God: it is both a return to the beginning, to a rightly ordered and renewed creation, and an anticipation of the eternal kingdom to come. Thus both marriage and virginity exist within the horizon established by the prayer that Jesus taught his disciples: "Our Father in heaven, hallowed be your name. Your kingdom come. Your will be done, on earth as it is in heaven" (Matt. 6:9–10). This is a plea for the kingdom of God, including God's will and name, to be fully established on earth as it is in heaven. This neces-

---

19. See Raniero Cantalamessa, OFM Cap., *Virginity: A Positive Approach to Celibacy for the Sake of the Kingdom of Heaven*, trans. Charles Serignat (Staten Island, NY: Alba House, 1995).

sarily implies a plea for a new heaven and a new earth as spoken of by Isaiah and in Revelation (Isa. 66:22; Rev. 21:1).

Jesus' teachings on marriage and virginity take on their full meaning within this great desire for a new heaven and a new earth. If this world is all there is, then why make the sacrifices entailed by vows of marriage and celibacy? Even Jesus' disciples ask whether marriage is worth it without the option of divorce. Yet if the life to come is real, and if our desires are so great and deep that they will only be fulfilled in the eternal embrace of God our Father, then the sacrifices entailed by vows are worthwhile. As Paul observes, "I consider that the sufferings of this present time are not worth comparing with the glory about to be revealed to us" (Rom. 8:18). Fidelity to vows may well cause great suffering, but so may our fidelity to the baptismal vows to renounce Satan and believe in God alone. Looking back to vows is at the same time looking forward to the God who wants to welcome us into his eternal kingdom, saying, "Well done, my good and faithful servant; you have been faithful over a little, I will set you over much; enter into the joy of your master" (Matt. 25:21).

Jesus explains to his disciples that his kingdom includes those who freely forgo marriage. Some of his followers, both men and women, will choose apostolic celibacy. Jesus teaches this new truth by referring to "eunuchs"—namely, those in ancient societies who could not engage in sexual relations: "Not all men can receive this precept, but only those to whom it is given. For there are eunuchs who have been so from birth, and there are eunuchs who have been made eunuchs by men, and there are eunuchs who have made themselves eunuchs for the sake of the kingdom of heaven. He who is able to receive this, let him receive it" (Matt. 19:11–12).

Virginity thus emerges in Jesus' teaching as a higher calling alongside marriage. At the beginning and end of his discussion of it,

Jesus makes particular reference to the reality that not all can follow the path of virginity. He opens up the idea that all are called to follow him and yet not all are called in the same way (see Mark 5:18–20). Some will follow him through their use of earthly goods and marriage to benefit others; some will follow him in a direct imitation of his poverty and virginity. All will discover, despite ongoing trials and temptations, that if we follow Jesus' way, we will flourish: "Come to me, all you that are weary and are carrying heavy burdens, and I will give you rest. Take my yoke upon you, and learn from me; for I am gentle and humble in heart, and you will find rest for your souls. For my yoke is easy, and my burden is light" (Matt. 11:28–30). Living in accord with Jesus' way brings spiritual rest; breaking with his way causes unrest.

Paul faithfully carries forward Jesus' teachings on marriage and virginity. In one of the few times when he makes direct reference to a specific teaching of Jesus in his letters, he states Jesus' prohibition of divorce. He writes, "To the married I give this command—not I but the Lord—that the wife should not separate from her husband (but if she does separate, let her remain unmarried or else be reconciled to her husband), and that the husband should not divorce his wife" (1 Cor. 7:10–11). To make the point even clearer, he adds, "A wife is bound as long as her husband lives" (1 Cor. 7:39). Jesus' teaching on marriage and the prohibition against divorce was such a foundational element of the apostolic preaching that Paul explicitly says that it came from the Lord.

Paul also teaches that the married state and the unmarried state are both good and acceptable within the New Covenant community. Nonetheless, he encourages Christians to take seriously the option of refraining from marriage. He summarizes his teaching when he says, "He who marries his fiancée does well; and he who refrains from marriage will do better" (1 Cor. 7:38). In addressing the Corinthians, he writes that he wants them to be free from worldly concerns and available for the Lord. "The unmarried man," Paul explains, "is anxious about the affairs of the Lord, how to please the Lord; but the married man is anxious about affairs of the world, how to please his wife, and his interests are divided. And the unmarried woman and the virgin are anxious about the affairs of the Lord, so that they may be holy in body and spirit; but the married woman is anxious about the affairs of the world, how to please her husband" (1 Cor. 7:32–34). The Apostle's point is true: married people are called to focus on their own families.

We must put aside tendencies to put down the married state in order to elevate the unmarried state, or, what is more common today, to put down the spiritual privileges of the unmarried state in order to ensure that the married feel fully welcome in the mission of the Church. Our modern minds are often suspicious of any hierarchical order, so we want to impose sameness on valid modes of difference. Paul himself warns Timothy against those who "forbid marriage" and so deny the goodness of God's creation (1 Tim. 4:3). The Apostle's teaching is rather straightforward: the married and the unmarried states are both good and holy; and the unmarried state is better. Apostolic celibacy leaves people freer to dedicate themselves to the affairs of the Lord. There is one call to holiness but multiple ways in which that holiness is lived in this age.

The shared call to holiness is shown in the "more excellent way" of charity or love that Paul puts before the Corinthians, both the married and the unmarried. Paul writes:

> If I give away all my possessions, and if I hand over my body so that I may boast, but do not have love, I gain nothing. Love is patient; love is kind; love is not envious or boastful or arrogant or

rude. It does not insist on its own way; it is not irritable or resentful; it does not rejoice in wrongdoing, but rejoices in the truth. It
bears all things, believes all things, hopes all things, endures all
things. . . . For now we see in a mirror, dimly, but then we will see
face to face. Now I know only in part, even as I have been fully
known. And now faith, hope, and love abide, these three; and the
greatest of these is love. (1 Cor. 13:3–7, 12–13)

What a beautiful description of the Christian life as a life of the perfection of love! Despite the fact that this passage on love is a popular choice for weddings, it is not uniquely about marriage but rather
about the love that ought to shape the entire Church. Yet it reveals the
love of marriage as well since the love of Christ that gathers together
the New Covenant community is the same love that renews marriage
to be what it was "from the beginning."

Marriage on a Mission: Priscilla and Aquila

Let us close this chapter by putting before our minds Christian marriage when it is fully participating in the mission of Christ to spread
the Good News of his kingdom. In Acts, we are introduced to a couple named Priscilla and Aquila. Paul meets these faithful Jews in
Corinth after the Roman Emperor Claudius exiled Jews from Rome.
Since Paul, Priscilla, and Aquila were all tentmakers, they worked
together, and Paul stayed with them (Acts 18:1–3). In Corinth, Paul
persuaded many Jews and Greeks that Jesus was indeed the Messiah who had been crucified and risen from the dead. Priscilla and
Aquila, impressed by Paul's preaching and life, came to share this
belief in Jesus as the one in whom the promises of God had been
fulfilled.

When Paul left Corinth and journeyed to Syria, he was "accompanied by Priscilla and Aquila" so they could help him in his missionary

endeavors (Acts 18:18). Confident of their fidelity and support, Paul then left this couple in Ephesus to help the young Christian community. There, as recorded in Acts, they met an eloquent Jew named Apollos who believed that Jesus was the Christ and was learned in the Scriptures. Despite his learning and zeal, however, Apollos did not fully understand the new Christian faith. He only knew about the baptism of John and not the baptism of the Holy Spirit. Thus, "when Priscilla and Aquila heard him, they took him aside and explained the Way of God to him more accurately" (Acts 18:26). After this correction, Apollos became a more effective preacher, "showing by the Scriptures that the Messiah [Christ] is Jesus" (Acts 18:28).

Here we see the unmarried and the married working alongside one another in the spread of the Gospel. Priscilla and Aquila play an integral role in helping Paul in his apostolic ministry. They are persuaded by him about the truth that Jesus of Nazareth is indeed the Christ. They work alongside him as tentmakers. They host him in their home and so support his ministry. They host the church in their home. They journey with him on some of his apostolic journeys. However, they do not accompany him on all his journeys, since they set up a household in a new city. Once they have established their new home, they help share the Gospel more fully with another early and prominent convert, Apollos.

Priscilla and Aquila become well known in the early Church and appear frequently in the New Testament. In addition to Acts, Paul mentions them explicitly in three of his letters. At the end of Paul's First Letter to the Corinthians, he writes, "Aquila and Prisca, together with the church in their house, send you hearty greetings in the Lord" (1 Cor. 16:19). (Note that "Prisca" is the more formal version of "Priscilla.") Aquila and Priscilla used their marriage and their home to support the Church. They had not given up all of their possessions as had some of the disciples. Nonetheless, as a married couple, Priscilla and Aquila put their possessions in the service of the local Christian community, so much so that that the early Christians met in their home to celebrate the Eucharist.

Paul concludes his Letter to the Romans by mentioning many Christians known both to him and to the Christians in Rome. It is striking that he begins his greetings by listing Priscilla and Aquila first: "Greet Prisca and Aquila, my fellow workers in Christ Jesus, who risked their necks for my life, to whom not only I but also all the churches of the Gentiles give thanks; greet also the church in their house." (Rom. 16:3–5 RSV-CE). Again, Paul speaks of the local church that meets in their house. Paul praises their sacrifices for him and for all the churches and describes them as his "fellow workers in Christ Jesus." Their lives and possessions are fully in the service of the Lord. Finally in a letter to Timothy, Paul again singles out Priscilla and Aquila, mentioning them first among only seven names that are mentioned in the letter. Once more he writes, "Greet Prisca and Aquila" (2 Tim. 4:19). Both married people and dedicated virgins are called to be "fellow workers" in Christ's mission.

Conclusion

This chapter has considered the good news of the Bible's teaching on sexuality and marriage. Both the Old and New Testaments emphasize the fundamental goodness of marriage—as we saw for example in the opening chapters of Genesis, the story of Tobias and Sarah, and Jesus' blessing of marriage at the wedding at Cana.

The Bible also uncovers the many sexual practices across societies and cultures that have twisted this original goodness in the image of our disordered desires and confused inclinations. Leviticus thus powerfully condemns incest and sexual abuse. Jesus likewise calls us to see the image of God in each person and warns us that "everyone who looks at a woman with lust has already committed adultery with her in his heart" (Matt. 5:28). He reveals the danger of turning other persons into objects for gratification, whether imaginatively or physically. And he uses arresting language to challenge us not to look at others lustfully: "If your right eye causes you to sin, tear it out and throw it away" (Matt. 5:29)—not literally but in the sense of returning to chastity.

Paul calls the new Christians of his day to turn away from the disordered sexual practices so common in Greco-Roman society and likewise calls Christians today to do the same. As preached by Jesus and Paul, the good news about marriage and sexuality is not a rigid set of rules that enslave and limit freedom. Instead, the teachings of the Church liberate human beings to live in accord with our created natures now renewed in Jesus Christ. The teachings on marriage and sexuality do not condemn but offer the forgiveness of past sins and hope for healing by the grace of the Holy Spirit.

The New Covenant reveals that marriage is called to be an indissoluble sign of the union of Christ and his Church. Heaven is shown to be the marriage of the Lamb and his Bride. Marriage looks forward to something greater than itself. The New Covenant likewise presents the call to lifelong virginity as a witness to the coming consummation of the kingdom of God. The New Covenant opens up the beauty and dignity of marriage and virginity as complementary ways to follow Christ and manifests to the world creation in its renewed form. In living our vocation, let us answer Paul's call: "Glorify God in your body" (1 Cor. 6:20).

CHAPTER 9

Why Do Catholics Fight So Much with Each Other?

"Do not speak evil against one another"
(James 4:11)

Catholics appear at times to be unable to get along with each other. Even in the New Testament itself we find arguments and disputes among Christians. All too frequently over the course of history, Catholics have fought bitterly with each other over points of doctrine and practice. Even saints have disagreed with each other sharply, and certainly the average Catholic may seem as inclined to gossip and complain as anyone else. Why be a Catholic, however, if it is going to be such an experience of tension and arguments? As a Catholic who left the Church expressed her frustration, "About a year ago, I was in the local pub, sat near a priest, and was listening to him bitch about a fellow priest—not for me."[1]

The sociologist William D'Antonio and his co-authors report that Catholics who practice their faith seriously often have deep concerns about the present state of the Church. They write that such Catholics "are genuinely troubled by some past behaviors, some current conditions, and some scary projections for the future."[2] Such worries are not conducive to handing on the faith to the next generation.

---

1. Stephen Bullivant, Catherine Knowles, Hannah Vaughan-Spruce, and Bernadette Durcan, *Why Catholics Leave, What They Miss, and How They Might Return* (New York: Paulist Press, 2019), 28.

2. William V. D'Antonio, James D. Davidson, Dean R. Hoge, and Mary L. Gautier, *American Catholics Today: New Realities of Their Faith and Their Church* (Lanham, MD: Rowman & Littlefield, 2007), 67.

According to sociological studies, people with strong faith are more likely to "have experienced a miracle, committed their lives to God, had prayers answered, and/or had a moving spiritual experience."[3] To some degree at least, the joy of these powerful experiences is dampened when Catholics fight with each other.

It is not enough, however, to avoid unpleasant speech. Another problem is that many Catholics are reluctant to speak in ways that might make them unpopular. In *Blessed are the Bored in Spirit: A Young Catholic's Search for Meaning*, Mark Hart reports on the basis of his extensive experience with Catholic young people: "They want to be heard, but are reluctant to speak. It has become more important to be liked than to be respected, to be tolerant than to be truthful."[4] Of course the desire to find social acceptance is powerful, but so too is the discovery of the truth that God has a plan for each of us and has revealed his plan for the world's salvation in Christ.

The people who make up the Church are often tempted to conform to the world. Sharp speech can therefore be necessary at times, as a corrective to a false assimilationism. Even so, under the desire to correct the errors of others, Catholics may easily slide into speech that is unnecessarily divisive and confrontational. The line between speech that builds up and speech that tears down is sometimes difficult to discern.

Can the Bible offer guidance on this matter, which is becoming urgent in our era defined not only by conflict between different visions of Christian faith and life, but also by the extremes of incivility and strict political correctness in the broader culture? This chapter examines teachings and examples from the Old and New

---

3. Christian Smith, Kyle Longest, Jonathan Hill, and Kari Christoffersen, *Young Catholic America: Emerging Adults In, Out of, and Gone from the Church* (Oxford: Oxford University Press, 2014), 185.

4. Mark Hart, *Blessed are the Bored in Spirit: A Young Catholic's Search for Meaning* (Cincinnati, OH: Servant Books, 2006), 3.

Testaments to explore the harm that evil speech does, the need to speak out against evil, and the ultimate purpose of speech in giving praise to God.

Doing Evil and Speaking Evil

Language has been corrupted by sin. The Psalmist will go so far as to complain, "Everyone is a liar" (Ps. 116:11). The story of the fall in Genesis depicts this corruption of speech. When Adam and Eve commit the first sin, God comes to them and asks them to confess what they have done. But instead of confessing honestly, they strive to separate themselves from blame. Most tragic in this regard are the words used by Adam. Having freely rebelled against God's Law, he complains to God, "The woman whom you gave to be with me, she gave me fruit of the tree, and I ate" (Gen. 3:12). His way of putting it blames Eve entirely as though he simply ate what Eve put before him. Whereas once Adam rejoiced in the sight of his beloved Eve, proclaiming her to be "flesh of my flesh" (Gen. 2:23), now he blames her for his own crime against God. This kind of speaking evil, in which we assign to others the blame for our own deeds, often results in terrible harm. Such words show a refusal to take responsibility and to repent. Our tendencies to lie and to cover up our betrayals may fool human beings but do not fool God. Such language therefore not only fails to love our neighbor but also lacks awareness of the God who will judge us and who will extend to us his mercy if we turn to him with repentance.

Perhaps the paradigmatic examples of the fragmenting power of evil speech arise during the exodus from Egypt. Due to the difficulty of the exodus journey in the wilderness, as well as due to the desire to gain power, the people often complain against Moses and attack his leadership. Soon after escaping from the Egyptians, "the people complained against Moses, saying, 'What shall we drink?'"

(Exod. 15:24). Later, when faced with the difficulty of leaving the wilderness, "all the Israelites complained against Moses" (Num. 14:2). This complaining and criticism sows deep discord and division. At one stage, even Moses' brother Aaron and his sister Miriam go so far as to speak against Moses and undermine his authority. They suggest that Moses' main concern is his own power rather than the people's true good. They ask rhetorically, "Has the LORD indeed spoken only through Moses? Has he not spoken through us also?" (Num. 12:2). Although they aim to foment a rebellion, God immediately puts a stop to it.

Less easily stopped is a rebellion that arises not from within Moses' own family but from among the people and specifically from certain leaders of the tribes of Levi and Reuben. Korah, Dathan, On, and Abiram lead this rebellion against Moses' authority. They make their rallying cry the claim that the whole congregation is as holy as Moses. This claim, quite laughable by this stage in the exodus— since the people have repeatedly proven their lack of holiness— causes Moses great alarm due to his commitment to the mission he has received from God.

Insofar as the rebellion involves Korah (a Levite), Moses sees it primarily as a challenge to the authority of Aaron as the chief priest. Dathan and Abiram, neither of whom are Levites, attack Moses himself, questioning, "Is it too little that you have brought us up out of a land flowing with milk and honey to kill us in the wilderness, that you must also lord it over us?" (Num. 16:13). Their words make the false claim that Moses, in leading the people out of Egyptian slavery and toward the Promised Land, has been motivated by a desire for power, to "lord it over us." But in speaking these evil words against Moses, they are ironically revealing the truth about their own motives—namely, they want power. Their words have a devastating impact upon many lives.

The Ten Commandments that God gives to Moses on Mount Sinai include a warning against speaking evil. The commandment states, "You shall not bear false witness against your neighbor" (Exod. 20:16). The fundamental component of harmful speech against another person consists in the lie about the person. We distort what someone else has said or done, or we accuse someone without a sufficient basis for the accusation. We falsely impugn the reputation of someone else. In what must ultimately be seen as a kind of hatred of the other person, we do not care that we are either deliberately lying or that we have no secure knowledge to back up our criticism. In the words of the Ten Commandments, insinuating something that harms another person's reputation unjustly is a case of "bearing false witness."

Exodus 23 presents another set of laws against distorting the truth with our speech. Here the Law states: "You shall not spread a false report. You shall not join hands with the wicked to act as a malicious witness. You shall not follow a majority in wrongdoing; when you bear witness in a lawsuit, you shall not side with the majority so as to pervert justice. . . . Keep far from a false charge" (Exod. 23:1–3, 7). In the decisions of the communities of early Israel, great weight was given to the reports of neighbors against neighbors. The perversion of false speech might be seen in our day in the workplace, when employees speak falsely of other employees in order to carry out a grudge, to get promoted ahead of someone else, or simply to enjoy the diversion of repeating unverified rumors. In all these ways, the Bible reminds us that false reports cause true harm.

Israel's proverbs, which provide instruction for everyday ethics, are filled with warnings against speaking evil about another person. For example, Proverbs 6 describes how "a villain" will exhibit "crooked speech" and, often through insinuation, will be continually devising evil and "sowing discord" (Prov. 6:12, 14). In addition to the discord that the wicked person stirs up through speech that bends the truth, there is a further harm when people reveal secrets without due cause. Proverbs advises us to stay away from a "gossip" who "reveals secrets" (Prov. 20:19). The more we speak with untrustworthy people, the more we become entangled in their harmful speech.

Proverbs makes clear that the source of evil speech is the broken and sinful human heart. We would not slander our neighbor if we possessed real healing, authentic charity, or interior justice. This biblical truth affirms a popular saying from the field of psychology: "Hurt people hurt people." Proverbs therefore warns that evil speech will bring about not only the harm of the person spoken against but also the harm of the one who speaks. Proverbs 10:31 cautions, "the perverse tongue will be cut off." Proverbs 12:13 states, "The evil are ensnared by the transgression of their lips." We need to ask for the Lord's healing of our inner woundedness so that our outer speech reflects inner peace. Proverbs is well aware that evil speech brings harm as well to those whose reputations are sullied. Thus, Proverbs 12:18 compares "rash words" to "sword thrusts" in contrast to the healing words of the wise. Evil speech breaks down the bonds of love and justice.

False speech may be motivated by the desire to gain power and influence. Israel's history includes not only many faithful prophets but also many false prophets. A notable instance comes in Jeremiah 28 in the story of the false prophet Hananiah. After a limited first exile of some leaders to Babylon, the prophet Hananiah shared a prophecy that was pleasing to the remaining rulers of Jerusalem and thus put him in good stead with them. Jeremiah later confronted

Hananiah: "Listen, Hananiah, the LORD has not sent you, and you made this people trust in a lie" (Jer. 28:15). In validation of his word, Jeremiah prophesied that Hananiah would die that very year—and he did. The story of this false prophet demonstrates the temptation to manipulate speech for the sake of securing favor and personal gain.

It is not accusation against another person, in itself, that is forbidden. After all, an accusation can be truthful. For instance, Jeremiah's love for the good of God's people made it right for him to answer Hananiah with sharp words. Hananiah was proclaiming exactly what the political rulers wanted the people to hear. Jeremiah found himself in a situation of leadership rooted in lies and chose to risk personal harm by speaking the truth.

Jeremiah shows us that unwelcome speech may be for the good of the community. On another occasion, the prophet Jeremiah obeyed God's command to tell the truth about the people of Israel. Standing in the court of the temple, Jeremiah proclaimed the evil that the people were doing in order to give them a chance to repent. But instead of repenting, "the priests and the prophets and all the people laid hold of him, saying, 'You shall die!'" (Jer. 26:8). They imprisoned him in the depths of a cistern for his prophetic truth-telling about their evil. Jeremiah's challenging words were an expression of great courage and great love. Had the people listened to Jeremiah, the final stage of the exile of the people of Judah may well have been avoided.

Jeremiah could have made his own the words of Psalm 27:12: "Do not give me up to the will of my adversaries, for false witnesses have risen against me, and they are breathing out violence." Likewise, the Psalmist in Psalm 35 is fighting for his life; his enemies are stealthily hunting him, seeking to destroy him. They are "malicious witnesses" who encourage others to slander him, as soon as he appears weak in any way (Ps. 35:11, 15). The Psalmist eloquently depicts a campaign of evil speech: "For they do not speak peace, but they conceive deceitful words against those who are quiet in the land. They open wide their mouths against me; they say, 'Aha, Aha, our eyes have seen it'" (Ps. 35:20–21). Such persons employ lies in order to destroy a person whose power they want and who are made vulnerable by present weakness.

As there are false prophets, there are also false leaders. The book of Daniel tells a story of how false leaders use devious speech to prey upon others. There was a faithful woman named Susannah who would take walks each day in her garden. Two nearby elders of Israel made plans to force themselves on her. When they secretly entered her garden, they threatened her with false words: "If you refuse, we will testify against you that a young man was with you" (Dan. 13:21). Susannah refused, and the elders called the assembly of the people together and falsely accused her of adultery. When Susannah cried out to God for deliverance from these false witnesses, God roused a young man named Daniel who had the people examine each of the elders separately in order to catch them in their lies. Having discovered the false accusations of the elders, the assembly then punished the two elders with the very punishment that they had corruptly tried to impose on Susannah. Although God does not often intervene miraculously, God is always on the side of truthful speech. He condemns those who abuse and intimidate others through false speech.

The Power of the Tongue

The Letter of James has strong words against speaking unjustly against our neighbor. James states, "If any think they are religious, and do not bridle their tongues but deceive their hearts, their religion is worthless" (James 1:26). If we speak out of hatred or unrighteous anger, we can only do harm. Such words, lacking truth, harm our relationship with God and neighbor. James teaches, "Let everyone be quick to listen, slow to speak, slow to anger; for your anger does not produce God's righteousness" (James 1:19). How often we are not "quick to listen" but instead quick to anger, quick to criticize, quick to speak ill of others either behind their backs or to their faces.

James compares our tongues to the rudder of a ship. Just as a small rudder steers a large ship, so also can a person's small tongue steer the course of events with tremendous impact upon people's lives. He compares the tongue to a little fire that can set ablaze a great forest. He warns that, in our speech, we do not easily avoid lies and false insinuations. Therefore, as he says, "The tongue is an unrighteous world among our members, staining the whole body, setting on fire the cycle of nature, and set on fire by hell" (James 3:6). This may seem to be a bit strong!

Fortunately, James helps us to understand his rationale more clearly. He observes that human beings have immense abilities for taming creation. We have tamed some animals and birds; we have even tamed the ocean so as to be able to make good use of it. But taming our own tongue is much more difficult. As he points out, we use the tongue—speech—to "bless the Lord and Father" while at the same time we may be using this very same instrument to "curse those who are made in the likeness of God" (James 3:9). There is indeed something gravely wrong here. Why cannot the instrument of praise—namely, our tongue or speech—be kept pure?

James uses images drawn from nature to help us see the problem more acutely. He asks rhetorically, "Does a spring pour forth from the same opening both fresh and brackish water? Can a fig tree, my brothers and sisters, yield olives, or a grapevine figs? No more can salt water yield fresh" (James 3:11–12). The point is that, if indeed our mouths are both praising God and slandering human beings, then our mouths are not pure because our hearts are not pure.

In contrast to words that lash out in unjust anger and hurtful criticism, James exhorts Christians to seek wisdom first in order to have speech grounded in the truth. He writes, "the wisdom from above is first pure, then peaceable, gentle, willing to yield, full of mercy and good fruits, without a trace of partiality or hypocrisy" (James 3:17). Such wisdom from above opens up a new perspective on our speech since we are invited to see situations as God sees them and not merely as our egos initially react to them. Such peaceable and gentle wisdom allows us to be straightforward in our communications with others. Thus, we become more open to reason and full of mercy. Taking care with words is crucial for the well-being of persons and communities. He calls upon those who speak to do so with humility, calling upon God's transformative gift of wisdom.

Jesus likewise emphasizes frequently the importance of our inner dispositions in shaping our communication with one another. He helps us to understand that we have a hard time perceiving the world as it is, when he teaches in his Sermon on the Mount: "The eye is the lamp of the body. So, if your eye is healthy, your whole body will be full of light; but if your eye is not unhealthy, your whole body will be full of darkness. If then the light in you is darkness, how great is the darkness!" (Matt. 6:22–23). Jesus is not talking merely about physical eyes or physical sight but about moral perception, our ability to perceive truth and goodness. When anger or pride blinds us to truth, we will be "dark" interiorly—that is, in terms of our openness to and expressiveness of the light of truth.

Jesus also teaches about the source of evil speech by reflecting upon what makes a person clean before God. God intended the Mosaic food laws to separate the Israelites from their idolatrous neighbors. In his divine authority as the Messiah, Jesus reveals the symbolic meaning of these food laws and indicates that they will not be needed in his inaugurated kingdom.[5] He states, "There is nothing outside a person that by going in can defile," given that what truly defiles us is what comes from our broken interior life, from our heart (Mark 7:15). We must contend with the thoughts and temptations that we experience in our hearts and that all too easily flow forth into actions—such as evil speech or slander.

Jesus warns against "evil intentions, . . . fornication, theft, murder, adultery, avarice, wickedness, deceit, licentiousness, envy, slander, pride, folly" (Mark 7:21–22). All of these things deeply harm the persons who harbor them as well as those whom they afflict. It may seem that, on this list, slander or deceit or evil speech against our neighbor are among the least sins that we have to worry about. Certainly, speaking falsely about our neighbor or insinuating that our neighbor has done something of which he or she is actually innocent causes harm to our neighbor. But at least such speech is obviously far better than murder! Or is it?

In his Sermon on the Mount, Jesus reveals the path of living rightly with God and neighbor. In a telling manner, the first moral teaching he addresses concerns evil speech. Jesus says, "You have heard that it was said to those of ancient times, 'You shall not murder'; and 'whoever murders shall be liable to judgment.' But I say to you that if you are angry with a brother or sister, you will be liable to judgment; and if you insult a brother or sister, you will be liable to the council; and if you say, 'You fool,' you will be liable to the hell of fire" (Matt. 5:21–22). The tongue is assigned a foundational role in the new kingdom of God. Living well in the kingdom of God is incompatible with our all-too-habitual patterns of gossip, insults, and rash judgments. The inner desire to harm another person may

---

5. For further discussion, see Matthew Levering, *Engaging the Doctrine of Israel: A Christian Israelology in Dialogue with Ongoing Judaism* (Eugene, OR: Cascade, forthcoming).

well be quite strong in a person who lacks the power to do external damage.

Such a perspective helps us to hear Jesus' teaching that speech is a matter for our eternal judgment. He teaches, "I tell you, on the day of judgment you will have to give an account for every careless word you utter; for by your words you will be justified, and by your words you will be condemned" (Matt. 12:37). Let us place this role of speech in judgment alongside Jesus' parable of the sheep and the goats in which our eternal judgment is determined by what we did to the least of our brothers and sisters and so did to him. Who we become, and thus how we will be judged, is a combination of our deeds and words. Our words matter. They express who we are and indeed shape who we become. The renewed kingdom of God is a kingdom of rightly-ordered actions and speech. After all, "the Spirit is the truth" (1 John 5:6) and believers are to be "walking in the truth" (3 John 4).

The Gospels powerfully disclose how harmful speech easily leads to harmful deeds against the most innocent among us. In the Gospel of Mark, for example, we find that the Jewish leaders, in seeking evidence against Jesus that could justify his execution by the Romans, succeeded in finding many who "gave false testimony against him" even though "their testimony did not agree" (Mark 14:56). Their words played a decisive role in the eventual Crucifixion of Jesus. Paul points out that, if the Jewish leaders had recognized the Lord, "they would not have crucified the Lord of glory" (1 Cor. 2:8). We might well imagine that the Jewish leaders would have done better if fewer scribes and Pharisees had chosen to speak with Jesus only "to trap him in what he said" (Mark 12:13), rather than with a real desire to learn from him.

Painful Speech

Truthful speech nonetheless may require painful speech. Paul tells the Corinthians that "there have to be factions among you, for only so will it become clear who among you are genuine" (1 Cor. 11:19). Jesus himself says, "I have not come to bring peace, but a sword. For I have come to set a man against his father, and a daughter against her mother, and a daughter-in-law against her mother-in-law; and one's foes will members of one's own household" (Matt. 10:34–36). Even though the Church is the inaugurated kingdom, the Church is also a fully human community, which means that truth often emerges from the midst of a painful debate, in which even families and friends may become divided. Responding to distortions of truth and love may well lead to pain and even division.

In his prophetic role, Jesus himself used painful speech to sharply correct some of the leaders of his people Israel—as well as some of the future leaders of his Church. With regard to the latter, for instance, Jesus commends Peter for recognizing him as the Messiah, but when Peter tries to persuade Jesus not to accept the cross, Jesus sharply rebukes him. Jesus tells Peter, "Get behind me, Satan! You are a stumbling block to me; for you are setting your mind not on divine things but on human things" (Matt. 16:23). Peter does not turn away after Jesus' sharp correction but continues to follow Jesus.

Jesus speaks sharply against the scribes and Pharisees of his day, many of whom do not listen to his words. Accusing the leaders of being "hypocrites" or "blind guides," Jesus lists seven "woes" (Matt. 23). He accuses the leaders of focusing on their own power and prestige, valuing human things over divine things, pretending to be righteous, and so on. All this is unfortunately recognizable in religious leadership across the centuries—and not only among the clergy but also among laypeople who partake in leadership. Jesus' speech is appropriately biting. We need to remember that our hearts lay open before God's sight.

Due to human fallenness, false prophets and false leaders will continue within the Church. In 2 Peter, we encounter the grim news that "there will be false teachers among you, who will secretly bring in destructive opinions. They will even deny the Master who bought them. . . . And in their greed they will exploit you with deceptive words" (2 Pet. 2:1–3). As noted earlier, in Paul's farewell address to the Christians in Ephesus, he warns that "savage wolves will come in among you, not sparing the flock. Some even from your own group will come distorting the truth in order to entice the disciples to follow them" (Acts 20:29–30). We cannot assume that all Christians will be genuinely "filled with the Holy Spirit" and speak "the word of the Lord with boldness" (Acts 4:31). But this news should not make us live in paranoid fear as though such false teachers can be greater than Christ. We must simply keep our eyes on "Jesus Christ, and him crucified" (1 Cor. 2:2), trusting that he will guide his Church through trials.

God ensures that the Church, indwelt by the Holy Spirit and governed by the ascended Christ at the right hand of the Father, does not fail in speaking the truth of the Gospel. In "the faithful city" (Zech. 8:3) that Christ inaugurates, God promises that the people will "speak the truth to one another, render . . . judgments that are true and make for peace, . . . and love no false oath" (Zech. 8:16–17). We know that "the gates of Hades shall not prevail" against the Church built by Christ upon the foundation-stone of Peter's faith and office (Matt. 16:18).

We should always heed Paul's advice: "Let no evil talk come out of your mouths, but only such as is good for edifying, as fits the occasion, that it may impart grace to those who hear" (Eph. 4:29).

Although there will be occasions when we must acquaint our audience with negative things about another person, such occasions and audiences should be chosen carefully and should be likely much rarer than our common practice. Otherwise a proclivity toward gossip and slander develops—a proclivity toward enjoying "evil talk" perhaps as a means of exercising power over others or simply trying to maintain illusory control over situations. But lest a Christian become so averse to speaking negative things that the Christian refuses to hold others accountable, Paul reminds us only several verses later that we must "take no part in the unfruitful works of darkness, but instead expose them" (Eph. 5:11).

Paul calls the followers of Jesus to a spiritual maturity in light of our knowledge "of the full stature of Christ" (Eph. 4:13). We must strive to relinquish deceit and instead excel in "speaking the truth in love" (Eph. 4:15). True love requires "speaking the truth" even when painful. By speaking truth to each other in love, we strengthen the bonds of charity that unite us in Christ. With respect to strengthening the unity of the Body of Christ, Paul exhorts us, "Therefore, putting away falsehood, let all of us speak the truth to our neighbors, for we are members of one another" (Eph. 4:25). Truthful and loving speech builds up the Body of Christ.

Speech that Glorifies God

What is speech ultimately for? We have seen the corruption of speech in the name of domination and control of others. We have seen the call to truthful speech even to the point of challenging others. Let us consider here the role of speech in proclaiming the truth of God and glorifying him. Here we shift from considering speech *about* God to considering speech *to* God.

The Psalms guide Israel and the Church in faithfully addressing God. How should a creature properly speak to its Creator? To do so, the creature has to set aside its illusion of power and control and recognize that the Creator alone is God. Psalm 27 depicts the absolute trust that we should have in God. It begins, "The Lord is my light and my salvation; whom shall I fear? The Lord is the stronghold of my life; of whom shall I be afraid?" (Ps. 27:1). Similarly, Psalm 121 describes the creature's great desire for help from the Creator: "I will lift up my eyes to the hills—from where will come my help? My help comes from the LORD, who made heaven and earth" (Ps. 121:1–2). Psalm 73 emphasizes that the Lord alone suffices: "Whom have I in heaven but you? And there is nothing on earth that I desire other than you. My flesh and my heart may fail, but God is the strength of my heart and my portion forever" (Ps. 73:25–26). In praying these Psalms, the renewed community speaks from the truth of its position as humble creatures depending on God for everything.

The renewal of speech reaches its climax in the praise of God. Psalm 92 begins, "It is good to give thanks to the LORD, to sing praises to your name, O Most High" (Ps. 92:1). Psalm 117 begins, "Praise the LORD, all you nations! Extol him, all you peoples" (Ps. 117:1). The call of all of the nations of the earth is to praise the Lord. The role of the creature is to render thanksgiving and praise to God the Creator and Redeemer of the human race. Given the importance of giving praise to God, the last Psalm acts as a fitting conclusion to all of the Psalms by reiterating the power and beauty of letting our speech glorify God. In the six verses of Psalm 150, the expressions "Praise the LORD," "Praise God," and "Praise him" appear thirteen times! Fittingly, the Psalmist concludes, "Let everything that breathes praise the LORD! Praise the LORD!" (Ps. 150:6).

Praise of God is the supreme mode of speech and will remain in heaven. In heaven, gone will be the perverted desire to hide ourselves from the truth or to exploit others through false speech. Also gone will be the need to confess our sins or to call others to abandon theirs. The only thing left will be for intelligent creatures to sing forever of the glories of God.

The book of Revelation helps us to imagine heavenly speech. The first speech we witness is that of four spiritual creatures worshiping God: "Holy, holy, holy, the Lord God Almighty, who was and is and is to come" (Rev. 4:8). After praising God simply for who he is, the four creatures praise God for being the Creator: "You are worthy, our Lord and God, to receive glory and honor and power, for you created all things, and by your will they existed and were created" (Rev. 4:11). Next, the creatures are joined by twenty-four elders, the prayers of the saints, and the voices of many angels to praise not only God the Creator but also the Lamb that was slain: "Worthy is the Lamb that was slaughtered to receive power and wealth and wisdom and might and honor and glory and blessing!" (Rev. 5:12). To show that the Lamb shares in God's unique honor, all of creation cries out, "To the seated on the throne and to the Lamb be blessing and honor and glory and might forever and ever!" (Rev. 5:13). Here is speech in its heavenly form, speech perfected, speech that sings the goodness of God the Creator and of the Lamb for all eternity. Here is truthful speech indeed.

Conclusion

Toward the end of his great prayer in the upper room, Jesus prays to his Father on behalf of his disciples: "Sanctify them in the truth" (John 17:17). He elsewhere tells his disciples, "You will know the truth, and the truth will make you free" (John 8:32). To be his followers, we need to be sanctified in the truth and we need to know the truth—the truth of his divine love, a truth whose profession requires humility. Through the Holy Spirit, we need to live this truth by obeying his commandment to "love one another as I have loved you"—namely, even at the cost of our own life (John 15:12).

Thus, the Catholic vocation in the world involves the countercultural refusal to malign and complain about one another. It also involves the equally countercultural willingness to witness to unpopular truths, when God calls us to do this. Above all, we must bear testimony to Jesus and the truth of divine love, divine justice, and divine mercy. We can begin by being willing to affirm the Gospel publicly, for, as Jesus says, "Whoever denies me before others will be denied before the angels of God" (Luke 12:9). To acknowledge Jesus' Lordship publicly cannot be done, however, if we are spewing hateful speech, since this would be a counter-witness.

In a world that is often governed by our disordered passions rather than by justice and truth, speaking the truth in love may involve a cross. Jesus, the crucified Lord, teaches that we should "have no fear" of the powerful persons who seek to suppress the truth, since "nothing is covered up that will not be uncovered, and nothing secret that will not become known" in the final judgment (Matt. 10:26). He assures us that we can trust the Holy Spirit to give us the words that we need in order to speak both boldly and charitably, while avoiding any prideful sense that we ourselves know everything (see Matt. 10:19–20). In living in this way, we show our allegiance to Jesus.

By contrast, the devil "does not stand in the truth" and "is a liar and the father of lies" (John 8:44). Speaking the truth in love, then, we show that we truly are no longer in our sins (see 1 Cor. 15:17). Evil speech may be able to add something to our worldly power, but by separating us from Christ and by harming others, it is ultimately a refusal to love whose consequences will redound upon ourselves and our communities. Since Christ has been raised and has poured out his Spirit, we are called to renounce the "father of lies" and no longer seek to destroy each other by means of denigration and detraction. We are called instead to testify in love with our tongue to the Lord who deserves all praise.

Today, having received the healing power of Jesus Christ, we may choose to react no longer from our wounded nature but now to speak from the renewed image of God in us. Let us hasten to heed James's call: "Do not speak evil against one another" (James 4:11).

CHAPTER 10

Are the Saints of the Church
Too Strange to Be Relevant?

"So great a cloud of witnesses"
(Hebrews 12:1)

Today, we admire the achievements of doctors, scientists, artists, and entrepreneurs because of the concrete ways that they have enhanced human lives. Likewise, we follow the activities of people in music, films, and sports who exhibit creativity and excellence. Their lives attract us because they seem to be lived to the full, often with the privileges of wealth, fame, and so on. If the saints enter our minds, however, our first thought may be of a strange and constricted lot, leading unappealing lives of self-sacrifice, religious zeal, and the seeming refusal of every pleasure.

Even for those who admire the deeds of the canonized saints of the Church, there may seem to be no reason to emulate their *faith*. Stephen Bullivant and his co-authors asked self-identified lapsed Catholics what they miss about the Church, and "many respondents . . . singled out the saints, in several cases mentioning them by name."[1] But for these respondents, emulating the saints' belief in Christ and devotion to the Church is no longer viewed as reasonable—as shown by the fact that these respondents are ex-Catholics. Furthermore, for more than a few Catholics, the saints are not really human but

---

1. Stephen Bullivant, Catherine Knowles, Hannah Vaughan-Spruce, and Bernadette Durcan, *Why Catholics Leave, What They Miss, and How They Might Return* (New York: Paulist Press, 2019), 74.

rather are perfect people who did not struggle with personal failings or defects. On this view, the saints are *them* and not even possibly *us*.

In fact, such views miss out on what a saint really is. Christians speak generally of the faithful, both the living and those who have gone before us, as the "communion of saints." A saint in the strict sense is simply someone who is in heaven—not necessarily someone who was canonized. The Church assumes that the vast majority of saints have never been officially recognized. That is why we celebrate All Saints Day on November 1—to honor the countless people who, by the grace of the Holy Spirit, lived lives of self-sacrificial love in configuration to Christ, and are now with him in glory.

Jesus himself, as the Savior, is the only one about whom it can be said that "from his fullness have we all received, grace upon grace" (John 1:16). His life is the model for every saint, although every saint can also say with John the Baptist that he is not even worthy to untie Christ's sandals (John 1:27). Given that the Spirit was present in Old Testament times—and indeed has been at work since the creation of all things—there have *always* been saintly people whose lives point to Christ. Through their faith, the saints have discovered that our true vocation is love,[2] embodied in an infinite number of ways in accord with the particular talents of the person and needs of the era.

At Mundelein Seminary in the Archdiocese of Chicago, there is a chapel where the seminarians pray and where Mass is celebrated for the community. In the chapel are stained-glass windows containing iconographic images of saints from around the world. The images not only radiate heroic faith and love but also manifest the truly "catholic" or global presence and impact of saints. The chapel includes saints from almost every continent and from many different periods of history. Simply sitting in this chapel is a very moving

2. See Thérèse of Lisieux, *Story of a Soul: The Autobiography of St. Thérèse of Lisieux*, 3rd ed., trans. John Clarke, OCD (Washington, DC: ICS Publications, 1996).

experience when one appreciates how powerfully Christ has worked in these lives throughout the world.

Likewise, Brandon Vogt, in *Saints and Social Justice*, tells the stories of beatified or canonized Christians, including Teresa of Kolkata, Peter Claver, Frances of Rome, Anne Marie Jahouvey, Roque González, Thomas More, Pier Giorgio Frassati, Vincent de Paul, Benedict of Nursia, Dorothy Day (recognized as a "Servant of God"), John Paul II, Damien of Molokai, Giles, and Isidore the Farmer.[3] One comes away with a profound sense of the breadth and beauty of the vocation of love that is open to all of us.

Nevertheless, the saints today are not particularly popular even among many Catholics. By comparison to the famous leaders and celebrities in our society, the saints may seem far less notable or interesting. Can the Bible give us any assistance in valuing the saints and making them a meaningful part of our lives?

In answer, we will suggest that the saints are *witnesses*, just as we are called to be. The lives of the saints focus our attention upon the death and Resurrection of Jesus Christ. They thus point us to the true *source* of hope, mercy, love, and life. In ways unique to each saint, they show us how Christ bears fruit in every generation and, indeed, in our own lives too.

Witnesses in the Times before Christ

The Letter to the Hebrews proclaims, "Since we are surrounded by so great a cloud of witnesses, let us also lay aside every weight and sin that clings so closely, and let us run with perseverance the race that is set before us" (Heb. 12:1). Who are these witnesses, and to what are they witnessing? According to Hebrews, they are people who have known the God of Israel and who have responded to God with faith.

---

3. Brandon Vogt, *Saints and Social Justice: A Guide to Changing the World* (Huntington, IN: Our Sunday Visitor, 2014).

Faith involves "the assurance of things hoped for" and "the conviction of things not seen" (Heb. 11:1). The witnesses have believed in something that cannot be seen—namely, that "the world was created by the word of God" (Heb. 11:3 RSV-CE). What is more, they have hoped, with the assurance of faith, in the saving providence of the Creator. People who have faith believe in the invisible God and believe that God "rewards those who seek him" (Heb. 11:6).

Hebrews 11 depicts a kind of hall of fame—or, rather, a hall of faith—of great heroes from the Old Testament. Abel is praised for his faith in God, a faith giving rise to Abel's righteous sacrifice. Enoch's faith led God to spare him death. Noah's faith led God to approve him and to spare him from the flood. Abraham's faith made him willing to leave his country and journey to the Promised Land. As we noted above, Abraham even was willing to sacrifice his son Isaac—which in the end God ensured did not happen—because the patriarch knew that God has power over all life, including the power to raise the dead.[4] Sarah's faith led her to believe God's promise that she would bear a child despite her advanced age. Moses' faith enabled him to renounce the privileges of Pharaoh's court and instead to share in the suffering of God's people. In all of these examples, Hebrews makes clear that faith is the source of—and is expressed in—heroic deeds. Hebrews observes that "righteousness . . . comes by faith" and "without faith it is impossible to please [God]" (Heb. 11:6–7 RSV-CE). Faith here is the act of completely entrusting oneself to God. The fruit of such faith is that we become right with God.

Hebrews emphasizes that the faithful witnesses of Old Testament times sought a goal beyond this world. They were blessed to realize that this world was not their true home and to acknowledge that "they were strangers and foreigners on the earth" (Heb. 11:13).

---

4. For further discussion, see Leroy A. Huizenga, *The New Isaac: Tradition and Intertextuality in the Gospel of Matthew* (Leiden: Brill, 2009).

They hoped for the new creation, described in Hebrews as the city with lasting foundations "whose architect and builder is God" (Heb. 11:10). In this city, suffering, sin, and death will be no more. Although they died before seeing the consummation of their hope, they were already "witnesses" of its reality. In faith, they spiritually saw and welcomed their true homeland. Rather than cleaving to earthly things, they cleaved to God and "desire a better country, that is, a heavenly one" (Heb. 11:16). By cleaving to God and desiring to be with him in his city, they heroically risked their lives in order to serve God above anything else.

It must be acknowledged that the list of witnesses in Hebrews includes not only biblical figures known for great faithfulness but also biblical figures known for great faithlessness. The book names Gideon, Barak, Samson, Jephthah, David, Samuel, and the prophets, along with unnamed Israelites who accepted martyrdom for the sake of God's name. One might wonder how notable sinners such as Samson and Jephthah made it onto a list of witnesses to faith. Hebrews does not deny that Israel's heroes were often sinners. For political reasons within the royal courts, Abraham twice pretended that Sarah was his sister, essentially giving her to someone else for sexual purposes, though God ensured that no adultery ensued. Sarah was cruel to her slave Hagar. Jacob cheated his foolish brother Esau. Moses was banned by God from crossing the Jordan. David committed sins with the eventual result that his own son Absalom raised an army against him.

In the Bible, even the greatest believers still need a savior. To say this is not to excuse the toleration of sin in ourselves or in the people of God. Hebrews also exhorts Christians to strive for "the holiness without which no one will see the Lord" (Heb. 12:14). Witnesses to faith are not perfectly faithful; they are witnesses ultimately to God's perfect faithfulness. Even with their defects and sins, Israel's heroes accomplished great deeds in God's plan of salvation in distinction from their sin. By their faith, they cooperated with God's Spirit and power to accomplish great deeds and to desire God and his plan above all things even if they had not done so throughout their lives. This is surely comforting for us who hear of these great witnesses of faith.

The Witness of Risking Everything for God

Let us see what further we might learn about these heroic witnesses to God and his promises. The book of Genesis commends a faith in God that means risking one's own earthly security and status. We see this expressed in the story of God's covenant with Noah.

While Noah's neighbors went about their regular lives, Noah built a great ark at God's command. Even building a house, let alone an ark, is a project that requires significant resources. Noah's faith in God's word enabled him to take this risk. In contrast to Noah and his ark stands the story of the citizens of the land of Shinar, who built the city and tower of Babel. They had no command from God but only sought to fulfill their desire for power and honor. While making their preparations, they told each other, "Come, let us build ourselves a city, and a tower with its top in the heavens, and let us make a name for ourselves; otherwise we shall be scattered abroad upon the face of the whole earth" (Gen. 11:4). They thus labored to elevate themselves to the divine regions by their own strength, and to avoid being scattered in a way that would ruin their worldly security and status.

Whereas Noah's faithfulness saved the human race, the proud tower of Babel led only to the earthly dispersion and chaos that are so feared by earthly citizens. The Bible unveils a counterintuitive pattern here: seeking earthly security with earthly resources is bound to end in failure. Jesus speaks with the same voice as Genesis as he echoes the same truth: "For those who want to save their life will lose it, and those who lose their life for my sake will save it" (Luke 9:24).

When God called Abraham—who was at the time called "Abram"—he gave the patriarch a command. Every command given by God assigns the dignity of choice to the recipient of the command. God does not force Abraham to obey but calls him to do so. In this case, the command to Abraham was rather stark: "Go from your country and your kindred and your father's house to the land that I will show you" (Gen. 12:1). God promised that, if Abram did this, he would make Abram's descendants into a great nation and Abram's name a blessing. Abram freely chose to trust God and believe in him. According to Genesis 15:6, Abram "believed the LORD; and the LORD reckoned it to him as righteousness." It was Abram's faith—his willingness to believe God's word and to suffer for it—that became the patriarch's most distinctive character trait. Obeying God's will led to much suffering for Abraham as he sojourned among strangers, but Abraham obeyed because he trusted in God.

Moses is another great faithful witness. Moses was a Hebrew who had been raised in Pharaoh's courts and had access to all of the privileges that were denied to the Hebrews in Egypt. After killing an Egyptian who was beating a Hebrew slave, Moses fled from Pharaoh. He lost everything and ended up in the land of Midian, exiled not only from the riches of Egypt but also from his own people, the Israelites. His new job was to tend the sheep of his Midianite father-in-law.[5] But while Moses was in the wilderness, God came to him. The angel of God instructed Moses, "Remove the sandals from your feet, for the place on which you are standing is holy ground" (Exod. 3:5).

---

5. For background, see Keith Bodner, *An Ark on the Nile: The Beginning of the Book of Exodus* (Oxford: Oxford University Press, 2016), 155–167.

We might think that Moses has hit the jackpot—God calls him and commissions him for a glorious task! But in fact, the grueling hardships that are to come make God's commission very difficult for Moses to accept. Having fled from Egypt where Pharaoh sought to kill him, Moses' task is now to return to Egypt and, without any military power, to lead away a throng of Israelite slaves that are doing heavy labor for their Egyptian masters. A doubtful venture indeed. Moses asks God, "Who am I that I should go to Pharaoh, and bring the Israelites out of Egypt?" (Exod. 3:11). This may seem like modesty, but it is also common sense in the face of an almost impossible mission.

Moses is not even sure that the Israelites remember their God after all the years of Egyptian slavery. He asks God's name, so as to be able to give it to the Israelites if he agrees to go speak to them. God tells him, "Thus you shall say to the Israelites, 'I AM has sent me to you,'" and God adds, "Thus you shall say to the Israelites, 'The LORD, the God of your ancestors, the God of Abraham, the God of Isaac, and the God of Jacob, has sent me to you'" (Exod. 3:14–15). He instructs Moses to tell the Israelites that God himself has seen their suffering and that God intends to remove them from Egypt and bring them to "a land flowing with milk and honey" (Exod. 3:17). And he promises that he himself will provide the compelling force that will persuade Pharaoh to set the large mass of Hebrew slaves free: "I will stretch out my hand and strike Egypt with all my wonders that I will perform in it; after that he will let you go" (Exod. 3:20). Moreover, God will make it so that the Israelites do not leave empty-handed but with rich gifts given them by the Egyptians.

Moses, however, knows well what Egypt is. At that time, it was one of the wealthiest and most powerful societies the world had ever known. Therefore, before believing God's word, Moses asks a few more questions as he seeks to point out that no one, let alone the Israelites, will believe what he says or follow him. For example, he complains that the Israelites will simply deny that God ever appeared to him, and he further bemoans that, because he is not eloquent in speech, no one will listen to him. The Lord responds with a demonstration of power: he transforms Moses' rod into a serpent; and he makes Moses leprous and then immediately heals him. God suggests that miracles such as these will persuade the people. With regard to Moses' lack of eloquence, God promises that, as the Creator, he can easily make Moses' speech persuasive.

But because of the extent of the risk and suffering involved—greater than even Moses himself could have anticipated—Moses still does not respond with faith. Instead, he tells God what any typical person would say. He says, "O my Lord, please send someone else" (Exod. 4:13).[6]

At this stage of the story, God becomes angry with Moses. After all, God has just performed miracles for Moses. Why can't Moses trust God in faith? But God does not give up on the man whom he has chosen to liberate his people. Instead, he gives Moses more help so that the reluctant liberator does not have to act alone. Moses' brother Aaron will do the public speaking for him.[7] This is enough to persuade Moses. He now fully gives himself in faith to the mission that God has for him.

Moses' "yes" to God does not take away suffering from his life. In fact, his "yes" results in great suffering. He will suffer Pharaoh's refusal to let Israel go and worship the Lord, and later he will suffer the complaining of the people of Israel in their wanderings in the

---

6. See Thomas B. Dozeman, *Exodus* (Grand Rapids, MI: Eerdmans, 2009), 143; he points out that the Hebrew of this verse is difficult to translate with certitude.

7. For historical-critical discussion of the figure of Aaron in relation to Moses, see Dozeman, *Exodus*, 143–145.

wilderness. But during his lifetime, Moses' intimacy with the Lord grows so much that we are told "the LORD used to speak to Moses face to face, as one speaks to a friend" (Exod. 33:11). Moses went from being unwilling and hesitant to being perhaps the greatest example of faith in God in Israel's history. And as with all the biblical patriarchs and matriarchs, he is considered a saint in the Catholic Church. To this day, the Roman Martyrology—the Holy See's official calendar of saints' feasts—lists his feast day: September 4.

Dwelling with God

When considering the biblical understanding of saints, we should not overlook the Maccabean martyrs, to whom Hebrews 11:35 likely refers when it states, "Others were tortured, refusing to accept release, in order to obtain a better resurrection." In the second century BC, many Jews chose to die at the hands of their Hellenistic persecutors rather than to violate the Mosaic Law by honoring false gods, eating unclean foods, and so on. The pagan king Antiochus, desiring to compel religious uniformity in the lands he had conquered, made even circumcising a baby or observing the sabbath a capital crime for the Jewish people. Those Jews who embraced the punishment of death rather than disobeying God's Law recognized that, although disobeying Antiochus might lead to their execution, God would reward their obedience eternally. The aged martyr Eleazar proclaimed, "Whether I live or die I will not escape the hands of the Almighty" (2 Macc. 6:26).

The second book of Maccabees recounts how a mother of seven sons willingly watched all her sons freely die rather than eat food forbidden by God. We read that "the brothers and their mother encouraged one another to die nobly, saying, 'The Lord God is watching over us and in truth has compassion on us'" (2 Macc. 7:5–6). The mother reminds her sons that it is more reasonable to die for one's

Creator than it is to live a few more years in shame and wickedness. She recounts her faith that "the Creator of the world . . . will in his mercy give life and breath back" to her sons in the world to come, because of the greatness of their love for God (2 Macc. 7:23). Each of her sons accepts death as part of the discipline that God justly inflicts for Israel's sins and their own sins. In faith, they place their "whole trust in the Lord" (2 Macc. 7:40).[8]

The witnesses of faith are part of the history by which God has been preparing his everlasting dwelling of peace. In Revelation, we find the goal of history in John's vision of "the holy city, the new Jerusalem, coming down out of heaven from God, prepared as a bride adorned for her husband" (Rev. 21:2). This is the homeland to which we look forward in faith: the intimate and everlasting dwelling of God with his people, in which "nothing accursed will be found" (Rev. 22:3).

Through the divine indwelling, believers even now experience a foretaste of this reality. In Revelation, we see the image of an eternal city in which God himself will dwell: "And I heard a loud voice from the throne saying, 'See, the home of God is among mortals. He will dwell with them; they will be his peoples, and God himself will be with them; he will wipe every tear from their eyes. Death will be no more; mourning and crying and pain will be no more, for the first things have passed away.'" (Rev. 21:3–4). This reality is not simply something that is to come in the future. The saints who have gone before us are already living with Christ, if not yet in the fullness of the new creation. On earth, Christians who live in faith and love also already belong to the inaugurated kingdom, which is the Church.

Faith seeks a home with God. In making a covenant with Abraham, God promised to build up a people who will dwell with God

---

8. For background to 2 Maccabees 7, see Jonathan A. Goldstein, *II Maccabees: A New Translation with Introduction and Commentary* (Garden City, NY: Doubleday, 1983), 291–317.

in the Promised Land. Abraham's grandson Jacob also received the promise of the covenant and, at the same time, saw a still greater vision: "A ladder set up on the earth, the top of it reaching to heaven; and behold, the angels of God were ascending and descending on it" (Gen. 28:12). Jacob's dream portrays God dwelling with his people with the dramatic result that the divide between heaven and earth is overcome. The earth is now suffused with the active presence of God. In the Gospel of John, Jesus presents himself as the fulfillment of Jacob's dream and therefore as the center of the everlasting covenant between God and his people. We see this image of fulfillment when Jesus tells Nathanael, "You will see heaven opened, and the angels of God ascending and descending upon the Son of Man" (John 1:51).

Faith bears witness that God has entered into a radically new relationship with the human race. God promises, "I will take you [Israel] as my people, and I will be your God" (Exod. 6:7); and "I the LORD dwell among the Israelites" (Num. 35:34). The cloud of witnesses is united by receiving this promise and by knowingly living in God's presence.

We read in the prophets that, after the exile, there will come a glorious day on which God will accomplish a wondrous restoration of Israel. Isaiah affirms to the people of Israel, "You shall be called My Delight Is in Her, and your land Married; for the LORD delights in you, and your land shall be married" (Isa. 62:4). On that day, God will dwell in stunning intimacy with his formerly faithless people. In the prophecy of Hosea, we find a similar promise: "On that day, says the LORD, you will call me, 'My husband.' . . . And I will take you for my wife forever; I will take you for my wife in righteousness and in justice, in steadfast love, and in mercy. I will take you for my wife in faithfulness; and you shall know the LORD" (Hosea 2:16, 19–20; see

Isa. 54).[9] The heroes of the faith give a shared witness to God's plan to dwell with us and to have us dwell with him.

Christ's Witness and the Witness of Christians

Jesus Christ fulfills the desire of the faith-filled witnesses of the Old Testament to dwell with God. In his Incarnation, he is revealed to be "Emmanuel" or "God is with us" (Matt. 1:23). Through his cross and Resurrection, Jesus brings about the long-desired and faithfully witnessed divine indwelling on an even greater level than could have been imagined. In the Gospel of John, his last words on the cross are "it is finished" (John 19:30). He is the perfect "bridegroom" (Mark 2:19–20; John 3:29). His "hour" (John 2:4) is the hour of the marriage of God and his people, foreshadowed by Jesus' miracle at the wedding at Cana. As noted above, Paul recognizes that the marriage of a man and a woman, who become "one flesh" (Gen. 2:24), is a sign that refers to the marital union of Christ and the Church (see Eph. 5:25–32).[10] The Bible could not express God's dwelling with us in any greater terms.

This new creation marked by supreme divine indwelling comes about in us as we are configured to the Lord by self-sacrificial love. According to Paul, we must die with Christ and be "dead to sin and alive to God" (Rom. 6:11). Dying with Christ involves sharing in his suffering. Thus Paul boasts in his own suffering, not for suffering's sake, but because his bodily witness to self-sacrificial love spreads the Gospel. He tells the Corinthians, "We are afflicted in every way, but not crushed; perplexed, but not driven to despair; persecuted, but not forsaken; struck down, but not destroyed; always carrying in the body the death of Jesus, so that the life of Jesus may also be visible

9. See Bo H. Lim and Daniel Castelo, *Hosea* (Grand Rapids, MI: Eerdmans, 2015), 74, 77.

10. See Rudolf Schnackenburg, *The Epistle to the Ephesians: A Commentary*, trans. Helen Heron (Edinburgh: T & T Clark, 1991), 254–256.

in our bodies" (2 Cor. 4:8–10). Death and suffering have been transformed in Jesus' own death and Resurrection. They are now ways of
witnessing to the new life of Jesus. Paul reiterates his point to help
his reader not miss this profound new truth: "While we live we are
always being given up to death for Jesus' sake, so that the life of Jesus
may be made visible in our mortal flesh" (2 Cor. 4:11).[11] Thus, in the
Christian understanding, Jesus Christ transforms death and suffering so they may bear witness to the glory of his risen life. Indeed,
throughout our life, we are to bear witness to the power of Christ's
saving death and his glorious Resurrection.

Christ teaches his disciples, "Servants are not greater than their
master. If they persecuted me, they will persecute you" (John 15:20).
But why should self-surrendering love lead to rejection and persecution? It is not solely that some people respond well to the witness of Christians whereas others do not. We can never know why
particular people reject Jesus. More deeply, we must ask why self-
surrendering love generates resistance even in our own hearts. Faith
and self-sacrificial love challenge us, and for that same reason they
can be repellent to us. The heroes of faith in the Old Testament and
Jesus Christ himself show that faith and love require fully trusting
God and pouring out oneself for others. This is very hard for us to do,
though it is possible through the Holy Spirit.

Christ therefore exhorts his disciples, "In the world you face persecution. But take courage; I have conquered the world" (John 16:33).
And he displays his victory, encouraging his followers in the most
dramatic way possible, by rising from the dead. Yet even if Christ
has already triumphed over sin and death, there will be an ongoing
tribulation that Christ's followers must patiently endure. The times
between Christ's Ascension and his return in glory will be marked

---

11. See Frank J. Matera, *II Corinthians: A Commentary* (Louisville, KY: Westminster John
Knox, 2003), 108–11.

by ongoing sufferings such as the world has always known, including natural disasters, wars, and persecutions (Luke 21). In this context, it can be difficult to hold fast to the claim that Christ has overcome this fallen world and has inaugurated a new creation. Christ cautions, "Be on guard so that your hearts are not weighed down with dissipation and drunkenness and the worries of this life" (Luke 21:34). He knows how easily our hearts become distracted and overwhelmed and turn away from the new reality made possible by his Resurrection. This is why we need to remember not only the life of Christ but also the life of so many saints who have lived between his time and our own. The saints are ongoing witnesses to the reality and power of Jesus' Resurrection.

In order to appreciate the saints with greater realism, it is helpful to contrast their lives with the lives of those who reject God and his guidance for living. To see the two ways of living in greater contrast, let us turn to the teachings of the Wisdom of Solomon. The author, after observing that God "does not delight in the death of the living," makes the paradoxical point that some humans make "a covenant" with death (Wis. 1:13, 16). Why would anyone "make a covenant" with death? People do so perhaps when they choose to believe that death is the end of everything, and so death paradoxically becomes a "friend" in reassuring them that nothing done in this life has lasting significance. In this nihilistic worldview, good deeds and evil deeds alike appear equally transient. Life becomes a quest for avoiding pain and seeking pleasure. We may without compunction eliminate anything that gets in our way.

For those holding this mistaken but common perspective, the meaning of life is to experience all the pleasures that we can before we are swallowed up by annihilation. Since "reason is a spark kindled by the beating of our hearts" rather than evidence of an intelligent

Creator, the answer is to "enjoy the good things that exist" and to
"crown ourselves with rosebuds before they wither" (Wis. 2:2, 6, 8).[12]
Nothing ultimately has any meaning one way or another, so it is fair
to conclude that "our might [should] be our law of right, for what is
weak proves itself to be useless" (Wis. 2:11). Those who live in this
manner have indeed "made a covenant" with the disordered desires
and death associated with this present life. They have chosen to be at
home in the fallen world.

By contrast, the saints, as witnesses of faith, guide us to "set [our]
minds on things that are above" (Col. 3:2). They demonstrate that
the goal of life is not found in seeking one's own comfort in this
world but in seeking to live in accord with God's plan by the power of
his Spirit. Not every way of seeking one's own comfort and avoiding
one's own pain is appropriate for the human person. Some actions
are wrong, and some ways of living harm us and others. Thus, lovers
of the fallen world will inevitably fall into conflict with those who
love God. Wisdom speaks of this conflict from the point of view of
those in love with earthly power: "The righteous man . . . is incon-
venient to us and opposes our actions" (Wis. 2:12). In the end, the
worldly, who may well be professed Christians, may even go so far as
to "condemn [the righteous man] to a shameful death" (Wis. 2:20).
Those who fail to trust God fail to see the truth of reality as disclosed
by faith. Faith knows that God is on the side of those who trust in
him and that this life is not the end.

The Wisdom of Solomon holds that, in the end, the wicked will
discover their terrible error. They will ask, "What has our arrogance
profited us? And what good has our boasted wealth brought us?" They
will finally come to recognize that "all those things [their pleasures]
have vanished like a shadow, and like a rumor that passes by"

---

12. See David Winston, *The Wisdom of Solomon: A New Translation with Introduction and Commentary* (Garden City, NY: Doubleday, 1979), 114–119.

(Wis. 5:8–9). By contrast, the saints, the great "cloud of witnesses," are able to see the truth that will eventually be made manifest to all. They live in accordance with this knowledge, even if this new way of living seems strange to worldly eyes. In this way, the saints live—and so encourage us to live—"on earth as it is in heaven."

Witnesses of Hope in the Midst of Suffering and Death

Faithful Christians witness to the hope of resurrection to eternal life and they desire that everyone share in that hope. This hope calls us to refuse to restrict our love. Paul tells the early Christians in Corinth, "We have spoken frankly to you Corinthians; our heart is open wide to you. There is no restriction in our affections, but only in yours" (2 Cor. 6:11–12). For the witnesses of Christ, there is no desire that any enemy perish. Quite the opposite: the witnesses of Christ imitate Christ's great love for sinners and his desire for the salvation of sinners. All of us have experienced what sin is like; we know the internal misery that sinners endure. We therefore rejoice in Christ's mercy toward sinners and seek to emulate it. Paul calls himself "the very least of all the saints" (Eph. 3:8) and yearns that every person will come to "know the love of Christ which surpasses knowledge" (Eph. 3:19). Yet even when we have entrusted our lives to Christ, each of us still needs to pray with the Psalmist: "Do not remember the sins of my youth or my transgressions; according to your steadfast love remember me, for your goodness' sake, O LORD!" (Ps. 25:7).

To sustain such repentance and love in the midst of an often-hostile world, the Christian needs courage or determination. A strong impediment to imitating the way of the saints is the natural fear of suffering and death. To say the least, even believers are often reluctant to follow the path of the cross insofar as it entails personal risk in the present life. One of the ironies is that tribulations are a fixture of this life whether we follow Christ or not. Christ does not promise that we will avoid suffering but that he will help us to over-come fear with faith.

The Letter to the Hebrews speaks of people "who all their lives were held in slavery" due to "fear of death" (Heb. 2:15). Such fear can indeed hold a person in a vise, causing him or her to experi-ence hidden or overt despair about the possibility of faith and hope. Job expresses the roots of this despair when he complains to God, "Your hands fashioned and made me; and now you turn and destroy me" (Job 10:8; cf. 16:7–14). Even for those who strive to believe in life after death, fear of suffering and death may be so overwhelming that it is difficult to remember any principles other than trying to avoid suffering and prolong this earthly life at whatever cost. But Jesus instructs his disciples in his Farewell Discourse in John: "This is my commandment, that you love one another as I have loved you. No one has greater love than this, to lay down one's life for one's friends" (John 15:12–13). It is not a question of *whether* we will expe-rience suffering and death but of *how* we will choose to encounter those realities.

In response to our natural fear of suffering and death, Paul calls us to see that death has been changed once and for all by Christ cru-cified. When we receive the gift of Christ's self-sacrificial love, we will find that the Spirit has released our hearts and minds from the slav-ery of cleaving to our own bodily life in this world. Paul says of him-self, "We are treated as imposters, and yet are true; as unknown, and yet are well known; as dying, and see—we are alive; as punished, and yet not killed; as sorrowful, yet always rejoicing; as poor, yet making many rich; as having nothing, and yet possessing everything" (2 Cor. 6:8–10). Christian life experienced from the inside is far richer than it may appear to those outside. Paul appears as though he must be the most miserable of human beings, but in fact he possesses "everything." In faith, he is truly free to pour himself out in love. He has received a participation in Christ's own life.

Paul lived with such courage and determination, in the face of many persecutions, because he let Christ live in him. Even his immense bravery was not merely his own. In the book of Acts, when he has been harassed and jailed for preaching the Gospel, Paul turns to the Lord for comfort and strength. "That night," Acts tells us, "the Lord stood near him and said, 'Keep up your courage! For just as you have testified for me in Jerusalem, so you must bear witness also at Rome'" (Acts 23:11; emphasis added). The Lord promised Paul and promises us strength and perseverance as long as we, rather than trusting in our own strength, continually turn to him. He speaks to us personally as he says, "Keep up your courage!"

Not only may Christians find courage to suffer *for* Christ, they also find courage to do so *with* Christ. Christians no longer suffer alone. They are members of one Body that extends across time, place, and even into heaven. Moreover, they are members with Christ as their Head. Christ thus suffers in them and with them. Paul teaches this mystery of suffering when he writes to the early Christians that he even rejoices in his sufferings, for through them he shares intimately in the sufferings of his Lord and Savior. "In my flesh," he writes, "I am completing what is lacking in Christ's afflictions for the sake of his body, that is, the church" (Col. 1:24). Christ's suffering is complete in himself but not yet in his Body—namely, in us. When we suffer, since we no longer suffer alone, Christ suffers with us, we suffer with Christ. As Christ's suffering redeemed the whole world, so also Christian suffering helps to share the fruits of that redemption with his Body. The saints show us how to bear our sufferings with greater endurance, knowing that no suffering is in vain since

Christ dwells in us. When joined to Christ, even our sufferings have redemptive value. Nothing in our life is wasted.

Because the Spirit has poured the love of Christ into Paul's heart and mind, nothing external can separate the Apostle from his hope in God's promises. His whole life has been reshaped by the coming glory made available through the death and Resurrection of Jesus Christ. He no longer fears "hardship, or distress, or persecution, or famine, or nakedness, or peril, or sword" (Rom. 8:35). So long as he has faith, none of this can separate him from the Lord who has conquered sin and death. The source of Paul's faith and love flows not from his own meager power but from the power of the living God who has called and chosen him as a witness by grace.

In his First Letter to Corinthians, Paul shows the strength of his hope in Christ's Resurrection by comparing it to life without such hope. In the early Church, to be an Apostle one had to have accompanied Jesus in his ministry or been a "witness . . . to his resurrection" (Acts 1:22). To be a Christian today shares in that same reality: to be a witness to the Resurrection, to live a life that is different because Jesus rose from the dead so that we might be saved. Let us listen carefully to Paul's blunt language. Paul draws out the logic for his readers: "If Christ has not been raised, then our proclamation has been in vain and your faith has been in vain" (1 Cor. 15:14). As a gifted preacher, Paul repeats the same truth: "If Christ has not been raised, your faith is futile and you are still in your sins" (1 Cor. 15:17). Christ's Resurrection removes our sins and makes our faith efficacious.

Moreover, Christ's Resurrection unlocks the door to heaven. Paul leads his readers to recognize that Christian hope rests in eternal life: "If for this life only we have hoped in Christ, we are of all people most to be pitied" (1 Cor. 15:19). As if that were not enough, he draws the counterfactual conclusion, "If the dead are not raised, 'Let us eat and drink, for tomorrow we die'" (1 Cor. 15:32; cf. Wis. 2:6–9). Everything we do in this life is changed by belief in Christ's Resurrection and the resulting hope in our resurrection unto eternal life.

The witness of the saints reminds us that it is not only life that has been changed by the Paschal Mystery; Christ's Passion and Resurrection have changed death as well. Death is especially hard to understand in our contemporary culture. We tend not to want to talk about death. Almost any actions are justified as long as they prolong life. At the same time, paradoxically, assisted suicide has come to be respected by some because it is seen as the final (even if ultimately pointless) self-assertion of a person who refuses to remain passive in the face of all-powerful death. The hero of such assisted suicide or euthanasia could be the disgraced King Saul, who "took his own sword and fell upon it" (1 Sam. 31:4). Death hangs over the modern imagination as the supposed greatest evil.

Paul exhorts Christians to view death differently. Death is no longer the greatest evil. In 1 Thessalonians, he counsels Christians not to "grieve as others do who have no hope" (1 Thess. 4:13). Paul does not intend that Christians should not grieve, but we should not grieve "as others do who have no hope." The biblical tradition is full of lamenting and weeping over earthly death. Even Jesus wept at the tomb of Lazarus (John 11:35).[13] Christians ought to grieve because death still remains an evil, as shown by its pain, loss, and separation. God did not create our soul and body to be rent asunder; for "God did not make death" (Wis. 1:13).

Christian grief, however, remains a hopeful grief. Paul gives the reason for grieving with hope: "Since we believe that Jesus died and rose again, even so, through Jesus, God will bring with him those

---

13. See Rebekah Eklund, *Jesus Wept: The Significance of Jesus' Laments in the New Testament* (London: Bloomsbury, 2015).

who have died" (1 Thess. 4:14). As Jesus rose from the dead, so he will raise up those who die united to him. Paul recalls the prophecy of Hosea to show that the power of death has been overcome: "Where, O death, is your victory? Where, O death, is your sting?" (1 Cor. 15:55). Fulfilling the prophets, Christ has transformed death in the inaugurated-but-not-yet-consummated kingdom of God. Paul teaches, "The sting of death is sin, and the power of sin is the law. But thanks be to God, who gives us the victory through our Lord Jesus Christ" (1 Cor. 15:56–57; cf. Hosea 13:14). Christians are invited to witness to this victory and share it with others. This world and its suffering and death are not all there is. No longer are we blinded by darkness and doubt, for we now live in the light of the Christ's victory over death. The saints lived their lives boldly since they struggled to overcome their natural fear of death with their confidence in Christ's victory and the new world to come.

In the familiar verse from the First Letter of John, "God is love," John describes the newness of God's love that we come to see in faith. We come to know that God is love as we abide in his love. This love fills us with confidence and overcomes fear. John writes, "We have known and believe the love God has for us. God is love, and those who abide in love abide in God, and God abides in them. Love has been perfected among us in this: that we may have boldness on the day of judgment. . . . There is no fear in love, but perfect love casts out fear" (1 John 4:16–18). God's revelation of himself as love is meant to transform us. When we give in to hatred of our neighbor, we are no longer abiding in—or giving witness to—God's love. Instead, we are abiding in worldly rebellion against God and giving witness to our own disordered desires and judgments, separating ourselves from the "cloud of witnesses." John calls us instead to join that company filled with confidence and love.

Confidence and love in the face of death is perhaps nowhere better expressed that in the first martyr for faith in the Resurrection, Stephen. The word *martyr* is Greek for "witness," and Stephen was indeed a great witness to the love and mercy of Christ. He was known among the Apostles to be a "man full of faith and the Holy Spirit" and was selected to serve the Christian community in Jerusalem as a deacon (Acts 6:5–6). Soon afterward, he was arrested for his faith in Jesus Christ. He gave a stirring speech in which he narrated God's saving plan throughout the history of Israel and how the prophets of Israel foretold the "coming of the Righteous One," of whom the authorities "have become his betrayers and murderers" (Acts 7:52). The authorities, including the high priest and Saul, who would be later known as the great Apostle Paul, condemned Stephen and had him stoned.

Let us witness Stephen's final words and his stunning witness to trust and love in the face of his death. Acts emphasizes that he was "filled with the Holy Spirit"—not merely his own strength. Stephen spoke aloud, "Look, I see the heavens opened, and the Son of Man standing at the right hand of God!" (Acts 7:55–56). He thus witnessed to the truth of his faith in the face of intense opposition. And he prayed, "Lord Jesus, receive my spirit" (Acts 7:59). Facing death with hope, he trusted in Jesus Christ to receive him into his arms.

Even more powerful is that Stephen witnessed to the reality of love in the face of his executioners. Echoing Jesus' request to the Father from the cross, "Father, forgive them; for they do not know what they are doing" (Luke 23:34), Stephen pleads to the Lord Jesus, "Lord, do not hold this sin against them" (Acts 7:60). As a faithful witness, Stephen gives us a concrete example of facing suffering and death with faith in Christ, hope in Christ, and love in Christ.

World Upside Down

Stephen's witness in the face of death may seem impractical. But Paul reminds us that what the world considers wisdom—or what the world considers practical—may in fact be foolish. Indeed, Paul urges each of us to "become fools so that you may become wise," since "the wisdom of this world is foolishness with God" (1 Cor. 3:18–19). To the world, the path of the great "cloud of witnesses" may seem strange. Paul recognizes, however, that even in terms of what is practical, "God's foolishness is wiser than human wisdom, and God's weakness is stronger than human strength" (1 Cor. 1:25).

This "foolishness" and "weakness" of God has been shown to the world as the cruciform love of Jesus Christ, whom God raised from the dead. Again, the "witness" or "testimony" to the truth of Christ is discovered in love. The First Letter of John makes the same connection between our witness and Christ: "Those who believe in the Son of God have the testimony in their hearts. . . . And this is the testimony: God gave us eternal life, and this life is in his Son" (1 John 5:10–11). Faith in Christ allows us to live as an embodied testimony to the self-surrendering love of God.

The call to be faithful witnesses is not a call to be rash or reckless. Jesus instructs us to be "wise as serpents and innocent as doves" (Matt. 10:16). He thus makes clear that, if we are going to bear witness in faith to him, this will mean accepting persecution, even perhaps at times from those within the Church. We are sent out as "sheep into the midst of wolves" (Matt. 10:16). This does not mean that persecution is evidence that we are always in the right! There may be times when we are persecuted by others because we have failed in our duties or been incorrect in our judgments. Discernment is always required. We may need to overcome a worldly form of cleverness that is really a matter of saving one's one skin and status. Christ teaches us to follow him to the point of suffering for bearing witness to his truth. Such perseverance, however, is not foolishness but ultimate wisdom. Christ makes the path clear: "For those who want to save their life will lose it; and those who lose their life for my sake, and for the sake of the gospel, will save it. For what will it profit them to gain the whole world and forfeit their life?" (Mark 8:35–36).

In a fallen world, each of us must struggle against inclinations to hold onto our pleasures, status, and security, all of which we must eventually let go of anyway. In such a world, a lived witness to the truth of Christ's teachings on faith and morals as witnessed by the Church may well give offense. Sometimes we ourselves will fail. In the Gospels, the disciples themselves recoil from the words of Christ, who calls them to be perfect or become whole through following him (Matt. 5:48). But in the end, true life will be found in taking up our cross. We must begin with saying "yes" to the Good News of the salvation offered us in Jesus Christ. The Gospel's teachings should not be felt as ever-heavier burdens, for the Gospel also includes the Blood of Jesus that washes away our sins. As Jesus says so truly, "Come to me, all you that are weary and are carrying heavy burdens, and I will give you rest. Take my yoke upon you, and learn from me; for I am gentle and humble in heart, and you will find rest for your souls. For my yoke is easy, and my burden is light" (Matt. 11:28–30). We, having received the free gift of God's mercy, may then seek to give witness to Christ in our lives.

The Cloud of Witnesses Cares for Us

Do saints united to Jesus in heaven care for us and pray for us? We have biblical evidence that the answer is yes. Recall that Paul frequently expresses his will to pour himself out in love for his churches. At the same time, Paul also says that for him "living is Christ and dying is gain" and that to "depart and be with Christ . . . is far better"

(Phil. 1:21, 23). Paul grants that in the flesh he can be of more direct, earthly service to his flock. But how could it really be "far better" or "gain" for Paul to die and be with Christ, if this would mean that Paul had utterly to cease loving and praying for those to whom he is united in Christ? If Paul is alive in heaven—and he is—then we know that he continues to love and care for us unceasingly, united to Christ's love and prayer for us.

We know, too, that "there is joy in the presence of the angels of God over one sinner who repents" (Luke 15:10). Why would we suppose, then, that the holy souls who dwell with Jesus would not share in the joy of the angels or that they would not be united with Jesus in his intercession? Recall that, in "the heavenly Jerusalem" that now exists, there are not only "innumerable angels in festal gathering" but also "the spirits of the righteous made perfect" (Heb. 12:22–24). Hebrews depicts these holy "spirits" as conscious, not asleep. And, if so, they must be dwelling in the joy of Christ's self-surrendering love and prayer for the salvation of God's people. In the book of Revelation, the Seer describes a vision of "the souls of those who had been slaughtered for the word of God and for the testimony they had given" (Rev. 6:9). These witnesses cry out for justice on earth.[14] Obedient to God's call for patience, these witnesses pray for their fellow members of the Body of Christ who are now bearing witness on earth.

The book of Revelation describes the saints alive with Jesus Christ in heaven. Revelation depicts a vision of "the twenty-four elders" (Rev. 5:8)—symbolic of the twelve tribes of Israel and the twelve Apostles—singing a song of praise to the Lamb. The Seer also sees "a great multitude that no one could count, from every nation, from all tribes and peoples and languages, standing before

---

14. See Peter S. Williamson, *Revelation* (Grand Rapids, MI: Baker Academic, 2015), 127–130.

the throne and before the Lamb, robed in white, with palm branches in their hands," all joined in praising Christ (Rev. 7:9). Certainly this is an image of heavenly worship rather than literalistic description. But it makes clear that, even now, the heavenly realm (the beginning of the new creation) is filled with the souls of the blessed, conscious and awake in giving praise to God and the Lamb. They are the great "cloud of witnesses" who have gone before us.

Not only do the heavenly saints praise God, they also intercede on our behalf and pray for us. Using further imagery, Revelation depicts how prayers come to God through these heavenly hosts. The twenty-four elders are described as holding "bowls full of incense, which are the prayers of the saints" on earth (Rev. 5:8; cf. 8:3). These elders in heaven bear the prayers of God's holy ones on earth to God and the Lamb. God cannot be outdone in generosity. He has chosen to allow his sanctified creatures to share in intercession as a way of giving glory to himself. These witnesses thus dwell in the presence of God in heaven and help us in our worship of God.

At the right hand of the Father, Christ "holds his priesthood permanently" and "always lives to make intercession" for "those who approach God through him" (Heb. 7:24–25). Since the heavenly saints live in Christ, they also share in some way in his priestly intercession for us. Surely they could not forget about the Body of Christ on earth, the Church in its earthly pilgrimage. United to Christ's intercessory prayer, the prayers of the "cloud of witnesses" sustain us in our earthly life as we "go to him [Christ] outside the camp and bear the abuse he endured" (Heb. 13:13).

Among this "cloud of witnesses" who live everlastingly in union with Jesus Christ, one member stands out as uniquely "full of grace"—Mary of Nazareth (Luke 1:28 RSV-CE). "All generations will call me blessed," she says, "for the Mighty One has done great things for me, and holy is his name" (Luke 1:48–49).[15] When we name Mary as "blessed," we are invited to recall the Beatitudes in which Jesus declares "blessed" the poor, the meek, the suffering, the pure in heart, the peacemakers. When we treated the Beatitudes earlier, we suggested that the Beatitudes are a self-portrait of Jesus. Given that Mary is configured to her Son, we may also consider them a portrait of Mary. In fact, Mary's cousin Elizabeth has already declared both Jesus and Mary "blessed": "Blessed are you among women, and blessed is the fruit of your womb" (Luke 1:42). During her life on earth, she shared in Christ's blessedness as one who did not yet see heaven but trusted as we must trust. Thus, Elizabeth continues, "And blessed is she who believed that there would be a fulfillment of what was spoken to her from the Lord" (Luke 1:45). Mary's faith serves as an example for us, that we too may believe that the promises of our Lord will be fulfilled for us in the consummation of his kingdom.[16]

Mary also exemplifies what it means to be blessed by sharing in the death and Resurrection of her Son. With her, we may draw close to her Son and to his saving cross by which Mary remained in self-sacrificial love (John 19:25). On the cross, Jesus gave Mary to us not only as an example but as a mother: "When Jesus saw his mother and the disciple whom he loved standing beside her, he said to his mother, 'Woman, here is your son.' Then he said to the disciple, 'Here is your mother'" (John 19:26–27).[17] With the unveiling of the heavenly liturgy in Revelation, we recognize that Mary is the true "ark of [the] covenant" now dwelling in "God's temple in heaven,"

---

15. See Pablo T. Gadenz, *The Gospel of Luke* (Grand Rapids, MI: Baker Academic, 2018), 42, 52.

16. See Edward Sri, *Rethinking Mary in the New Testament: What the Bible Tells Us about the Mother of the Messiah* (San Francisco: Ignatius Press, 2018).

17. See Francis Martin and William M. Wright IV, *The Gospel of John* (Grand Rapids, MI: Baker Academic, 2015), 320–321.

the beginning of the new creation (Rev. 11:19; cf. 12:1).[18] She is the "woman clothed with the sun, with the moon under her feet, and on her head a crown of twelve stars"; she is the mother of the one who rules all the nations (Rev. 12:1, 5). She is persecuted with all her children, those who keep the testimony of Jesus. Just as she interceded before her son Jesus on earth, she now intercedes before her son Jesus, the eternal king, as the mother of the king in heaven. Her prayers help us to adopt the self-sacrificial love of the cross rather than the self-centered paths of the fallen world. The paths of our disordered inclinations will pass away; the paths of trusting in God and in what he has done in Jesus Christ and his saints will endure forever (see 1 John 2:17; 1 Cor. 7:31).

Conclusion

The saints become relevant to us when we remember that they are fellow Christians who gave exemplary witness to the power of Jesus' cross and Resurrection. In faith, all Christians are invited to bear witness to what we have "received from the Lord" (1 Cor. 11:23). We know "that Christ died for our sins in accordance with the scriptures" and "that he was raised on the third day in accordance with the scriptures" (1 Cor. 15:3–4). Jesus has ascended to the Father to prepare a place for those who receive his gift of mercy and share in his love, and he prepares this place through his witnesses. Seeking to draw us into the new creation, he has inaugurated his kingdom by pouring out his Spirit.

Recognizing our own weakness, let us ask God to unite us more and more with his great cloud of witnesses. We are not alone! Let us call upon their prayers in Christ, inspired by their faith, hope, and love. Let us join Christ's kingdom of witnesses, as together we

---

18. See Williamson, *Revelation*, 202–10; and Matthew Levering, *Mary's Bodily Assumption* (Notre Dame: University of Notre Dame Press, 2014).

"live . . . in him, rooted and built up in him and established in the faith, . . . abounding in thanksgiving" (Col. 2:6–7). Though the life of self-sacrificial love embodied by the saints on earth may appear strange and risky to the eyes of the world, in fact this way of life—and this way of life alone—will establish us securely. As Christ proclaims at the end of his Sermon on the Mount, where he pronounced the Beatitudes that characterize the lives of the saints: "Everyone then who hears these words of mine and acts on them will be like a wise man who built his house on rock. The rain fell, the floods came, and the winds blew and beat on that house, but it did not fall, because it had been founded on rock" (Matt. 7:24–25). The saints are those faithful witnesses who built their lives on the rock of Jesus Christ. When we look at their love, we rejoice, for they are indeed "so great a cloud of witnesses" (Heb. 12:1).

CONCLUSION

The Catholic writer and evangelist Brandon Vogt encapsulates the questions the Church faces from many people today—questions that we have sought to address with this book: "Isn't Catholicism a backward, intolerant, bigoted religion? Isn't it run by pedophile priests and full of scandals? Doesn't it degrade women and LGBT people and obsess about sex? Isn't it plagued by pointless rules that stifle real faith?"[1]

Vogt knows that these are questions that Catholics sometimes struggle to answer. To these we could add the notions that modern science or philosophy has disproven God and that the stories about Jesus are now outdated in a technological and pluralistic world. As Vogt remarks, during his journey to Catholic faith, one of the key things that helped him to answer these questions for himself was being "exposed . . . to the fascinating world of the Bible."[2] We have sought in this book to expose that fascinating world.

Let's quickly review the terrain we have covered. We started with a question that young Catholics often pose as they begin to wonder about their faith: Does God exist? If so, how would we be expected to know this? How could we truly know it, beyond simply having an irrational belief that there is Someone out there? In addition, although people say that Jesus is God, how could this make sense, given that he was obviously a man? Surely this was just an instance of ancient Jews getting carried away, just like ancient Romans did when they deified and worshiped their emperors?

---

1. Brandon Vogt, *Why I Am Catholic (And You Should Be Too)* (Notre Dame, IN: Ave Maria Press, 2017), 1.

2. Vogt, *Why I Am Catholic*, 2.

In response, our first chapter pointed out that God has revealed himself to us in two ways. The first way is through the cosmos and through all things that exist. We tend to think that things "just exist" and always will exist—the cosmos will just go on forever, and its existence is self-explanatory. But in fact finite things require a source of being. The cosmos itself, in all its vastness as the sum total of all existing things, is a finite existent. It therefore depends upon a source of being; its being is dependent, caused being. This source is sheer being—or, better, infinite and unfathomable act of "to be," God. As Paul says in Romans 1, from the things that are made, especially in their order and beauty, we should know that there must be an eternal and unrestricted cause, a Creator who is not dependent upon another for being and who indeed is the transcendent, infinite source of all finite being.

Although knowing that God exists is a good start, it is not enough on its own. God recognizes that even though we should be able to know that he exists, we can doubt the logic and can easily ignore it. Besides, we need to know God personally, not just to know that there is a divine source of the universe. So God calls and forms a people to whom he reveals himself as Creator, as "I AM WHO I AM," as the covenantal Redeemer. He thus reveals himself as merciful and committed to save.

In Jesus, God comes as Messiah, the King of the whole world. He demonstrates his true kingship by establishing his people in justice. Not by power or by violence does he establish his reign, but by taking the lowest place and becoming the servant of all, in self-surrendering love. He claimed divine authority, and his purpose was to inaugurate the fulfillment of God's promise to dwell with his people, to redeem them from the sin and death that alienated them from God, to establish the kingship of God amidst his people and all nations, to pour out the divine Spirit so that all people would know the living God, and to establish the new law of love. Jesus did all this, supremely revealing the Father to be pure mercy and love.

Furthermore, the apostolic testimony is clear: Jesus rose from the dead, so that he is no longer a corpse but living, having ascended in the flesh to his Father. When we are united to him in love, the reign of God advances in the world, a reign of self-sacrificial love whose goal is everlasting sharing of the Trinitarian life. Our Savior Jesus is worth knowing, because he is none other than the divine Son, communing with the Father through the Spirit in the unity of God. Coming to know Jesus is a joy because he is "the Author of life, whom God raised from the dead" (Acts 3:15).

But if Jesus is all this, why do we need the Church to tell us? Aren't the Bible and the Church basically other people's experiences of God? Shouldn't we rather trust our own insights into God and the meaning of the universe? Isn't our own reading of the Bible or, for that matter, of any spiritual book enough? Why should we listen to the teaching of the Church?

In response, our second chapter called to mind the central testimony of the Bible—namely, that God has revealed himself for our salvation. God has the power to speak. The news that the Bible brings is that God is infinitely personal in his wisdom and love. God has chosen to communicate himself and his saving love personally. He does this not only by forming a people, Israel, but also by becoming flesh as a man among his beloved people. Jesus himself, having lived his life entirely for us, also chose to communicate himself personally: he made himself, the truth of his Word, available to all humanity precisely within a community. This community is structured so as to enable us to hear God's Word and to receive the saving power of his merciful love.

Human fallenness means that we feel threatened by having to listen to anyone, whether God or our fellow humans. But in a community, we must learn to listen—to humble our pride so that we no longer live simply for ourselves—in order to contribute fully to the life of the community. Thus, Jesus unites us to himself within a "Body," the Church, where we enter into personal communion with him and others precisely by learning to receive him rather than to grasp him on our own terms. This is why we should "listen to the Church"—because Jesus himself, who makes known the glory of the divine Love, speaks through it. Paul describes this attitude as "the obedience of faith" (Rom. 1:5).

Yet despite the testimony to Jesus' Resurrection, and despite the wondrous way in which Jesus revealed God's merciful love for his creatures and consummated the covenants and promises of God, it may seem that Christ can't be taken seriously because his community, his inaugurated kingdom, has been seemingly a failure. What is the Church's history, after all, but a history of division, hypocrisy, foolishness, oppression, and self-aggrandizement? On this view, Jesus might have been interesting, but the Holy Spirit's failure to transform human hearts reveals that Jesus was not what he claimed to be and that Christians never really received the "Holy Spirit." It was a noble dream, but two millennia of history show us that it failed to deliver.

In response, our third chapter investigated the sending of the Holy Spirit upon believers. We examined the holy pattern of life of the justified and sanctified believer, and reflected upon what it means no longer to bear the guilt of past transgressions, for Christ has borne all sins. The reality of divine mercy is striking. In a world where it is hard to forgive ourselves and hard to forgive our neighbors, God has established a fountain of forgiveness. This mercy is rooted in divine love, a love that God shares with us. United to Christ by faith that he is our Redeemer, we experience redemption and sanctification through his Spirit. Yet, in this same chapter we reflected upon the biblical testimony to the fact that at present the Church is filled with sinners, and that we can turn away from Christ and resist the Spirit's work. Christ indicated his Church would be comprised of wheat and weeds, but he expressed this in the hope that the "weeds" (those in the Church who have turned to sin) would repent and return. Such a return is possible through the channels of divine mercy that Christ provides his Church through Scripture and the sacraments.

A more careful look at the history of the Church reveals extraordinary deeds of love and humble acts of profound hope. At times, entire societies have been transformed so as no longer to be based upon cruelty and domination. The reality of the Spirit's work depends upon looking for it in the right place. Countless people have been transformed in love and have exhibited the marks of Jesus Christ—which is to say, the marks of selfless love—in themselves and their families and communities. Furthermore, the Church has faithfully handed on the means of salvation, the holy teachings, holy Scriptures, and holy sacraments. This is the real truth about the Church, which those who deface it by their sins (whether they be laity or clergy) cannot destroy. Those who love the Lord remain burdened by sin, but they experience the power of God working within them and within his Church to configure God's people to the image of Christ's love. Not worldly power, but the power of real hope and self-sacrificial love is what was promised and is still given in abundance today: "You shall receive power when the Holy Spirit has come upon you" (Acts 1:8).

Even so, is there not a major problem with all this talk about love? If Jesus is the divine Son, then why did the divine Father decide to manifest his love for the world by sending his own Son to be tortured and killed? By comparison to the beauty and grace of the Greek gods and goddesses, or the serenity of the Buddha, or the military conquests and spiritual trances of Muhammad, all Christians have for public show is a bloody cross. Is God a child abuser? It seems that salvation bought by an innocent person's blood is not worth accepting. Human dignity requires that salvation not be acquired on the back of an innocent person, killed in the most gruesome manner. In addition, the Eucharist is a communion in Christ's Body and Blood. This seems to make the cross of Christ even worse. Are we cannibals?

In response, our fourth chapter investigated the cross and the Eucharist. The Bible reminds us that when we sin, we are turning our back upon the giver of life. We decide to live according to our desires and according to our self-will. And we want what we want, no matter what the cost to others; and we don't care if God doesn't like it. To live in this way is actually to shake one's own foundation as a creature. We are intrinsically relational, personal beings made for communion in knowing and loving. We are made for friendship. When we turn away from the life-giver, we expose ourselves to the loss of personality and communion through death. Death is a profound threat to us, and yet sin, with its rejection of real communion and its focus on living for self, has within it already the seed of the radical alienation that is death.

Jesus, when he comes to redeem us from sin and to draw us everlastingly into glorious communion with God and the blessed, does not shy away from going to the heart of things. From within our deepest wound—the penalty of death—he heals us. He takes on the most terrible death so as to turn it into the path of life. He pours his love out in dying. He heals the relational wound that alienated us from God and from our neighbors against whom we have sinned.

All this was prepared for by the Old Testament history of sacrifices—from the near-sacrifice of Isaac, to the Passover lamb and the temple cult—and the way these sought to overcome the depth of sin. Jesus does not cling to his life, much less does he live to advance his own interests. Rather, he and the Father and the Holy Spirit are perfectly united in the absolute love that he makes manifest on the cross. In this love, he does what we want to do but could not: he offers himself, and everything that he is, to his Father. Instead of cleaving to his earthly existence, he gives it up freely for us.

The injustice of sin is so deep within human history that it is undone only through the justice and superabundant love found in Jesus' perfect gift of himself. In this perfect self-offering, he reveals the selflessness of the divine Trinitarian communion, and he reveals our everlasting vocation: to share in his self-offering in love, a self-offering rooted in the Trinitarian selflessness that is infinite wisdom, infinite love, infinite joy, infinite interpersonal communion. The Eucharist is none other than our sharing in Christ's self offering on the cross, in a sacramental mode. We come to share in the greatest possible love! It follows that the communion of the Church is none other than a communion or "sharing in the blood of Christ" (1 Cor. 10:16).

Still, there seems to be a problem. Even if we are grateful for the loving sacrifice of Christ, we might yet ask: Does the Creator of the universe really care about what you or I do on any given day? Even if he does, why would he hold our faults against us? It seems to us that when we sin or make mistakes, we are just humans acting in human ways. If God is merciful, why doesn't he just say we're okay as we are, without all the complications of religion? Why do we need to be reconciled to God?

In response, our fifth chapter recalled the hard truths about sin and the good news of God's mercy. The Bible portrays sin in a deeply realistic and personal way. It knows that we are all sinners, and it does not shy away from the personal and communal harm caused by various kinds of sins. Indeed, it narrates in vivid detail what it means to be caught in our sins and enslaved to them.

Yet to our eyes, these very sins often seem unavoidable. We adamantly defend these sins, even if part of our mind knows well that they are indefensible. We are caught in a vise of interior division, embarrassment, and misery. When we reach out to God, we do so half-heartedly because we focus more on cleaving to our own desires and to our own will.

The Bible helps us to discover the source of this struggle: our exile from being in communion with God. We have become, frankly, enemies of God because we want God to serve us—to supply us with power and prestige, or physical pleasures, or health and security. Our sinful condition is a very serious matter because we stand against our own good; we are frightened by that which could save us. The prophets speak of a time in which God will end our exile so that we might again dwell with him and he with us.

Even as we stand in this very condition in which we are enemies of God, Christ reveals that he loves us and is willing to die for us. Jesus tells many parables of God's mercy for sinners and of how God delights in bringing us home from our exile. The greatness of this realization—God actually loves us and has unlocked the cage in which we find ourselves—should bring us to tears. The redemption offered by Christ is a sheer gift to be received in faith and love. This great good news is that Jesus Christ is personally calling us through his Church: "Be reconciled to God" (2 Cor. 5:20).

Does this mean, however, that we cannot live normally among our friends and peers? Are we to be like the caricature of the puritan, perpetually repressed by the straitlaced norms of his or her fanatical religion? After all, in the twenty-first century, the Bible's morality cuts sharply against the grain. The public image of Christians is often of buffoons who deserve to be persecuted because they are haters. In a nutshell, it seems better to go with the times and to live and think like everyone else in our society.

In chapter six, we showed that the Bible recognizes this temptation to worldliness. In fact, Sacred Scripture makes clear that those who wish to experience reconciliation with God and neighbor must pursue a path of conversion. Christianity cannot be a religion of living in accord with the desires of the flesh. That is what the world does, but Christianity cannot be a religion of the illusion of worldly security. Rather, the Bible reveals that just as Christ went to the cross, so too we will have to be configured to his cruciform love. It teaches that we find our deepest meaning in reflecting and imitating the goodness and beauty of the God who created us. We were not made in the image of a fallen world but in God's image. The call to conversion present throughout the Bible is a call to leave behind disordered ways. This conversion cannot be done with our own strength, but is the fruit of Christ's redemption and the sending of his Holy Spirit.

The key point is that Christ came to bring a way of life that is distinctive. It is a way of life in which we do not cleave to this world and its glories. It is an invitation rather to cleave to the infinite Source and Creator of the world's glories, to the one who knows how to fulfill our desires. We are to be conformed to the love of God so that we can love all his renewed creation in and with him. No wonder Paul commands, "Do not be conformed to this world" (Rom. 12:2).

If we look at things through the lens of loving our neighbor, another question arises. We may ask, if Christianity is about caring for others, then isn't Christianity's purpose now mainly to assist governments in caring for the poor? In that case, it doesn't really matter whether people believe in Christ so long as they care for the poor. On this view, the Vatican should sell all its treasures and distribute the money to good causes. Likewise, the true Christianity would be an ideal modern state in which the poor were given the dignity they deserve via food, clothing, housing, health care, and the like.

In chapter seven, we made clear that the Bible takes a different viewpoint. The purpose of Jesus' coming among us was not to deliver an economic program. As the Son of God, he could have done a lot of things. He might have outlined the best possible economic or political model, or he might have invented modern medicine and saved countless lives. He could have instituted better methods of farming and thereby allowed his hungry fellow Israelites a full meal. But he did none of this. What he came to bring was the truth about God and the truth about the human person.

At the same time, Christ reveals that Christian love calls for constant concern about our neighbors, including their material needs. The poor are God's beloved children, and if we care for them, it is the same as caring for Christ. At the final judgment, Christ will call to himself those who have fed the hungry, cared for the sick, clothed the naked. All those who are the "least" among us are *Christ* for us. It is a sign of a true Christian community when one finds that, due to beneficent love, "there was not a needy person among them" (Acts 4:34).

All this may be so, and yet surely we might justifiably complain that the Church is far too strict about sex. After all, if two people love each other, they often will feel the need to express their love physically. According to the Church, only a man and woman united in marriage can rightly enjoy the fullness of sexual pleasure. This seems archaic at best or discriminatory at worst. Besides, the Church also condemns sexual expressions such as pornography, yet countless men and women use pornographic means of gratification.

In chapter eight, we addressed this thorny question from the perspective of the Bible. According to the Bible, our bodies are not merely our instruments. It is one thing to say, "I want a drink," and then to go get a glass of water. But it is another thing to say "I want to have sex," and then to go get a random male or female partner. This is because our sexual organs and sexual drives are connected, biologically and psychologically speaking, to procreation and the raising of children. Sexual intimacy, in our body-soul constitution, touches a very deep nerve. It has a deeply inscribed relational dimension. In fact, the Bible reveals that we are created for nothing less than the marriage of God and creation, and human marriage is a sign of this glorious everlasting marriage.

The Bible shows moreover that the world's practice of marriage and sexuality is in need of healing. Families and the good of children depend upon the permanency and unity shaped by the love between the man and the woman. Against the untrustworthy desires and abuses of power that shape our experience of marriage and sex, God recalls sexuality and marriage to what it was created to be, when the two become one for life, and for children. Furthermore, in Christ, although human marriage and sexuality remain good, they are not the final and ultimately defining reality. The ultimate reality is a union with God and the blessed so intimate as to be marital, even while being beyond the union that we would call sexual in worldly terms. Christ's followers thus can be called to give up marriage and sex, or even simply to endure its loss, as part of being conformed to this greater call of the everlasting marriage of God and creation. In the end, God is greater than every earthly creature or experience—including sexual intercourse. No wonder Paul commands: "Glorify God in your body" (1 Cor. 6:20).

Even if the above is persuasive, a quick glance at the blogosphere reveals the presence of Catholics who are condemning each other, condemning popes, condemning people who condemn popes, and generally bickering with a fervor that one might almost call "religious." There is a barrage of negative and critical language pouring forth from people who identify as Catholics. This situation seems to show that Christianity in general, and Catholicism in particular, does not work. Best to abandon it to the haters, and to seek kinder, gentler pastures for oneself.

Given this problem, chapter nine sought to tease out the various issues at stake in Christian speech. On the one hand, the Bible clearly teaches that Christians must be careful in the use of words, since slandering others and causing division and enmity by our words are so easy to do and are such grave sins against our neighbor. If we are carried away by our self-assurance, we can easily become divisive and condemn others in profoundly anti-Christian ways. On the other hand, sometimes charity requires bold and challenging speech, as the biblical prophets, Jesus, Paul, and others show. Lest we get too comfortable and allow injustices to be done by the powerful inside and outside the Church, we must realize that we may sometimes need to speak very sharp words. But the Bible calls us to do so with utmost care and charity, recognizing the bitter consequences that even well-directed sharp words may have and heeding the call not to "speak evil against one another" (James 4:11).

A final issue needs to be addressed. Are the saints really models of a life well lived? Over the centuries, the saints have been busy preaching the Gospel, going out into the desert, studying Scripture, getting martyred, giving spiritual counsel, contemplating God, practicing ascetic disciplines, caring for the poor, and at times even leading the Church. What kind of life is this? Most normal people have a completely different life. Rather than waking up on a hard bed in the middle of the night to pray and do penance, we get out of our soft warm beds to take a comfortable shower and go downstairs for a bowl of cereal. We watch television, go to movies, and eat at good restaurants. The saints seem disconnected from the actual life that we lead. If these are the people to whom we belong, then maybe the whole Christian thing is a mistake for us. Surely the saints are too strange to be relevant.

In chapter ten, we sought biblical wisdom on this final point. The saints are heroic and faithful witnesses, and yet, like us, they are also sinners. Hebrews displays this in listing among the great saints of ancient Israel people known not only for their saintly acts of leadership, self-sacrifice, and love of God and neighbor, but also for some particularly ugly sins. The Bible likewise makes clear that there are many vocations or many missions in the Church, and therefore many paths to sainthood. Marriage is one of these paths, as the example of Priscilla and Aquila shows. God calls some people to positions of spiritual greatness, but they arrive there by the path of humility and even humiliation, as with Peter, who was the rock on which Christ founded his Church but who also denied Christ three times. Many saints are like the tax collector Zacchaeus, whose humiliation was imposed upon him by his stature. He was too short to be noticed, but he was nonetheless called by Christ. The key to the holiness of all these saints, normal people though they were, is that their lives were built upon the Redeemer, in whom they placed their trust. Christ enabled them to exhibit the truth of his love, even though this meant suffering—as exemplified by the Virgin Mary at the foot of the cross.

Just as Christ is trustworthy, so too are his great witnesses. Even when they die, they are alive in Christ. These witnesses are our greatest friends, and we are right to ask them for their prayers, just as we ask our friends down the street to pray for us. The Church is not a communion of power, but a communion of love rooted in God's grace. The Bible shows that the saints, after their deaths, continue to pray and intercede for us. In Christ's mystical body, inclusive of all who have died in Christ, we share in the joy of Christ. Let us rejoice, since we belong to "so great a cloud of witnesses" (Heb. 12:1).

❀ ❀ ❀

We began this book by noting the urgent call of Vatican II and recent popes for Catholics to be instructed by Sacred Scripture. We also noted the pressing problems that have jeopardized the handing on of the Catholic faith. In recent decades, pastors and scholars have proposed various solutions to these problems. Christians should undertake more works of mercy; Christians should celebrate the liturgy with greater solemnity and devotion; Christians should recognize the urgency of evangelization for the salvation of souls; Christians should reclaim the great treasures of culture and spirituality built up over the centuries; Christians should seek a personal encounter with Jesus Christ; Christians should perceive and care for the beauty of creation and the dignity of the human person; Christians should strengthen the creedal instruction given to believers.

We agree with all these solutions. Each of them, however, can benefit from a renewal of the Word of God in our midst. Christians are part of a people whom God has been building up and instructing for millennia. In Christ, God has revealed himself in the profoundest way possible and reconfigured his people around himself as Lord and King, alive and at work in the world here and now. Through the Spirit, we are called to be configured to Christ's self-surrendering love that is true power and true life.

The Bible teaches us all this. As Bishop Robert Barron has remarked, however, "The Church has realized from the beginning that we need assistance if we are to read the Scriptures with profit."[3] Without the assistance of many teachers, past and present, and indeed, without the Church and its tradition, no one could read the Bible well. But the quest to discover who God is and who Christ is— and thereby to understand why the Catholic Church teaches what it does—requires of the whole Church an ever-deeper immersion in Sacred Scripture. We need to hear God's Word as contained in Scripture's stories, prayers, hymns, teachings, and testimonies.

The risen Jesus tells his disciples, who do not yet recognize him, "Was it not necessary that the Messiah should suffer these things and then enter into his glory?" (Luke 24:26). When they still do not understand, Jesus draws them into his scriptural word: "Then beginning with Moses [the Torah] and all the prophets, he interpreted to them the things about himself in all the scriptures" (24:27). He then opens their eyes to him in the "breaking of the bread" (24:35), so that they understand Scripture within the liturgical context of the Eucharist. Hearing God's Word, and tasting the wisdom, love, and mercy of Christ crucified, may we learn to proclaim with the disciples, "The Lord has risen indeed!" (Luke 24:34).

---

3. Bishop Robert Barron, "*The Word on Fire Bible:* A Bible for Restless Hearts," in *The Word on Fire Bible*, vol. 1, *The Gospels* (Park Ridge, IL: Word on Fire, 2020), 15.